TABLE 1.1

Index of Crime, United States, 1972-1991

Population[1]	Crime Index total[2]	Modified Crime Index total[3]	Violent crime[4]	Property crime[4]	Murder and non-negligent manslaughter	Forcible rape	Robbery	Aggravated assault	Burglary	Larceny-theft	Motor vehicle theft	Arson[3]
					Number of Offenses							
Population by year:												
1972-208,230,000	8,248,800		834,900	7,413,900	18,670	46,850	376,290	393,090	2,375,500	4,151,200	887,200	
1973-209,851,000	8,718,100		875,910	7,842,200	19,640	51,400	384,220	420,650	2,565,500	4,347,900	928,800	
1974-211,392,000	10,253,400		974,720	9,278,700	20,710	55,400	442,400	456,210	3,039,200	5,262,500	977,100	
1975-213,124,000	11,292,400		1,039,710	10,252,700	20,510	56,090	470,500	492,620	3,265,300	5,977,700	1,009,600	
1976-214,659,000	11,349,700		1,004,210	10,345,500	18,780	57,080	427,810	500,530	3,108,700	6,270,800	966,000	
1977-216,332,000	10,984,500		1,029,580	9,955,000	19,120	63,500	412,610	534,350	3,071,500	5,905,700	977,700	
1978-218,059,000	11,209,000		1,085,550	10,123,400	19,560	67,610	426,930	571,460	3,128,300	5,991,000	1,004,100	
1979-220,099,000	12,249,500		1,208,030	11,041,500	21,460	76,390	480,700	629,480	3,327,700	6,601,000	1,112,800	
1980-225,349,264	13,408,300		1,344,520	12,063,700	23,040	82,990	565,840	672,650	3,795,200	7,136,900	1,131,700	
1981-229,146,000	13,423,800		1,361,820	12,061,900	22,520	82,500	592,910	663,900	3,779,700	7,194,400	1,087,800	
1982-231,534,000	12,974,400		1,322,390	11,652,000	21,010	78,770	553,130	669,480	3,447,100	7,142,500	1,062,400	
1983-233,981,000	12,108,600		1,258,090	10,850,500	19,310	78,920	506,570	653,290	3,129,900	6,712,800	1,007,900	
1984-236,158,000	11,881,800		1,273,280	10,608,500	18,690	84,230	485,010	685,350	2,984,400	6,591,900	1,032,200	
1985-238,740,000	12,431,400		1,328,800	11,102,600	18,980	88,670	497,870	723,250	3,073,300	6,926,400	1,102,900	
1986-241,077,000	13,211,900		1,489,170	11,722,700	20,610	91,460	542,780	834,320	3,241,400	7,257,200	1,224,100	
1987-243,400,000	13,508,700		1,484,000	12,024,700	20,100	91,110	517,700	855,090	3,236,200	7,499,900	1,288,700	
1988-245,807,000	13,923,100		1,566,220	12,356,900	20,680	92,490	542,970	910,090	3,218,100	7,705,900	1,432,900	
1989-248,239,000	14,251,400		1,646,040	12,605,400	21,500	94,500	578,330	951,710	3,168,200	7,872,400	1,564,800	
1990-248,709,873	14,475,600		1,820,130	12,655,500	23,440	102,560	639,270	1,054,860	3,073,900	7,945,700	1,635,900	
1991-252,177,000	14,872,900		1,911,770	12,961,100	24,700	106,590	687,730	1,092,740	3,157,200	8,142,200	1,661,700	
Percent change: number of offenses:												
1991/1990	+2.7		+5.0	+2.4	+5.4	+3.9	+7.6	+3.6	+2.7	+2.5	+1.6	
1991/1987	+10.1		+28.8	+7.8	+22.9	+17.0	+32.8	+27.8	-2.4	+8.6	+28.9	
1991/1982	+14.6		+44.6	+11.2	+17.6	+35.3	+24.3	+63.2	-8.4	+14.0	+56.4	
					Rate per 100,000 Inhabitants							
Year:												
1972	3,961.4		401.0	3,560.4	9.0	22.5	180.7	188.8	1,140.8	1,993.6	426.1	
1973	4,154.4		417.4	3,737.0	9.4	24.5	183.1	200.5	1,222.5	2,071.9	442.6	
1974	4,850.4		461.1	4,389.3	9.8	26.2	209.3	215.8	1,437.7	2,489.5	462.2	
1975	5,298.5		487.8	4,810.7	9.6	26.3	220.8	231.1	1,532.1	2,804.8	473.7	
1976	5,287.3		467.8	4,819.5	8.8	26.6	199.3	233.2	1,448.2	2,921.3	450.0	
1977	5,077.6		475.9	4,601.7	8.8	29.4	190.7	247.0	1,419.8	2,729.9	451.9	
1978	5,140.3		497.8	4,642.5	9.0	31.0	195.8	262.1	1,434.6	2,747.4	460.5	
1979	5,565.5		548.9	5,016.6	9.7	34.7	218.4	286.0	1,511.9	2,999.1	505.6	
1980	5,950.0		596.6	5,353.3	10.2	36.8	251.1	298.5	1,684.1	3,167.0	502.2	
1981	5,858.2		594.3	5,263.9	9.8	36.0	258.7	289.7	1,649.5	3,139.7	474.7	
1982	5,603.6		571.1	5,032.5	9.1	34.0	238.9	289.2	1,488.8	3,084.8	458.8	
1983	5,175.0		537.7	4,637.4	8.3	33.7	216.5	279.2	1,337.7	2,868.9	430.8	
1984	5,031.3		539.2	4,492.1	7.9	35.7	205.4	290.2	1,263.7	2,791.3	437.1	
1985	5,207.1		556.6	4,650.5	7.9	37.1	208.5	302.9	1,287.3	2,901.2	462.0	
1986	5,480.4		617.7	4,862.6	8.6	37.9	225.1	346.1	1,344.6	3,010.3	507.8	
1987	5,550.0		609.7	4,940.3	8.3	37.4	212.7	351.3	1,329.6	3,081.3	529.4	
1988	5,664.2		637.2	5,027.1	8.4	37.6	220.9	370.2	1,309.2	3,134.9	582.9	
1989	5,741.0		663.1	5,077.9	8.7	38.1	233.0	383.4	1,276.3	3,171.3	630.4	
1990	5,820.3		731.8	5,088.5	9.4	41.2	257.0	424.1	1,235.9	3,194.8	657.8	
1991	5,897.8		758.1	5,139.7	9.8	42.3	272.7	433.3	1,252.0	3,228.8	659.0	
Percent change: rate per 100,000 inhabitants:												
1991/1990	+1.3		+3.6	+1.0	+4.3	+2.7	+6.1	+2.2	+1.3	+1.1	+.2	
1991/1987	+6.3		+24.3	+4.1	+18.6	+13.1	+28.2	+23.3	-5.8	+4.8	+24.5	
1991/1982	+5.3		+32.7	+2.1	+7.6	+24.4	+14.1	+49.8	-15.9	+4.7	+43.6	

[1]Populations are Bureau of the Census provisional estimates as of July 1, except 1980 and 1990 which are the decennial census counts.
[2]Because of rounding, the offenses may not add to totals.
[3]Although arson data are included in the trend and clearance tables, sufficient data are not available to estimate totals for this offense.
[4]Violent crimes are offenses of murder, forcible rape, robbery, and aggravated assault. Property crimes are offenses of burglary, larceny-theft, and motor vehicle theft. Data are not included for the property crime of arson.
All rates were calculated on the offenses before rounding.
Data for 1991 were not available for the State of Iowa; therefore, it was necessary that their crime counts be estimated.

Source: *Crime in the United States, 1991*, Federal Bureau of Investigation, (WDC, 1992)

- Climate;

- Effective strength of law enforcement agencies;

- Policies of other components of the criminal justice system (prosecutorial, judicial, correctional, and probational);

- Attitudes of citizenry toward crime;

- Crime reporting practices of citizenry.

CRIME IS ON THE INCREASE

Two main government sources collect crime statistics. The Federal Bureau of Investigation (FBI) annually compiles the Uniform Crime Reports, *Crime in the United States* (1992, WDC). The UCR collects data from law enforcement agencies representing approximately 98 percent of the total United States population. The second is the National Crime Survey discussed in detail in Chapter III, "Victimization."

TABLE 1.2

Index of Crime, United States, 1991

Area	Population[1]	Crime Index total	Modified Crime Index total[2]	Violent crime[3]	Property crime[3]	Murder	Forcible rape	Robbery	Aggra-vated assault	Burglary	Larceny-theft	Motor vehicle theft	Arson[2]
United States Total	252,177,000	14,872,883		1,911,767	12,961,116	24,703	106,593	687,732	1,092,739	3,157,150	8,142,228	1,661,738	
Rate per 100,000 inhabitants		5,897.8		758.1	5,139.7	9.8	42.3	272.7	433.3	1,252.0	3,228.8	659.0	
Metropolitan Statistical Area	195,233,844												
Area actually reporting[4]	96.9%	12,650,488		1,705,579	10,944,909	21,405	88,849	661,381	933,944	2,613,827	6,784,451	1,546,631	
Estimated totals	100.0%	12,915,670		1,727,995	11,187,675	21,594	90,661	665,905	949,835	2,670,592	6,949,546	1,567,537	
Rate per 100,000 inhabitants		6,615.5		885.1	5,730.4	11.1	46.4	341.1	486.5	1,367.9	3,559.6	802.9	
Cities outside metropolitan areas	22,775,569												
Area actually reporting[4]	88.2%	1,095,800		96,980	998,820	1,031	6,964	14,170	74,815	215,353	736,546	46,921	
Estimated totals	100.0%	1,238,034		109,575	1,128,459	1,155	7,839	15,923	84,658	244,616	830,686	53,157	
Rate per 100,000 inhabitants		5,435.8		481.1	4,954.7	5.1	34.4	69.9	371.7	1,074.0	3,647.3	233.4	
Rural Counties	34,167,587												
Area actually reporting[4]	85.5%	637,980		64,395	573,585	1,674	7,265	5,164	50,292	216,324	320,951	36,310	
Estimated totals	100.0%	719,179		74,197	644,982	1,954	8,093	5,904	58,246	241,942	361,996	41,044	
Rate per 100,000 inhabitants		2,104.9		217.2	1,887.7	5.7	23.7	17.3	170.5	708.1	1,059.5	120.1	

[1]Populations are Bureau of the Census provisional estimates as of July 1, 1991, and are subject to change.

[2]Although arson data are included in the trend and clearance tables, sufficient data are not available to estimate totals for this offense.

[3]Violent crimes are offenses of murder, forcible rape, robbery, and aggravated assault. Property crimes are offenses of burglary, larceny-theft, and motor vehicle theft. Data are not included for the property crime of arson.

[4]The percentage representing area actually reporting will not coincide with the ratio between reported and estimated crime totals, since these data represent the sum of the calculations for individual states which have varying populations, portions reporting, and crime rates.

Data for 1991 were not available for the State of Iowa; therefore, it was necessary that their crime counts be estimated.

Source: *Crime in the United States, 1991*, Federal Bureau of Investigation, (WDC, 1992)

The FBI reported that in 1991 an estimated 14.8 million crimes occurred in the United States, a 2.7 percent increase over 1990 and a 15 percent increase since 1982. Another way to measure the rate of crime is to compare the rates per 100,000 inhabitants. The rate in 1991 (5,898 per 100,000) was 1.3 percent higher than in 1990 (5,820) and 5.3 percent higher than in 1982 (5604) (Table 1.1).

Experts continue to debate whether the increase in crime, as shown by statistical reports, actually reflected an increasing number of local law enforcement agencies becoming part of the FBI crime reporting system and more accurate methods of maintaining their crime data, or was it really due to more crime? Others attributed the increase in the crime rate of the 1960s and 1970s to the growing up of the "baby boom" generation. As this bulge in the population entered their juvenile years, the age group most likely to commit crimes, it was only natural, they argued, that the crime rate would increase. (Most crimes are committed by males between the ages of 15 and 24.)

In fact, as almost all law enforcement agencies became part of the Uniform Crime Reports system, and the "baby boomers" outgrew their prime crime years, the crime rate began to decline, dropping 11 percent between 1981 and 1984. Some observers attributed this decline to the deterrent effect of more money being spent on law enforcement, stiffer sentences being handed out by the courts, and a growing number of neighborhood watch programs.

Based on these interpretations of the increase in crime in the 1970s and the decrease during the early 1980s, the decline should have continued. Unfortunately, according to FBI statistics, it has not. While neither the FBI nor the Bureau of Justice Statistics provides official interpretations as to why the crime rate has increased, unofficial observations generally attribute the increase to the influence of drug use and drug trafficking. As is noted in Chapter VI, a large proportion of criminals were on drugs when they committed the crimes for which they were sentenced.

Many crimes, including murder, were committed during drug transactions. While there are many reasons why youth gangs have developed, many support themselves through drug trafficking. For

CRIME — A SERIOUS AMERICAN PROBLEM

The Bureau of Justice Statistics (BJS) of the U.S. Department of Justice is the major source of information concerning crime and justice in America. The BJS compiles statistics on virtually every area of crime and reports that data in a number of publications. The annual BJS *National Crime Survey* produces data for a number of studies, the most important of which is the yearly *Criminal Victimization in the United States, 1990*, considered one of the most valuable sources on crime information.

Valuable BJS *Bulletins* include *Prisoners in 1991* (1992), *Probation and Parole 1990* (1991), *Jail Inmates 1990* (1991), *Survey of Youth in Custody* (1988), *Population Density in Local Jails 1988* (1990), *White Collar Crime* (1987), *Women in Jail 1989* (1992), *Crime and the Nation's Households, 1991* (1992), *Violent State Prisoners and Their Victims* (1990), *Drugs and Jail Inmates, 1989* (1991), and *Drugs and Crime Facts, 1990* (1991).

The *Uniform Crime Reports*, prepared by the Federal Bureau of Investigation (FBI), are an important source of data on crime. The annual *Crime in the United States*, along with the BJS survey, is considered the most important source on crime. *Law Enforcement Officers Killed and Assaulted* is another publication prepared from the *Uniform Crime Reports*.

The National Institute of Justice (NIJ) provides research on criminal issues, such as the problems of crime victims. Valuable NIJ publications include *Shock Incarceration Programs in State Correctional Juris-* *dictions* (1989), *Shock Incarceration: An Overview of Existing Programs* (1989), *Drugs and Crime 1990* (1991), and *Drug Use Forecasting* (1991).

The National Institute for Juvenile Justice and Delinquency Prevention publishes information on juvenile crime. Its publications include *Juvenile Court Statistics 1988* (1990) and *Children in Custody 1989* (1991).

Other publications used in producing this book include: *The Corrections Yearbook 1991* published by the Criminal Justice Institute; the Highway Loss Data Institute's *Insurance Theft Report* (1992); the quarterly *Violence and Victims* (1990) published by Spencer Publications; *Rural Drug Abuse* (1990), prepared by the United States General Accounting Office; and the *National Retail Security Survey '91*, a survey prepared by *Security Magazine*. The Sentencing Project conducts research on criminal justice issues and promotes sentencing reform. Information Plus thanks them for use of their reports, *Americans Behind Bars: One Year Later* (1992) and *Young Black Men and the Criminal Justice System: A Growing National Problem* (1990). Information for the chapter on white collar crime was supplemented by *Illegal Corporate Behavior*, published by the now defunct National Institute of Law Enforcement, and from Clifford Stoll's book *The Cuckoo's Egg*. Alcohol abuse information came from the National Highway Traffic Safety Administration's *Drunk Driving Facts* (1991). Thanks also go to the Gallup Organization, Princeton, New Jersey, for permission to use information from their surveys.

INFORMATION PLUS
WYLIE, TEXAS 75098
© 1980, 1982, 1984, 1988, 1990, 1992
ALL RIGHTS RESERVED

EDITORS:
ALISON LANDES, B.A.
CORNELIA B. CESSNA, B.A., M.S.
MARK A. SIEGEL, M.A., Ph.D.

CHAPTER I

CRIME - THE STATISTICS*

CRIME

The United States Department of Justice defines crime as all behaviors and acts for which a society provides formally sanctioned punishment. Written law, both federal and state, defines what is criminal and what is not. Some behaviors — murder, robbery, burglary — have always been seen as criminal, but other activities like driving under the influence of drugs or alcohol or domestic violence have only recently been added to the list of criminal offenses. Changes in our society have also had their influence on crime. Computers have provided another opportunity for white collar crime; the enticement to pad government contracts has proved too great a temptation for some companies. Crack cocaine has turned many inner cities into battle zones.

Crime can be as tragic and violent as murder or it can be as simple as taking gum from the store without paying. Most people have broken the law, wittingly or unwittingly, at some time in their lives. The true extent of criminality is impossible to measure; researchers can only keep records of what is reported by victims or what the police are aware of.

FACTORS IN THE RATE OF CRIME

The FBI lists many factors that influence the rate of crime. Their list includes:

• Population density and degree of urbanization;

• Variations in composition of the population, particularly youth concentration;

• Stability of population with respect to residents' mobility, commuting patterns, and transient factors;

• Modes of transportation and highway system;

• Economic conditions, including median income, destitution, and job availability;

• Cultural conditions, such as educational, recreational, and religious characteristics;

• Family condition with respect to divorce and family cohesiveness;

---

*Unless otherwise indicated, all charts in this chapter have been selected from *Uniform Crime Reports - Crime in the United States, 1991*, Federal Bureau of Investigation (WDC, 1992). For a comparison of crime statistics and another way of measuring them, see Chapter III, Victimization. This comparison is extremely important, because the Bureau of Justice Statistics (BJS) victimization statistics presented in Chapter III reach a different conclusion on whether crime is increasing than do the FBI Uniform Crime Report statistics which are presented in this chapter. Chapter III explains the differences in how the FBI and BJS data is collected.

some, the marketing of drugs is their reason for existence. The development of "crack" (a less expensive, smokeable form of cocaine) has allowed cocaine to be marketed to people who could not afford cocaine in its powdered form and, as a result, provided gangs throughout the United States with a lucrative commodity. Gang wars over "turf" have led to innumerable deaths to gang members and innocent bystanders. Some gangs, many with strong ethnic ties, such as the Chinese tongs or the Jamaican posse, are dedicated to the drug trade and have participated in increased, brutal crime.

THE UNIFORM CRIME REPORTS

The FBI keeps different sets of statistics relating to crime. The two major sets are: a breakdown of crimes reported to the police listed by type, the more serious of which are called the Crime Index; and how many offenses are "cleared," that is, a crime for which at least one person is arrested, charged and turned over to the court for prosecution (this does not necessarily mean that they were guilty). The Crime Index includes the violent crimes of murder, forcible rape, robbery, and aggravated assault; and the property crimes of burglary, larceny-theft, motor vehicle theft, and arson. (Chapter II gives further details on each of the Index crimes.) The arrest statistics include information on many different crimes as varied as fraud and vagrancy.

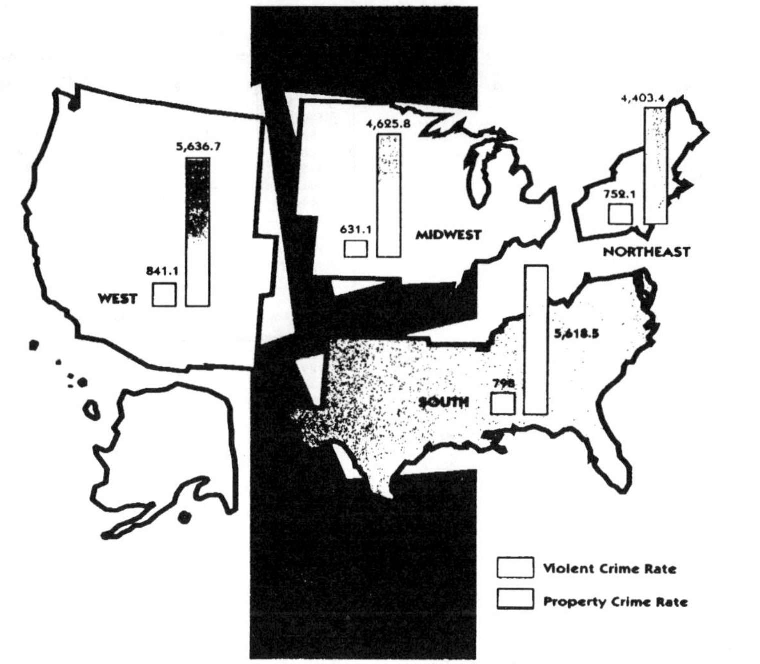

Source: *Crime in the United States, 1991*, Federal Bureau of Investigation, (WDC, 1992)

TABLE 1.3

Total Estimated Arrests[1], United States, 1991

Offense	Arrests	Offense	Arrests
TOTAL[2]	14,211,900	Embezzlement	14,000
Murder and nonnegligent manslaughter	24,050	Stolen property; buying, receiving, possessing	170,000
Forcible rape	40,120	Vandalism	335,100
Robbery	173,820	Weapons; carrying, possessing, etc.	232,300
Aggravated assault	480,900	Prostitution and commercialized vice	98,900
Burglary	436,500	Sex offenses (except forcible rape and prostitution)	108,000
Larceny-theft	1,588,300	Drug abuse violations	1,010,000
Motor vehicle theft	207,700	Gambling	16,600
Arson	20,000	Offenses against family and children	99,400
		Driving under the influence	1,771,400
Violent crime[3]	718,890	Liquor laws	624,100
Property crime[4]	2,252,500	Drunkenness	881,100
		Disorderly conduct	757,700
Crime Index total[5]	2,971,400	Vagrancy	38,500
		All other offenses	3,240,000
Other assaults	1,041,200	Suspicion (not included in totals)	18,400
Forgery and counterfeiting	103,700	Curfew and loitering law violations	93,400
Fraud	427,800	Runaways	177,300

[1]Arrest totals based on all reporting agencies and estimates for unreported areas.
[2]Because of rounding, figures may not add to totals.
[3]Violent crimes are offenses of murder, forcible rape, robbery, and aggravated assault.
[4]Property crimes are offenses of burglary, larceny-theft, motor vehicle theft, and arson.
[5]Includes arson.

Source: *Crime in the United States, 1991*, Federal Bureau of Investigation, (WDC, 1992)

TABLE 1.4

Total Arrests of Persons under 15, 18, 21, and 25 Years of Age, 1991

[10,148 agencies; 1991 estimated population 189,961,000]

Offense charged	Total all ages	Number of persons arrested				Percent of total all ages			
		Under 15	Under 18	Under 21	Under 25	Under 15	Under 18	Under 21	Under 25
TOTAL	10,743,755	614,063	1,749,343	3,244,997	4,908,560	5.7	16.3	30.2	45.7
Murder and nonnegligent manslaughter	18,654	302	2,626	6,722	10,192	1.6	14.1	36.0	54.6
Forcible rape	30,350	1,742	4,766	8,745	13,468	5.7	15.7	28.8	44.4
Robbery	139,182	9,979	35,632	61,981	86,098	7.2	25.6	44.5	61.9
Aggravated assault	368,483	16,029	52,653	100,001	158,203	4.3	14.3	27.1	42.9
Burglary	328,790	44,320	109,965	168,084	213,484	13.5	33.4	51.1	64.9
Larceny-theft	1,215,303	168,007	369,227	533,450	677,244	13.8	30.4	43.9	55.7
Motor vehicle theft	161,628	20,076	70,659	100,181	120,607	12.4	43.7	62.0	74.6
Arson	14,916	4,756	6,940	8,391	9,699	31.9	46.5	56.3	65.0
Violent crime[1]	556,669	28,052	95,677	177,449	267,961	5.0	17.2	31.9	48.1
Property crime[2]	1,720,637	237,159	556,791	810,106	1,021,034	13.8	32.4	47.1	59.3
Crime Index total[3]	2,277,306	265,211	652,468	987,555	1,288,995	11.6	28.7	43.4	56.6
Other assaults	789,144	50,026	122,624	211,150	335,600	6.3	15.5	26.8	42.5
Forgery and counterfeiting	77,066	1,221	6,866	19,272	33,297	1.6	8.9	25.0	43.2
Fraud	292,597	2,870	10,943	40,627	93,629	1.0	3.7	13.9	32.0
Embezzlement	10,602	158	784	2,505	4,441	1.5	7.4	23.6	41.9
Stolen property; buying, receiving, possessing	130,579	10,107	35,220	61,822	82,201	7.7	27.0	47.3	63.0
Vandalism	252,469	53,730	107,890	144,351	175,427	21.3	42.7	57.2	69.5
Weapons; carrying, possessing, etc.	178,955	10,693	37,575	70,785	102,070	6.0	21.0	39.6	57.0
Prostitution and commercialized vice	81,536	148	1,075	7,875	24,250	.2	1.3	9.7	29.7
Sex offenses (except forcible rape and prostitution)	82,228	7,406	14,417	21,565	31,052	9.0	17.5	26.2	37.8
Drug abuse violations	781,250	8,582	60,428	174,608	317,541	1.1	7.7	22.3	40.6
Gambling	12,913	143	912	2,243	3,550	1.1	7.1	17.4	27.5
Offenses against family and children	72,527	996	2,944	9,185	20,007	1.4	4.1	12.7	27.6
Driving under the influence	1,288,876	402	13,437	112,991	329,755	[4]	1.0	8.8	25.6
Liquor laws	453,807	9,320	104,210	311,161	357,216	2.1	23.0	68.6	78.7
Drunkenness	657,119	1,994	16,372	74,446	169,357	.3	2.5	11.3	25.8
Disorderly conduct	569,314	32,346	99,322	187,133	289,980	5.7	17.4	32.9	50.9
Vagrancy	31,262	596	2,257	5,186	8,276	1.9	7.2	16.6	26.5
All other offenses (except traffic)	2,480,902	74,706	247,853	586,947	1,026,278	3.0	10.0	23.7	41.4
Suspicion	14,707	1,253	3,150	4,994	7,042	8.5	21.4	34.0	47.9
Curfew and loitering law violations	73,125	21,859	73,125	73,125	73,125	29.9	100.0	100.0	100.0
Runaways	135,471	60,296	135,471	135,471	135,471	44.5	100.0	100.0	100.0

[1]Violent crimes are offenses of murder, forcible rape, robbery, and aggravated assault.
[2]Property crimes are offenses of burglary, larceny–theft, motor vehicle theft, and arson.
[3]Includes arson.
[4]Less than one-tenth of 1 percent.

Source: *Crime in the United States, 1991*, Federal Bureau of Investigation, (WDC, 1992)

Highest Rates in the City

While crime is certainly not limited to the cities, it is far more likely to occur in urban areas. In 1991, the Index crime rate per 100,000 inhabitants in metropolitan areas was over three times as high as that in rural areas, while in smaller cities it was 2.5 times the rural rate. The crime with the greatest difference was robbery, which occurs 21.4 times more often in metropolitan areas than in rural ones. Motor vehicle theft is also a crime that happens more frequently in cities, occurring more than six times the rate of rural car theft (Table 1.2).

Regional Differences

The Western states continued to have the highest crime rate in 1991, both for violent and property crimes (841 and 5,637 per 100,000 inhabitants respectively), while the Northeast had the lowest property crime rate (4,403), and the Midwest had the lowest violent crime rate (631) (Figure 1.1). The murder and burglary rates were highest in the South. Robbery and motor vehicle theft was highest in the Northeast, while the West led in rape, aggravated assault, and larceny-theft.

ARRESTS

The nation's police forces made an estimated 14.2 million arrests in 1991. Violation of laws dealing with alcohol (driving under the influence, liquor law violations, and drunkenness) accounted for 23 percent of all arrests, and drug abuse arrests were an additional 7 percent. Undoubtedly many of the arrests for disorderly conduct and vagrancy also involved substance abuse, and this still does not include those who committed other crimes

TABLE 1.5

Total Arrest Trends, 1982–1991

[7,073 agencies; 1991 estimated population 161,135,000; 1982 estimated population 147,670,000]

Offense charged	Number of persons arrested								
	Total all ages			Under 18 years of age			18 years of age and over		
	1982	1991	Percent change	1982	1991	Percent change	1982	1991	Percent change
TOTAL	7,873,899	9,337,403	+18.6	1,434,192	1,514,915	+5.6	6,438,907	7,822,488	+21.5
Murder and nonnegligent manslaughter	14,492	17,066	+17.8	1,279	2,465	+92.7	13,213	14,601	+10.5
Forcible rape	22,425	26,618	+18.7	3,299	4,094	+24.1	19,126	22,524	+17.8
Robbery	112,901	129,573	+14.8	29,892	33,510	+12.1	83,009	96,063	+15.7
Aggravated assault	203,868	331,693	+62.7	27,376	47,013	+71.7	176,492	284,680	+61.3
Burglary	345,952	291,980	−15.6	136,822	96,652	−29.4	209,130	195,328	−6.6
Larceny-theft	899,084	1,057,147	+17.6	293,404	316,142	+7.7	605,680	741,005	+22.3
Motor vehicle theft	90,418	145,869	+61.3	32,195	63,389	+96.9	58,223	82,480	+41.7
Arson	13,797	12,960	−6.1	5,304	6,041	+13.9	8,493	6,919	−18.5
Violent crime[1]	353,686	504,950	+42.8	61,846	87,082	+40.8	291,840	417,868	+43.2
Property crime[2]	1,349,251	1,507,956	+11.8	467,725	482,224	+3.1	881,526	1,025,732	+16.4
Crime Index total[3]	1,702,937	2,012,906	+18.2	529,571	569,306	+7.5	1,173,366	1,443,600	+23.0
Other assaults	348,814	686,175	+96.7	54,945	105,701	+92.4	293,869	580,474	+97.5
Forgery and counterfeiting	65,587	67,930	+3.6	6,295	5,528	−12.2	59,292	62,402	+5.2
Fraud	200,190	258,792	+29.3	17,561	9,765	−44.4	182,629	249,027	+36.4
Embezzlement	6,295	9,143	+45.2	501	685	+36.7	5,794	8,458	+46.0
Stolen property; buying, receiving, possessing	93,969	116,488	+24.0	23,839	31,422	+31.8	70,130	85,066	+21.3
Vandalism	160,991	218,345	+35.6	71,122	92,538	+30.1	89,869	125,807	+40.0
Weapons; carrying, possessing, etc.	130,144	159,045	+22.2	18,837	33,485	+77.8	111,307	125,560	+12.8
Prostitution and commercialized vice	89,036	75,870	−14.8	2,241	971	−56.7	86,795	74,899	−13.7
Sex offenses (except forcible rape and prostitution)	53,822	72,447	+34.6	8,925	12,575	+40.9	44,897	59,872	+33.4
Drug abuse violations	447,560	697,432	+55.8	61,598	54,025	−12.3	385,962	643,407	+66.7
Gambling	26,861	11,847	−55.9	816	783	−4.0	26,045	11,064	−57.5
Offenses against family and children	32,274	57,617	+78.5	1,233	2,523	+104.6	31,041	55,094	+77.5
Driving under the influence	1,125,068	1,065,062	−5.3	20,389	10,861	−46.7	1,104,679	1,054,201	−4.6
Liquor laws	308,157	358,966	+16.5	94,189	83,517	−11.3	213,968	275,449	+28.7
Drunkenness	869,450	605,262	−30.4	29,306	14,847	−49.3	840,144	590,415	−29.7
Disorderly conduct	434,625	491,227	+13.0	69,615	85,739	+23.2	365,010	405,488	+11.1
Vagrancy	27,287	29,530	+8.2	3,275	2,019	−38.4	24,012	27,511	+14.6
All other offenses (except traffic)	1,589,942	2,161,689	+36.0	259,844	216,995	−16.5	1,330,098	1,944,694	+46.2
Suspicion (not included in totals)	7,408	8,586	+15.9	2,191	2,751	+25.6	5,217	5,835	+11.8
Curfew and loitering law violations	69,551	62,656	−9.9	69,551	62,656	−9.9	....	....	....
Runaways	90,539	118,974	+31.4	90,539	118,974	+31.4	....	....	....

[1]Violent crimes are offenses of murder, forcible rape, robbery, and aggravated assault.
[2]Property crimes are offenses of burglary, larceny–theft, motor vehicle theft, and arson.
[3]Includes arson.

Source: *Crime in the United States, 1991*, Federal Bureau of Investigation, (WDC, 1992)

while under the influence. The most common Index crime was larceny-theft which accounted for approximately 11 percent of all crimes and 53 percent of Index crimes (Table 1.3).

Age

Age is a major determining factor in crime with almost half (46 percent) of all crimes committed by those under 25 years of age. This figure has been dropping in recent years, however, as the proportion of the population in those age groups declines. In 1984, 50.5 percent of all crimes were committed by those under age 25; in 1982, 53 percent; and in 1980, 56 percent. About 30 percent of all crime was committed by those under 21 years of age in 1991. That was also a decline from 32 percent in 1984, 34 percent in 1982, and 38 percent in 1980.

A large percentage of many crimes, including vandalism (70 percent), burglary (65 percent), liquor law violations (79 percent), and motor vehicle theft (75 percent) were committed by those under 25 years of age (Table 1.4). Generally, the older people get, the fewer crimes they commit. For a comparison of crimes committed by those under 18 (considered juveniles by most states) and those over 18 years old from 1982 to 1991, see Table 1.5.

Sex

Female arrests have risen by over 36 percent since 1982, compared to a 15 percent increase among men since 1982. Men were arrested 4.4 times more often than women; they accounted for 78 percent of Index crime arrests, 88 percent of

TABLE 1.6

Total Arrest Trends, Sex, 1982–1991

[7,073 agencies; 1991 estimated population 161,135,000; 1982 estimated population 147,670,000]

Offense charged	Males						Females					
	Total			Under 18			Total			Under 18		
	1982	1991	Percent change	1982	1991	Percent change	1982	1991	Percent change	1982	1991	Percent change
TOTAL	6,581,698	7,583,086	+15.2	1,135,879	1,171,409	+3.1	1,291,401	1,754,397	+35.9	298,313	343,506	+15.1
Murder and nonnegligent manslaughter	12,624	15,308	+21.3	1,178	2,352	+99.7	1,868	1,758	−5.9	101	113	+11.9
Forcible rape	22,216	26,318	+18.5	3,247	4,035	+24.3	209	300	+43.5	52	59	+13.5
Robbery	104,636	118,485	+13.2	27,908	30,559	+9.5	8,265	11,088	+34.2	1,984	2,951	+48.7
Aggravated assault	177,849	286,496	+61.1	23,223	39,942	+72.0	26,019	45,197	+73.7	4,153	7,071	+70.3
Burglary	322,005	265,410	−17.6	127,501	88,359	−30.7	23,947	26,570	+11.0	9,321	8,293	−11.0
Larceny-theft	629,462	717,967	+14.1	214,960	225,220	+4.8	269,622	339,180	+25.8	78,444	90,922	+15.9
Motor vehicle theft	82,343	131,346	+59.5	28,684	56,266	+96.2	8,075	14,523	+79.9	3,511	7,123	+102.9
Arson	12,028	11,261	−6.4	4,676	5,501	+17.6	1,769	1,699	−4.0	628	540	−14.0
Violent crime[1]	317,325	446,607	+40.7	55,556	76,888	+38.4	36,361	58,343	+60.5	6,290	10,194	+62.1
Property crime[2]	1,045,838	1,125,984	+7.7	375,821	375,346	−.1	303,413	381,972	+25.9	91,904	106,878	+16.3
Crime Index total[3]	1,363,163	1,572,591	+15.4	431,377	452,234	+4.8	339,774	440,315	+29.6	98,194	117,072	+19.2
Other assaults	298,435	573,138	+92.0	43,219	80,812	+87.0	50,379	113,037	+124.4	11,726	24,889	+112.3
Forgery and counterfeiting	44,233	44,213	[4]	4,344	3,686	−15.1	21,354	23,717	+11.1	1,951	1,842	−5.6
Fraud	121,657	149,977	+23.3	13,897	7,149	−48.6	78,533	108,815	+38.6	3,664	2,616	−28.6
Embezzlement	4,338	5,651	+30.3	365	447	+22.5	1,957	3,492	+78.4	136	238	+75.0
Stolen property; buying, receiving, possessing	83,088	102,699	+23.6	21,628	28,268	+30.7	10,881	13,789	+26.7	2,211	3,154	+42.7
Vandalism	145,775	194,424	+33.4	65,166	84,863	+30.2	15,216	23,921	+57.2	5,956	7,675	+28.9
Weapons; carrying, possessing, etc.	120,144	147,686	+22.9	17,609	31,339	+78.0	10,000	11,359	+13.6	1,228	2,146	+74.8
Prostitution and commercialized vice	24,065	25,628	+6.5	658	455	−30.9	64,971	50,242	−22.7	1,583	516	−67.4
Sex offenses (except forcible rape and prostitution)	50,045	67,215	+34.3	8,362	11,725	+40.2	3,777	5,232	+38.5	563	850	+51.0
Drug abuse violations	386,128	581,184	+50.5	51,647	48,153	−6.8	61,432	116,248	+89.2	9,951	5,872	−41.0
Gambling	23,969	10,265	−57.2	780	759	−2.7	2,892	1,582	−45.3	36	24	−33.3
Offenses against family and children	28,457	46,315	+62.8	782	1,668	+113.3	3,817	11,302	+196.1	451	855	+89.6
Driving under the influence	1,002,453	925,267	−7.7	18,009	9,364	−48.0	122,615	139,795	+14.0	2,380	1,497	−37.1
Liquor laws	260,854	290,936	+11.5	72,057	60,499	−16.0	47,303	68,030	+43.8	22,132	23,018	+4.0
Drunkenness	797,552	542,380	−32.0	25,181	12,573	−50.1	71,898	62,882	−12.5	4,125	2,274	−44.9
Disorderly conduct	366,052	391,517	+7.0	56,904	67,963	+19.4	68,573	99,710	+45.4	12,711	17,776	+39.8
Vagrancy	24,052	26,360	+9.6	2,720	1,753	−35.6	3,235	3,170	−2.0	555	266	−52.1
All other offenses (except traffic)	1,344,537	1,788,508	+33.0	208,473	170,647	−18.1	245,405	373,181	+52.1	51,371	46,348	−9.8
Suspicion (not included in totals)	6,313	7,117	+12.7	1,762	2,132	+21.0	1,095	1,469	+34.2	429	619	+44.3
Curfew and loitering law violations	54,526	45,931	−15.8	54,526	45,931	−15.8	15,025	16,725	+11.3	15,025	16,725	+11.3
Runaways	38,175	51,121	+33.9	38,175	51,121	+33.9	52,364	67,853	+29.6	52,364	67,853	+29.6

[1]Violent crimes are offenses of murder, forcible rape, robbery, and aggravated assault.
[2]Property crimes are offenses of burglary, larceny–theft, motor vehicle theft, and arson.
[3]Includes arson.
[4]Less than one-tenth of 1 percent.

Source: *Crime in the United States, 1991*, Federal Bureau of Investigation, (WDC, 1992)

violent crime, and 75 percent of the property crime. Men were arrested a greater percentage of the time than women for rape, robbery, burglary, weapons possession, drunkenness, and sex offenses. They were arrested most often for driving under the influence, larceny/theft, and drug abuse violations. These crimes were also the most frequent ones for women, but women were arrested much more often than men for prostitution, embezzlement, and running away. Since 1982, women have shown a huge increase in substance abuse arrests (89 percent for drug abuse and 44 percent for liquor law violations), in offenses against the family and children (196 percent), embezzlement (78 percent), motor vehicle theft (80 percent), and aggravated assault (74 percent) (Table 1.6).

Race

It is important to keep several factors in mind when comparing data on race. Although in total numbers, whites are arrested more often, in relation to their proportion of the population, blacks are overrepresented in almost all areas of crime. Hispanics are counted as an ethnic group, not a race, and therefore are not separated out in most statistics. Hispanics can be either white or black, although they are usually counted as white. Hispanics are also arrested more often in relation to their proportion of the population than non-Hispanics.

TABLE 1.7

Total Arrests, Distribution by Race, 1991

[10,075 agencies; 1991 estimated population 186,621,000]

Offense charged	Total arrests					Percent distribution[1]				
	Total	White	Black	American Indian or Alaskan Native	Asian or Pacific Islander	Total	White	Black	American Indian or Alaskan Native	Asian or Pacific Islander
TOTAL	10,516,399	7,251,862	3,049,299	115,345	99,893	100.0	69.0	29.0	1.1	.9
Murder and nonnegligent manslaughter	18,096	7,861	9,924	143	168	100.0	43.4	54.8	.8	.9
Forcible rape	29,767	16,306	12,960	259	242	100.0	54.8	43.5	.9	.8
Robbery	136,176	51,217	83,146	600	1,213	100.0	37.6	61.1	.4	.9
Aggravated assault	364,250	218,628	139,407	3,184	3,031	100.0	60.0	38.3	.9	.8
Burglary	323,670	222,817	94,688	2,844	3,321	100.0	68.8	29.3	.9	1.0
Larceny–theft	1,190,037	792,895	368,053	12,987	16,102	100.0	66.6	30.9	1.1	1.4
Motor vehicle theft	160,103	93,728	62,918	1,266	2,191	100.0	58.5	39.3	.8	1.4
Arson	14,738	11,309	3,164	132	133	100.0	76.7	21.5	.9	.9
Violent crime[2]	548,289	294,012	245,437	4,186	4,654	100.0	53.6	44.8	.8	.8
Property crime[3]	1,688,548	1,120,749	528,823	17,229	21,747	100.0	66.4	31.3	1.0	1.3
Crime Index total[4]	2,236,837	1,414,761	774,260	21,415	26,401	100.0	63.2	34.6	1.0	1.2
Other assaults	772,016	498,497	257,121	9,685	6,713	100.0	64.6	33.3	1.3	.9
Forgery and counterfeiting	74,869	48,535	25,264	418	652	100.0	64.8	33.7	.6	.9
Fraud	291,528	197,643	91,230	1,283	1,372	100.0	67.8	31.3	.4	.5
Embezzlement	10,565	7,202	3,195	74	94	100.0	68.2	30.2	.7	.9
Stolen property; buying, receiving, possessing	129,609	73,908	54,011	696	994	100.0	57.0	41.7	.5	.8
Vandalism	249,252	189,474	55,014	2,461	2,303	100.0	76.0	22.1	1.0	.9
Weapons; carrying, possessing, etc.	173,490	98,609	72,137	893	1,851	100.0	56.8	41.6	.5	1.1
Prostitution and commercialized vice	78,779	47,517	29,943	455	864	100.0	60.3	38.0	.6	1.1
Sex offenses (except forcible rape and prostitution)	80,838	63,185	15,985	828	840	100.0	78.2	19.8	1.0	1.0
Drug abuse violations	763,340	443,596	312,997	2,639	4,108	100.0	58.1	41.0	.3	.5
Gambling	12,464	5,581	5,843	16	1,024	100.0	44.8	46.9	.1	8.2
Offenses against family and children	70,945	47,304	20,942	763	1,936	100.0	66.7	29.5	1.1	2.7
Driving under the influence	1,270,713	1,129,876	115,724	14,846	10,267	100.0	88.9	9.1	1.2	.8
Liquor laws	448,880	391,991	43,576	10,610	2,703	100.0	87.3	9.7	2.4	.6
Drunkenness	625,127	507,571	102,307	13,544	1,705	100.0	81.2	16.4	2.2	.3
Disorderly conduct	558,504	365,765	182,414	7,185	3,140	100.0	65.5	32.7	1.3	.6
Vagrancy	30,755	15,735	14,341	605	74	100.0	51.2	46.6	2.0	.2
All other offenses (except traffic)	2,428,040	1,542,890	831,857	24,968	28,325	100.0	63.5	34.3	1.0	1.2
Suspicion	10,184	4,150	5,964	53	17	100.0	40.8	58.6	.5	.2
Curfew and loitering law violations	72,037	55,389	14,819	542	1,287	100.0	76.9	20.6	.8	1.8
Runaways	127,627	102,683	20,355	1,366	3,223	100.0	80.5	15.9	1.1	2.5

Source: *Crime in the United States, 1991*, Federal Bureau of Investigation, (WDC, 1992)

The 1990 U.S. census statistics show that blacks make up almost 12 percent of the total population, while Hispanics are 8 percent of the total. In 1991, (see Table 1.7) nearly seven out of 10 of all those arrested were white, almost three out of 10 were black, 1 percent were American Indian, and .9 percent were Asian or Pacific Islander. Whites were arrested 63 percent of the time for Crime Index offenses, and blacks were arrested almost 35 percent of the time. Blacks had a higher percentage of arrests than whites in the case of murder (54.8 percent versus 43.4 percent) and robbery (61.1 percent to 37.6 percent). Whites were much more likely be caught for driving under the influence, other liquor law violations, and running away. The proportion of American Indians arrested for vagrancy, drunkenness, and liquor law violations was well above their proportion of the population, while 8.2 percent of those arrested for gambling were Asian or Pacific Islanders.

Ethnic Origin

The FBI has stopped collecting data by ethnic origin, eliminating the statistics for Hispanic Americans. The most recent information is from 1986, when they represented 12.7 percent of those arrested. The proportion of Hispanics was particularly high among those arrested for motor vehicle theft (16.3 percent), murder (15.7 percent), aggravated assault (15.3 percent), gambling (24.8 percent), drunkenness (20 percent), and drug abuse violations (19.9 percent) (Table 1.8).

TABLE 1.8

—Total Arrests, Distribution by Ethnic Origin, 1986

[9,597 agencies; 1986 estimated population 176,840,000]

Offense charged	Total all ages					
	Number of arrests			Percent distribution		
	Total	Hispanic	Non-Hispanic	Total	Hispanic	Non-Hispanic
TOTAL	9,222,574	1,172,609	8,049,965	100.0	12.7	87.3
Murder and nonnegligent manslaughter	13,861	2,182	11,679	100.0	15.7	84.3
Forcible rape	26,502	3,054	23,448	100.0	11.5	88.5
Robbery	107,437	14,987	92,450	100.0	13.9	86.1
Aggravated assault	253,795	38,759	215,036	100.0	15.3	84.7
Burglary	322,847	47,466	275,381	100.0	14.7	85.3
Larceny-theft	1,028,864	123,821	905,043	100.0	12.0	88.0
Motor vehicle theft	113,642	18,472	95,170	100.0	16.3	83.7
Arson	13,674	1,068	12,606	100.0	7.8	92.2
Violent crime	401,595	58,982	342,613	100.0	14.7	85.3
Property crime	1,479,027	190,827	1,288,200	100.0	12.9	87.1
Crime Index total	1,880,622	249,809	1,630,813	100.0	13.3	86.7
Other assaults	538,228	50,477	487,751	100.0	9.4	90.6
Forgery and counterfeiting	68,348	4,612	63,736	100.0	6.7	93.3
Fraud	259,373	10,375	248,998	100.0	4.0	96.0
Embezzlement	9,805	514	9,291	100.0	5.2	94.8
Stolen property; buying, receiving, possessing	102,028	14,733	87,295	100.0	14.4	85.6
Vandalism	206,864	17,644	189,220	100.0	8.5	91.5
Weapons; carrying, possessing, etc.	138,869	21,043	117,826	100.0	15.2	84.8
Prostitution and commercialized vice	84,824	8,530	76,294	100.0	10.1	89.9
Sex offenses (except forcible rape and prostitution)	74,569	8,582	65,987	100.0	11.5	88.5
Drug abuse violations	611,414	121,422	489,992	100.0	19.9	80.1
Gambling	22,273	5,519	16,754	100.0	24.8	75.2
Offenses against family and children	40,206	2,052	38,154	100.0	5.1	94.9
Driving under the influence	1,313,726	186,220	1,127,506	100.0	14.2	85.8
Liquor laws	451,620	39,564	412,056	100.0	8.8	91.2
Drunkenness	711,143	142,129	569,014	100.0	20.0	80.0
Disorderly conduct	503,152	47,875	455,277	100.0	9.5	90.5
Vagrancy	30,768	4,585	26,183	100.0	14.9	85.1
All other offenses (except traffic)	1,976,669	219,622	1,757,047	100.0	11.1	88.9
Suspicion	7,002	715	6,287	100.0	10.2	89.8
Curfew and loitering law violations	65,663	5,649	60,014	100.0	8.6	91.4
Runaways	125,408	10,938	114,470	100.0	8.7	91.3

Source: *Crime in the United States, 1988*, Federal Bureau of Investigation, (WDC, 1989)

Offenses Cleared by Arrest

The more violent the crime, the more likely it is that a suspect will be arrested. Seven out of 10 murders, one-half of all rapes and aggravated assaults, and one-quarter of all robberies involved an arrest. (Remember, these are only the crimes that have been reported to the police.) On the other hand, in cases of burglary, larceny-theft, and motor vehicle theft, the chances of arrest were far less likely. In fact, since the vast majority of crimes are property crimes, overall, only one in five was cleared by arrest in 1991 (Table 1.9). Just because a crime is cleared by arrest, however, does not necessarily mean that the criminal has been found, since the person arrested may be innocent of the crime.

The "Take" From Each Crime

The value of the goods taken in the average crime varies dramatically (Table 1.10), although compared to the risk and consequences of crime, the value is usually disappointing. (For crime with real monetary potential, see "White Collar Crime" — Chapter VII.) Not surprisingly, motor vehicle theft has the highest average value at $4,983, making it the crime with best return. The typical

TABLE 1.9

Offenses Known and Percent Cleared by Arrest[1], Population Group, 1991

[1991 estimated population]

Population group	Crime Index total	Modified Crime Index total[2]	Violent crime[3]	Property crime[4]	Murder and non-negligent man-slaughter	Forcible rape	Robbery	Aggra-vated assault	Burglary	Larceny-theft	Motor vehicle theft	Arson
TOTAL ALL AGENCIES; 12,868 agencies; population 225,163,000:												
Offenses known	13,334,099	13,432,846	1,682,487	11,651,612	21,924	92,398	611,531	956,634	2,819,548	7,311,302	1,520,762	98,747
Percent cleared by arrest	21.2	21.2	44.7	17.8	67.2	51.8	24.3	56.5	13.5	20.3	13.9	15.9

Source: *Crime in the United States, 1991*, Federal Bureau of Investigation, (WDC, 1992)

TABLE 1.10

Offense Analysis, 1991, and Percent Change from 1990

[12,354 agencies; 1991 estimated population 222,105,000]

Classification	Number of offenses 1991	Percent change over 1990	Percent distribu-tion[1]	Average value
MURDER	19,782	+4.7	....	$87
FORCIBLE RAPE	93,084	+.9	....	30
ROBBERY:				
Total	636,185	+7.0	100.0	817
Street/highway	357,579	+6.3	56.2	627
Commercial house	74,418	+11.6	11.7	1,456
Gas or service station	16,493	+2.8	2.6	474
Convenience store	36,474	+2.2	5.7	387
Residence	62,526	+9.2	9.8	1,126
Bank	10,193	+17.2	1.6	3,177
Miscellaneous	78,502	+6.3	12.3	792
BURGLARY:				
Total	2,763,793	+1.9	100.0	1,246
Residence (dwelling):	1,828,151	+1.9	66.1	1,281
Night	581,263	+1.3	21.0	990
Day	787,997	+.4	28.5	1,463
Unknown	458,891	+5.4	16.6	1,335
Nonresidence (store, office, etc.):	935,642	+1.8	33.9	1,180
Night	438,962	+.4	15.9	1,039
Day	224,057	−3.1	8.1	1,141
Unknown	272,623	+8.8	9.9	1,438
LARCENY-THEFT (EXCEPT MOTOR VEHICLE THEFT):				
Total	7,150,692	+1.5	100.0	478
By type:				
Pocket-picking	73,010	−1.4	1.0	366
Purse-snatching	73,055	−1.4	1.0	280
Shoplifting	1,179,658	+3.0	16.5	104
From motor vehicles (except accessories)	1,605,003	+3.0	22.4	544
Motor vehicle accessories	1,010,373	−3.7	14.1	305
Bicycles	417,318	+6.9	5.8	233
From buildings	1,014,443	+1.4	14.2	788
From coin-operated machines	69,667	+26.9	1.0	139
All others	1,708,165	+.6	23.9	681
By value:				
Over $200	2,561,144	+1.4	35.8	1,234
$50 to $200	1,695,379	+1.2	23.7	115
Under $50	2,894,169	+1.8	40.5	22
MOTOR VEHICLE THEFT	1,521,958	+1.5	....	4,983

[1]Because of rounding, percentages may not add to totals.
Data for 1991 were not available for the State of Iowa;

Source: *Crime in the United States, 1991*, Federal Bureau of Investigation, (WDC, 1992)

TABLE 1.11

Type and Value of Property Stolen and Recovered, 1991

[12,354 agencies; 1991 estimated population 222,105,000]

Type of property	Value of property		Percent recovered
	Stolen	Recovered	
Total[1]	$14,972,819,000	$5,360,489,000	38.4
Currency, notes, etc.	911,708,000	45,979,000	5.0
Jewelry and precious metals	1,313,037,000	57,175,000	4.4
Clothing and furs	360,889,000	40,866,000	11.3
Locally stolen motor vehicles	7,671,285,000	4,866,216,000	63.4
Office equipment	320,434,000	29,072,000	9.1
Televisions, radios, stereos, etc.	1,106,944,000	51,848,000	4.7
Firearms	123,137,000	12,344,000	10.0
Household goods	256,096,000	15,571,000	6.1
Consumable goods	114,570,000	13,915,000	12.1
Livestock	28,014,000	3,237,000	11.6
Miscellaneous	2,766,706,000	224,268,000	8.1

[1]All totals and percentages calculated before rounding.

Source: *Crime in the United States, 1991*, Federal Bureau of Investigation, (WDC, 1992)

bank robbery nets $3,177, while the average burglary yields around $1,246. Robbing a gas station or convenience store, a risky, sometimes even fatal endeavor, produces approximately $400, less than pocket-picking ($366). When a criminal steals money, as in the case of a bank robber or purse-snatcher, he or she can usually spend the cash they have stolen. However, in the case of burglary or motor vehicle theft, the criminal almost never benefits from the total amount indicated in Table 1.10. While the value of the stolen goods in the typical burglary might be around $1,200, the thief has no way to sell it for its real value. He or she usually takes it to a "fence" (a person who buys and sells stolen goods), who pays around 10 cents on the dollar, depending upon how easily the fence feels he or she can find a buyer for the stolen property. Thus, if the television or VCR is worth $400, the fence will give the thief $40.

It may seem surprising that the "take" from a murder ($187) or rape ($30), the two most terrible crimes, is, by far, the lowest for any crime. However, in most cases of rape or murder, stealing is not the primary objective in the commssion of the crime.

Recovery Rate

Once a person's property is stolen, the likelihood of it being returned is small. With the exception of locally stolen motor vehicles (with a recovery rate of 63.4 percent, because many cases involve a young person stealing the car for a "joyride" and then abandoning the car), recovered property represents less than 40 percent of stolen property. However, recovery of such items as jewelry, precious metals, televisions, video cassette recorders, and stereos is highly unlikely (Table 1.11).

CHAPTER II

TYPES OF CRIME

In 1991, one crime was committed every two seconds — a dramatic increase from a rate of one crime every three seconds in 1984. Crimes against property were committed more frequently (once every two seconds) than violent crimes (once every 17 seconds). The time clock (Figure 2.1) does not imply that these crimes were committed with regularity; instead, they represent the relative frequency of occurrence. However, in several major crime categories, crime levels have dropped overall since 1981, the peak year for victimization ("Criminal Victimization," 1991, Bureau of Justice Statistics). The FBI *Uniform Crime Reports* publishes data for serious crimes in its Index of Crimes which includes murder, rape, robbery, aggravated assault, burglary, larceny-theft, motor vehicle theft, and arson. The following is their breakdown of offenses in 1991.

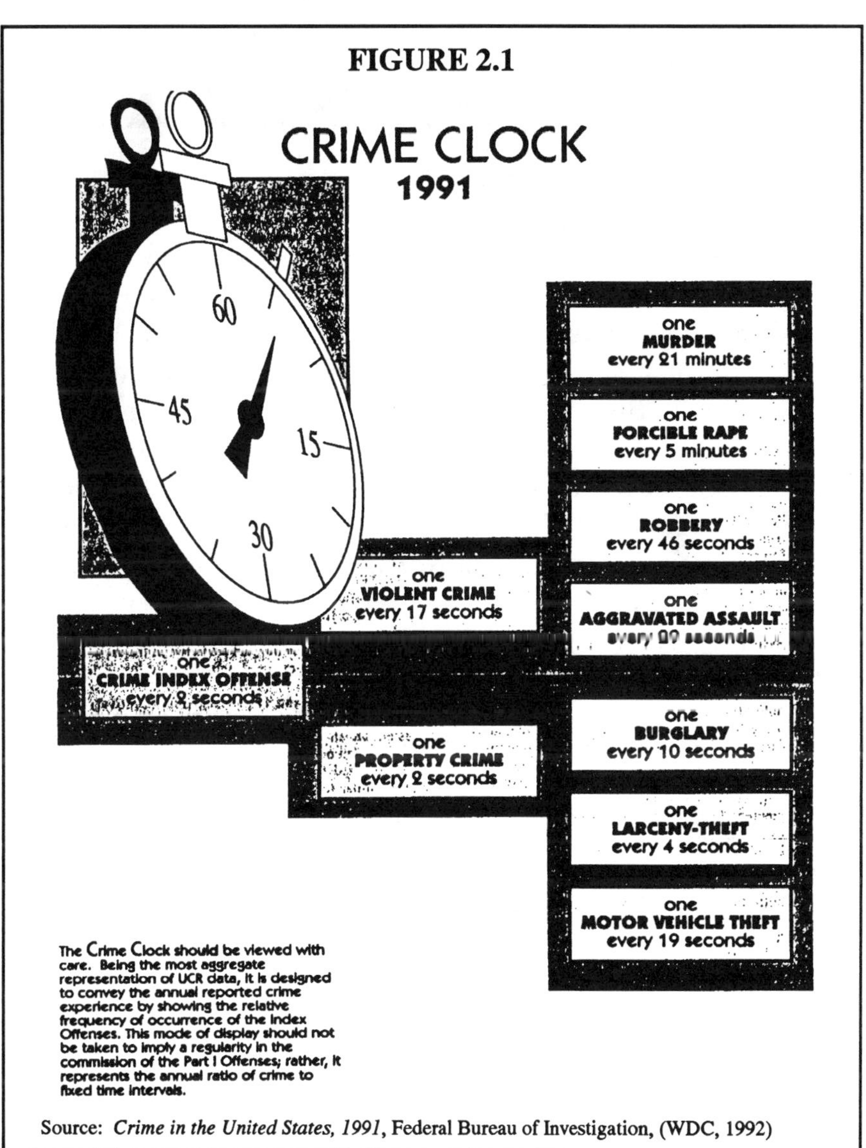

Source: *Crime in the United States, 1991*, Federal Bureau of Investigation, (WDC, 1992)

MURDER

Murder and nonnegligent manslaughter are defined by the Federal Bureau of Investigation (FBI) as "the willful (nonnegligent) killing of one human being by another." The figures do not include suicides, accidents, or justifiable homicides either by citizens or law enforcement officers. In 1991, a murder was committed every 21 minutes, a rate of 10 murders for every 100,000 inhabitants, resulting in an all-time high of 24,703 offenses. This represents a 5.4 percent increase over 1990. Murders were most likely to occur in July and August and least likely to occur in February (Figure 2.2).

Murder Rate By Area

Southern states averaged 12 murders per 100,000 people; the West, 10; and the Northeast and Midwestern states, eight per 100,000; and the Midwestern states, seven per 100,000. Cities had an 21 percent increase in murder since 1990, while suburban areas had increases of 2 percent. Rural counties registered a 1 percent decrease.

Sex and Race

More than three out of four murder victims were male. An average of 47 of every 100 victims were white, 50 were black, and three were of other races. Almost half (49 percent) were between the ages of 20 and 34 (Table 2.1). The offender and the victim were usually of the same race. About 93 percent of black murder victims were killed by black offenders, and 85 percent of the white murder victims were slain by white offenders. Eighty-seven percent of male victims were killed by males, but only one in 10 of the female victims was slain a by female (Table 2.2).

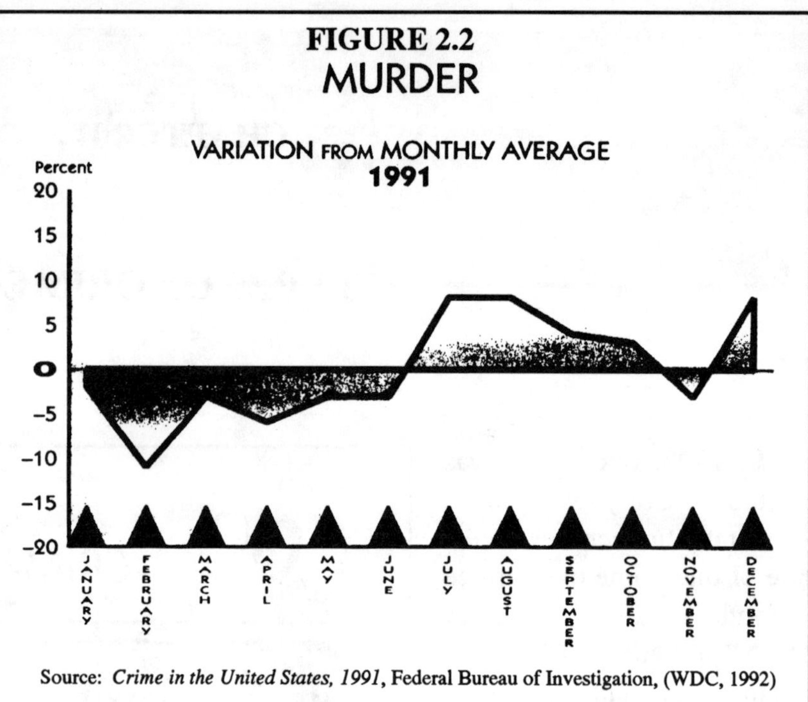

Source: *Crime in the United States, 1991*, Federal Bureau of Investigation, (WDC, 1992)

TABLE 2.1
Age, Sex, and Race of Murder Victims, 1991

Age	Total	Sex			Race			
		Male	Female	Unknown	White	Black	Other	Unknown
Total	21,505	16,781	4,693	31	10,135	10,660	531	179
Percent distribution[1]	100.0	78.0	21.8	.1	47.1	49.6	2.5	.8
Under 18[2]	2,233	1,595	637	1	1,038	1,131	52	12
18 and over[2]	18,898	14,925	3,971	2	8,943	9,376	473	106
Infant (under 1)	304	160	143	1	178	116	5	5
1 to 4	371	193	178		178	177	15	1
5 to 9	110	54	56		66	39	5	
10 to 14	290	201	89		152	129	7	2
15 to 19	2,702	2,335	367		1,035	1,600	49	18
20 to 24	3,948	3,312	636		1,571	2,278	76	23
25 to 29	3,362	2,703	659		1,450	1,806	90	16
30 to 34	2,898	2,237	660	1	1,355	1,455	76	12
35 to 39	2,145	1,689	456		1,074	994	66	11
40 to 44	1,496	1,148	347	1	775	666	48	7
45 to 49	981	744	237		574	374	26	7
50 to 54	658	515	143		399	226	27	6
55 to 59	459	346	113		289	155	11	4
60 to 64	421	302	119		255	154	12	
65 to 69	321	226	95		206	110	4	1
70 to 74	241	156	85		148	87	5	1
75 and over	424	199	225		276	141	3	4
Unknown	374	261	85	28	154	153	6	61

[1]Because of rounding, percentages may not add to totals.
[2]Does not include unknown ages.

Source: *Crime in the United States, 1991*, Federal Bureau of Investigation, (WDC, 1992)

TABLE 2.2

Victim/Offender Relationship by Race and Sex, 1991

[Single Victim/Single Offender]

Victim Race	Offender Race	Actual Number	Offender Sex	Actual Number
Total White Victims 5,194	White	4,399	Male	4,627
	Black	691	Female	523
	Other	60	Unknown	44
	Unknown	44		
Total Black Victims 5,433	White	347	Male	4,619
	Black	5,035	Female	781
	Other	18	Unknown	33
	Unknown	33		
Total Other Race Victims 239	White	72	Male	211
	Black	36	Female	22
	Other	125	Unknown	6
	Unknown	6		
Total Unknown Race 58	White	20	Male	33
	Black	16	Female	4
	Other	1	Unknown	21
	Unknown	21		
Sex				
Total Male Victims 8,149	White	3,447	Male	7,052
	Black	4,507	Female	1,043
	Other	141	Unknown	54
	Unknown	54		
Total Female Victims 2,717	White	1,371	Male	2,405
	Black	1,255	Female	283
	Other	62	Unknown	29
	Unknown	29		
Total Unknown Sex 58	White	20	Male	33
	Black	16	Female	4
	Other	1	Unknown	21
	Unknown	21		

Source: *Crime in the United States, 1991*, Federal Bureau of Investigation, (WDC, 1992)

Murder Circumstances

In 1991, approximately half of the murders were committed by a relative (12 percent) or acquaintance (34 percent) of the victim (Table 2.3). Among all female murder victims in 1991, 28 percent were slain by husbands or boyfriends. Four percent of the male victims were killed by their wives or girlfriends. Arguments led to 32 percent of the murders, while 21 percent resulted from felonies such as robbery, arson, etc. Three percent happened during brawls while the offenders were under the influence of alcohol or narcotics. The greatest increase in murder circumstances is murders involving narcotics (Table 2.4).

Handguns were the weapon used in 55 percent of all murders, while firearms of all kinds accounted for nearly 70 percent of the total. This percentage has remained relatively stable over the past few years (Table 2.5). A knife was used in 16 percent of murders; blunt instruments in 5 percent; personal weapons (fists, feet, and the like) in 6 percent; and other weapons such as poisons and explosives in the remainder (Table 2.6). Because murder is the most serious crime, it gets the most police attention and, therefore, has the highest arrest rate of all felonies. Sixty-seven percent of the 1991 murders were cleared (had an arrest made). An arrest, however, does not necessarily mean the person arrested was guilty or that he or she will be convicted.

THE KILLING OF LAW ENFORCEMENT OFFICERS

Sixty-five police officers were killed in the line of duty in 1990. All but one was male; 52 were white, 12 were black, and one was Asian. The largest number (28) were killed during arrest situations, most during a drug-related arrest (4) or a robbery or burglary (14). Nine officers died investigating suspicious persons or circumstances. Being on patrol duty in a one-officer vehicle is the most dangerous duty for a police officer, while just being alone raises the risk of death. In the past decade, 51 percent of the murdered officers were on single patrol duty (half in a one-officer car), and another 30 percent were unassisted on other types of assignments (Table 2.7).

Assailants

In 1990, 62 of the 65 murders of police officers were cleared by the arrest of 80 suspects; 75 were male, and five were female; 45 were white, 34 were black, and one, Asian. Forty-eight were under the age of 30 (Table 2.8). Among those charged, 72 percent were found guilty of murder; 8 percent were found guilty of a lesser offense related to murder; and 5 percent were found guilty of some crime other than murder. Ten percent had the charges against them dismissed, and 2 percent were committed to psychiatric institutions. The remainder died in custody before they were charged or tried. Of those found guilty of murder, 21 percent were sentenced to death, 49 percent received life imprisonment, 30 percent were given prison terms ranging from two months to 1,000 years, and the remainder were placed on probation or indeterminate sentence.

TABLE 2.3

Murder Circumstances by Relationship,[1] 1991

Circumstances	Total	Husband	Wife	Mother	Father	Son	Daughter	Brother	Sister	Other Family	Acquaintance	Friend	Boyfriend	Girlfriend	Neighbor	Stranger	Unknown Relationship
Total[2]	21,505	353	847	144	184	316	236	187	28	388	5,598	761	269	483	229	3,235	8,247
Felony type total	4,589	4	15	16	16	37	31	3	6	37	1,111	90	8	9	55	1,326	1,825
Rape	129						3				32	5		2	9	37	41
Robbery	2,201			7	8	1			1	19	380	36		1	19	874	855
Burglary	195		1		1	1				1	30	1	1		15	71	73
Larceny-theft	32			1							7				1	18	5
Motor vehicle theft	52										11	2		1		25	13
Arson	136	1	2	5	1	11	4		4	3	27	2	1		3	12	60
Prostitution and commercialized vice	20										8					4	8
Other sex offenses	47					1	1			1	24			1	1	6	12
Narcotic drug laws	1,344		1					3		2	493	34	2		4	184	621
Gambling	33									1	17	3				9	3
Other - not specified	400	3	11	3	6	23	23		1	10	82	7	4	4	3	86	134
Suspected felony type	209	1	1	1	1			1		3	20	3		2		22	154
Other than felony type total	11,115	322	752	105	150	256	186	165	21	303	3,984	616	248	432	164	1,558	1,853
Romantic triangle	312	7	25			1		1		6	175	29	9	29	3	20	7
Child killed by babysitter	31					3	1				22	4	1				
Brawl due to influence of alcohol	497	7	15	1	8	4	1	8		11	238	42	13	10	3	86	49
Brawl due to influence of narcotics	252	1	4	2	3					1	134	8		3	1	25	70
Argument over money or property	516	6	9	5	4	1		6		26	294	56	8	11	17	44	29
Other arguments	6,037	250	473	55	101	50	26	134	10	186	2,138	373	192	309	116	729	895
Gangland killings	204										85	3				73	43
Juvenile gang killings	838										242	9		1		254	331
Institutional killings	18										13	1				2	2
Sniper attack	12										4					3	5
Other - not specified	2,398	51	226	42	34	197	158	16	10	72	639	91	25	70	23	322	422
Unknown	5,592	26	79	22	17	23	19	18	1	45	483	52	13	40	10	329	4,415

[1] Relationship is that of victim to offender.
[2] Total murder victims for which supplemental homicide data were received.

TABLE 2.4

Murder Circumstances, 1987-1991

	1987	1988	1989	1990	1991
Total	17,963	18,269	18,954	20,273	21,505
Felony type total:	3,516	3,480	4,049	4,209	4,589
Rape	205	148	131	152	129
Robbery	1,676	1,522	1,728	1,871	2,201
Burglary	225	214	212	202	195
Larceny-theft	18	16	18	28	32
Motor vehicle theft	30	32	37	55	52
Arson	159	186	165	152	136
Prostitution and commercialized vice	22	15	12	27	20
Other sex offenses	32	62	58	90	47
Narcotic drug laws	885	1,027	1,402	1,367	1,344
Gambling	23	27	23	11	33
Other - not specified	241	231	263	294	400
Suspected felony type	202	229	150	148	209
Other than felony type total	9,772	9,706	10,270	10,889	11,115
Romantic triangle	365	314	385	407	312
Child killed by babysitter	23	23	24	34	31
Brawl due to influence of alcohol	488	422	432	533	497
Brawl due to influence of narcotics	114	197	306	242	252
Argument over money or property	471	486	551	514	516
Other arguments	5,766	5,460	5,736	6,044	6,037
Gangland killings	36	45	56	104	204
Juvenile gang killings	317	372	542	679	838
Institutional killings	23	21	22	16	18
Sniper attack	36	55	49	41	12
Other - not specified	2,133	2,311	2,167	2,275	2,398
Unknown	4,473	4,854	4,485	5,027	5,592

TABLE 2.5

Murder Victims, Type of Weapons Used, 1987-1991

Weapons	1987	1988	1989	1990	1991
Total	17,963	17,971	18,954	20,273	21,505
Total Firearms	10,612	10,895	11,832	13,035	14,265
Handguns	7,847	8,147	9,013	10,099	11,411
Rifles	776	753	865	746	741
Shotguns	1,101	1,105	1,173	1,245	1,113
Other guns	16	15	34	25	30
Firearms-not stated	872	875	747	920	970
Knives or cutting instruments	3,643	3,457	3,458	3,526	3,405
Blunt objects (clubs, hammers, etc.)	1,045	1,126	1,128	1,085	1,082
Personal weapons (hands, fists, feet, etc.)[1]	1,165	1,095	1,050	1,119	1,193
Poison	34	15	11	11	12
Explosives	12	34	16	13	16
Fire	200	255	234	288	194
Narcotics	24	36	17	29	22
Drowning	51	38	60	36	39
Strangulation	360	331	366	312	326
Asphyxiation	115	73	101	96	113
Other weapons or weapons not stated	702	616	681	723	838

[1] Pushed is included in personal weapons.

Source of all tables: *Crime in the United States, 1991*, Federal Bureau of Investigation, (WDC, 1992)

TABLE 2.6

Murder Victims—Weapons Used, 1991

Age	Total	Fire-arms	Knives or cutting instruments	Blunt objects (clubs, hammers, etc.)	Personal[1] weapons (hands, fists, feet, etc.)	Poison	Explosives	Fire	Narcotics	Strangu-lation	Asphyxia-tion	Other weapon or weapon not stated[4]
Total	21,505	14,265	3,405	1,082	1,193	12	16	194	22	326	113	877
Percent distribution[2]	100.0	66.3	15.8	5.0	5.5	.1	.1	.9	.1	1.5	.5	4.1
Under 18[3]	2,233	1,273	188	62	370	3	2	50	6	34	48	197
18 and over[3]	18,898	12,794	3,177	991	798	9	14	136	15	285	64	615
Infant (under 1)	304	9	5	10	163	2		2	5	2	29	77
1 to 4	371	57	14	27	171			24	1	4	13	60
5 to 9	110	37	20	5	7			13		9	5	14
10 to 14	290	209	37	9	7	1	2	7		5	1	12
15 to 19	2,702	2,252	252	49	43	1	1	11		23		70
20 to 24	3,948	3,116	490	99	81	1		9	1	52	8	91
25 to 29	3,362	2,435	533	115	100		1	9	4	47	6	112
30 to 34	2,898	1,966	517	134	120	1	1	13	2	41	11	92
35 to 39	2,145	1,363	407	128	124	1	2	21	2	30	7	60
40 to 44	1,496	918	284	102	87	2	3	17	2	23	4	54
45 to 49	981	609	196	62	52		1	9		15	3	34
50 to 54	658	346	163	68	42		2	6		13	2	16
55 to 59	459	243	93	54	32		1	6		8	2	20
60 to 64	421	195	94	44	32			14	1	14	4	23
65 to 69	321	132	84	44	19	1	1	3		10	1	26
70 to 74	241	96	70	27	24			3	1	6	3	11
75 and over	424	84	106	76	64	2	1	19	2	17	13	40
Unknown	374	198	40	29	25			8	1	7	1	65

[1]Pushed is included in personal weapons.
[2]Because of rounding, percentages may not add to totals.
[3]Does not include unknown ages.
[4]Includes drownings.

Source: *Crime in the United States, 1991*, Federal Bureau of Investigation, (WDC, 1992)

RAPE

The FBI defines forcible rape as, "the carnal knowledge of a female forcibly and against her will. Assaults or attempts to commit rape by force or threat of force are included, however, statutory rape (intercourse with a consenting minor) . . . and other sex offenses are excluded." Rape is a crime of violence in which the victim may suffer immediate, serious physical injury and long-term psychological pain. In 1991, 106,593 rapes were reported to law enforcement agencies. This represents approximately 83 out of every 100,000 women in the country. The statistics on rape are difficult to interpret, however, for several reasons. The crime often goes unreported. The Bureau of Justice Statistics (BJS) reported that only about half of the cases of completed or attempted rape were ever reported to the police. Because the BJS data is collected through interviews, they recognize that there is an unknown amount of underreporting in the BJS statistics as well. Homosexual rape and "date rape" (sex forced upon a woman by her escort) are not included in this data.

Public attitudes and legal definitions of rape are changing to encompass a wider range of sexual events, with varying degrees of violence, submissiveness, and injury, but all involving women having sex against their will. The majority of these cases involve acquaintance rape. Most states also now recognize marital rape, for which a husband can be charged with raping his wife. According to David Beatty, public policy director of the National Victims Center, "There is no question that acquaintance rape is more common than stranger rape. No one has the exact number, but the consensus is that probably in 80 to 85 percent of all rape cases, the victim knows the defendant." A more understanding attitude by law enforcement authorities and a greater awareness of women's rights has led to a significant change in the incidence of reported rape (a 115 percent increase) from 1965 to 1974. This growth in the rate of rape cases has now levelled off, and from 1987 to 1991, the rate increased 13 percent (Figure 2.3).

TABLE 2.7

LAW ENFORCEMENT OFFICERS FELONIOUSLY KILLED, 1990
CIRCUMSTANCES BY TYPE OF ASSIGNMENT

Circumstances at Scene of Incident	Total	2-Officer Vehicle	1-Officer Vehicle		Foot Patrol		Detective/ Special Assignment		Off Duty
			Alone	Assisted	Alone	Assisted	Alone	Assisted	
Total	65	12	16	9	0	0	4	9	15
Disturbance Calls	10	3	2	2	0	0	0	0	3
Bar fights, man with gun, etc.	5	1	1	1	0	0	0	0	2
Family quarrels	5	2	1	1	0	0	0	0	1
Arrest Situations	28	2	3	6	0	0	2	7	8
Burglaries in progress/ pursuing burglary suspects	1	0	0	1	0	0	0	0	0
Robberies in progress/ pursuing robbery suspects	13	1	1	3	0	0	1	1	6
Drug-related matters	4	1	0	0	0	0	0	3	0
Attempting other arrests	10	0	2	2	0	0	1	3	2
Civil Disorders (Mass disobedience, riot, etc.)	0	0	0	0	0	0	0	0	0
Handling, Transporting Custody of Prisoners	2	0	1	0	0	0	1	0	0
Investigating Suspicious Persons/ Circumstances	9	3	3	1	0	0	0	2	0
Ambush Situations	9	3	2	0	0	0	1	0	3
Entrapment/premeditation	2	1	0	0	0	0	0	0	1
Unprovoked attack	7	2	2	0	0	0	1	0	2
Mentally Deranged	1	0	1	0	0	0	0	0	0
Traffic Pursuits/Stops	6	1	4	0	0	0	0	0	1

TABLE 2.8

PROFILE OF PERSONS IDENTIFIED IN THE FELONIOUS KILLING
OF LAW ENFORCEMENT OFFICERS, 1981-1990

Persons Identified	1990	1981-1985	1986-1990	1981-1990
Total	80	564	466	1,030
Under 18 Years of Age	6	43	33	76
From 18 through 29 Years of Age	42	297	249	546
Male	75	548	445	993
Female	5	16	21	37
White	45	291	270	561
Black	34	253	182	435
Other Race	1	20	14	34
Prior Criminal Arrest	62	427	355	782
Convicted on Prior Criminal Charge	54	323	284	607
Prior Arrest for Crime of Violence	37	200	191	391
On Parole or Probation at Time of Killing	25	149	114	263
Prior Arrest for Murder	5	28	29	57
Prior Arrest for Drug Law Violation	26	124	119	243
Prior Arrest for Assaulting an Officer or Resisting Arrest	11	65	59	124
Prior Arrest for Weapons Violation	39	217	204	421

Source of both tables: *Law Enforcement Officers Kill and Assaulted*, 1990, (Federal Bureau of Investigation, (WDC, 1991)

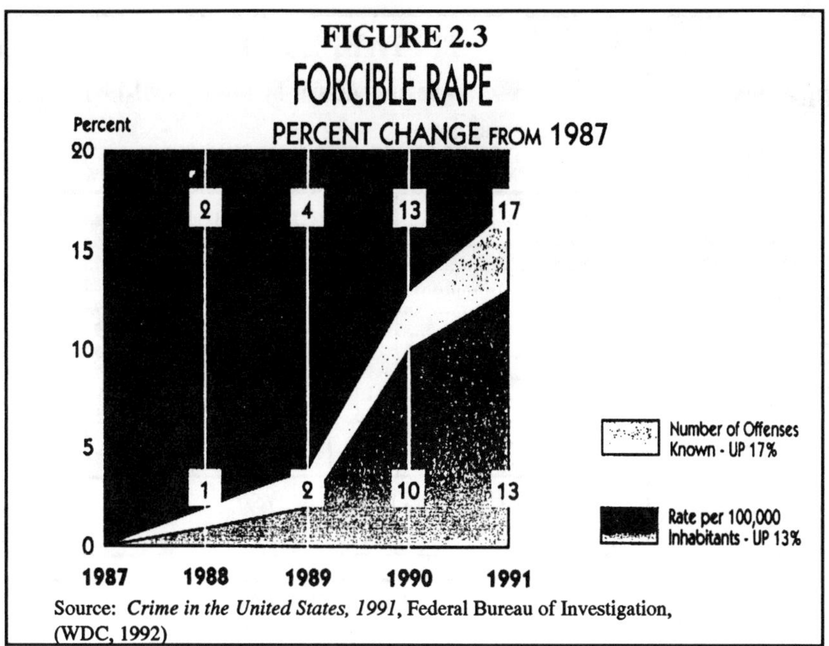

Source: *Crime in the United States, 1991*, Federal Bureau of Investigation, (WDC, 1992)

TABLE 2.9

Forcible Rape by Month, 1987-1991

[Percent of annual total]

Months	1987	1988	1989	1990	1991
January	7.2	7.4	7.4	7.6	7.1
February	6.8	7.3	6.3	6.7	7.0
March	8.1	8.0	7.7	7.9	7.9
April	8.2	8.0	8.3	8.1	8.3
May	8.9	9.0	8.6	9.1	9.2
June	9.3	8.7	8.9	9.0	9.2
July	9.7	9.9	10.0	9.6	9.5
August	9.8	9.8	9.5	9.4	9.7
September	8.9	9.0	8.8	9.1	8.8
October	8.1	8.4	8.9	8.4	8.6
November	7.7	7.6	8.3	7.7	7.8
December	7.3	6.8	7.3	7.4	6.8

Source: *Crime in the United States, 1991*, Federal Bureau of Investigation, (WDC, 1992)

When and Where

Rapes occurred most frequently during the summer months of July and August with the lowest incidence in February, December, and January (Table 2.9). The rate of rape was much higher in metropolitan areas (91 per 100,000 females) than in cities outside metropolitan areas (67 per 100,000) and rural counties (46 per 100,000). Regionally, the highest female rape rate occurred in the Western states (91 victims per 100,000 women), followed by the Midwestern states (89 per 100,000), the Southern states (88 per 100,000), and the Northeastern states (57 per 100,000).

Arrests

Over half of all rapes were cleared by arrest in 1991. Thirty percent of those arrested were under 25 years of age. Of those arrested, 55 percent were white and 43 percent were black. Rural areas cleared a greater number of offenses than did city and suburban law enforcement agencies.

ROBBERY

The FBI defines robbery as "the taking or attempting to take anything of value from the care, custody, or control of a person or persons by force or threat of force or violence and/or putting the victim in fear." Robbery is a particularly threatening crime because of the psychological and physical trauma suffered by its thousands of victims each year and because of the anxiety experienced from the mere threat of robbery. This threat can cause changes in how a person lives that are destructive to social life and the sense of community, especially in urban areas. Robbery is the only one of the seven traditional FBI Index crimes that is both a property crime and a violent crime. It shares with other crimes of property the primary motivation (money) and the likelihood that the perpetrators do not know their victims, while it shares with other types of violent crime a relatively high probability of victim injury or death.

Rate

An estimated 687,732 robberies were reported during 1991, for a robbery rate of 273 per 100,000 inhabitants, a 6 percent increase from 1990. Robbery is very much a big city crime with cities of populations which exceed one million suffering from a robbery rate of 1,189 robberies per 100,000 people. In metropolitan areas, the robbery rate was 341 per 100,000, and in cities outside metropolitan areas, it was 70 per 100,000. At only 17 per 100,000 inhabitants, robbery is not a common

TABLE 2.10

Robbery, Type of Weapons Used, 1991

[Percent distribution by region]

Region	Total all weapons[1]	Armed			
		Fire-arms	Knives or cutting instruments	Other weapons	Strong-armed
Total	100.0	39.9	11.0	9.3	39.8
Northeastern States	100.0	37.6	13.8	8.4	40.2
Midwestern States	100.0	42.3	8.4	10.4	38.9
Southern States	100.0	44.3	9.0	8.7	37.9
Western States	100.0	35.4	12.0	10.5	42.2

[1]Because of rounding, percentages may not add to totals.

Source: *Crime in the United States, 1991,*
Federal Bureau of Investigation, (WDC, 1992)

TABLE 2.11

Aggravated Assault by Month, 1987-1991

[Percent of annual total]

Months	1987	1988	1989	1990	1991
January	7.3	7.2	7.5	7.4	6.9
February	7.0	7.0	6.6	6.7	6.6
March	7.8	7.9	7.9	7.8	7.7
April	8.1	8.1	8.1	8.2	8.1
May	8.9	8.9	8.9	9.0	9.1
June	8.9	9.0	8.9	9.4	9.3
July	9.5	9.8	9.6	10.1	9.7
August	9.5	9.8	9.2	9.3	9.9
September	8.7	9.0	8.8	8.9	9.0
October	8.5	8.4	9.1	8.3	8.6
November	7.9	7.5	7.9	7.4	7.6
December	7.8	7.5	7.5	7.5	7.6

Source: *Crime in the United States, 1991,*
Federal Bureau of Investigation, (WDC, 1992)

TABLE 2.12

Aggravated Assault, Type of Weapons Used, 1991

[Percent distribution by region]

Region	Total all weapons[1]	Fire-arms	Knives or cutting instruments	Other weapons (clubs, blunt objects, etc.)	Personal weapons
Total	100.0	23.6	18.4	30.8	27
Northeastern States	100.0	17.1	21.2	31.6	30
Midwestern States	100.0	26.8	18.2	32.5	22.
Southern States	100.0	27.2	20.2	30.7	21.
Western States	100.0	21.3	14.4	29.5	34.

[1]Because of rounding, percentages may not add to totals.

Source: *Crime in the United States, 1991,*
Federal Bureau of Investigation, (WDC, 1992)

problem in rural areas. The Northeast had a robbery rate of 352 per 100,000; the West, 287 per 100,000; the South, 252; and the Midwest, 223 per 100,000.

Average Losses

An estimated $562 million was stolen during robberies for an average loss of $817 per incidence. Over half (56 percent) of the robberies occurred on the streets or highways. The greatest increase (17 percent) since 1990 has been in bank robberies, netting an average of $3,177. Private residences were involved in 10 percent of robberies. The impact of robbery on its victims cannot be measured simply in terms of loss of money. While the intention of a robber is to obtain money or property, the crime always involves the use or threat of force, and many victims suffer serious physical and/or psychological injury, sometimes even death. Strong-arm tactics were used in 40 percent of the robberies, firearms in another 40 percent, knives in 11 percent, and other weapons in the remainder (Table 2.10).

Arrests

In 1991, only 24 percent of the robbery offenses reported were cleared. Of those arrested in 1991, 62 percent were under 25 years of age, and 91 percent were male. Sixty-one percent of those arrested were black, and 38 percent were white.

AGGRAVATED ASSAULT

The FBI defines aggravated assault as, "an unlawful attack by one person upon another for the purpose of inflicting severe or aggravated bodily injury. This type of assault is usually accompanied by the use of a weapon or by means likely to produce death or great bodily harm." In 1991, 1,092,739 Americans were the victims of aggravated assault, a rate of 433 per 100,000 inhabitants. These figures represent a 28 percent increase in the rate per 100,000 since 1987. Metropolitan areas reported a rate of 487 per 100,000, compared to 372 per 100,000 in cities outside metropolitan areas and 170 per 100,000 in rural counties. Aggravated assault was much more likely in the

TABLE 2.13
Burglary by Month, 1987-1991

[Percent of annual total]

Months	1987	1988	1989	1990	1991
January	8.4	8.4	8.8	8.8	8.1
February	7.8	7.8	7.3	7.5	7.3
March	8.3	8.1	8.2	8.1	8.1
April	7.6	7.5	7.7	7.8	7.9
May	8.0	8.1	8.4	8.1	8.3
June	8.0	8.0	8.3	7.9	8.2
July	8.8	8.8	9.2	8.9	9.2
August	9.1	9.3	9.3	9.0	9.2
September	8.4	8.6	8.6	8.3	8.6
October	8.4	8.5	8.5	8.5	8.6
November	8.4	8.4	8.1	8.3	8.0
December	8.8	8.5	7.8	8.7	8.6

Source: *Crime in the United States, 1991*,
Federal Bureau of Investigation, (WDC, 1992)

use of force to gain entry is not required to classify an offense as burglary." An estimated 3,157,150 burglaries were reported in 1991, a rate of 1,252 per 100,000, a slight increase (1 percent) from the previous year but 16 percent below the rate in 1982. The burglary rate was highest in metropolitan areas (1,368 per 100,000), followed by cities outside metropolitan areas (1,074) and rural counties (708 per 100,000). The burglary rate was highest in the South (1,498 per 100,000) and the West (1,324), and lower in the Midwest (1,037) and Northeast (1,010). The highest burglary rates occurred in July and August and the lowest in February (Table 2.13).

South, accounting for 39 percent of the cases, and in the West (25 percent), followed by the Midwest and the Northeast (20 percent and 17 percent respectively). The highest rates of aggravated assault happened in July and August, while the lowest rate was in February (Table 2.11).

Weapons

About one-third (31 percent) of the aggravated assaults were committed with blunt objects or other dangerous weapons. Personal weapons such as hands, fists, and feet were used in 27 percent of the offenses; knives or cutting instruments in 18 percent; and firearms in 24 percent (Table 2.12).

Arrests

The police cleared an average of 57 percent of the reported cases of aggravated assault in 1991. About 11 percent of those arrested were under 18 years of age. Males (86 percent) were far more likely to be arrested than females (14 percent). Of all those arrested for aggravated assault, 60 percent were white, and 38 percent were black.

BURGLARY

The FBI defines burglary as, "the unlawful entry of a structure to commit a felony or theft. The

Losses

Two-thirds of the burglaries recorded were committed in residential dwellings. Forcible entry took place in 70 percent of the occurrences, 23 percent were unlawful entries (entering an open door without force), and the rest were forcible entry attempts. The offenses were equally distributed between the night and the day. Burglary victims suffered about $3.9 billion in losses in 1991, with an average loss per burglary of about $1,246. Residential property losses were listed as higher ($1,281) than nonresidential property losses ($1180). These values represent the loss to the owner of the property. The burglar usually collects only ten cents on the dollar from the "fence", the person who buys the stolen goods. A television set worth $400 nets the burglar only about $40. This means that most burglars are risking arrest for about $100.00.

Arrests

The police cleared only about 13 percent of the burglaries through arrest. Juveniles under age 18 accounted for 19 percent of those arrested. Ninety-one percent of those arrested for burglary in 1991 were males. Whites accounted for 69 percent of those arrested, while 29 percent were blacks.

TABLE 2.14

Larceny-Theft by Month, 1987-1991

[Percent of annual total]

Months	1987	1988	1989	1990	1991
January	7.6	7.6	8.0	8.2	7.8
February	7.5	7.5	7.2	7.4	7.5
March	8.3	8.2	8.2	8.2	8.2
April	8.0	7.8	8.0	7.9	8.1
May	8.2	8.3	8.6	8.3	8.4
June	8.5	8.5	8.7	8.3	8.5
July	9.1	9.0	9.2	8.9	9.2
August	9.2	9.5	9.5	9.1	9.3
September	8.4	8.5	8.3	8.2	8.3
October	8.6	8.7	8.6	8.7	8.7
November	8.1	8.2	8.0	8.1	7.9
December	8.4	8.3	7.7	8.4	8.2

Source: *Crime in the United States, 1991*,
Federal Bureau of Investigation, (WDC, 1992)

FIGURE 2.4

LARCENY-THEFT

Percent Distribution by Type of Theft

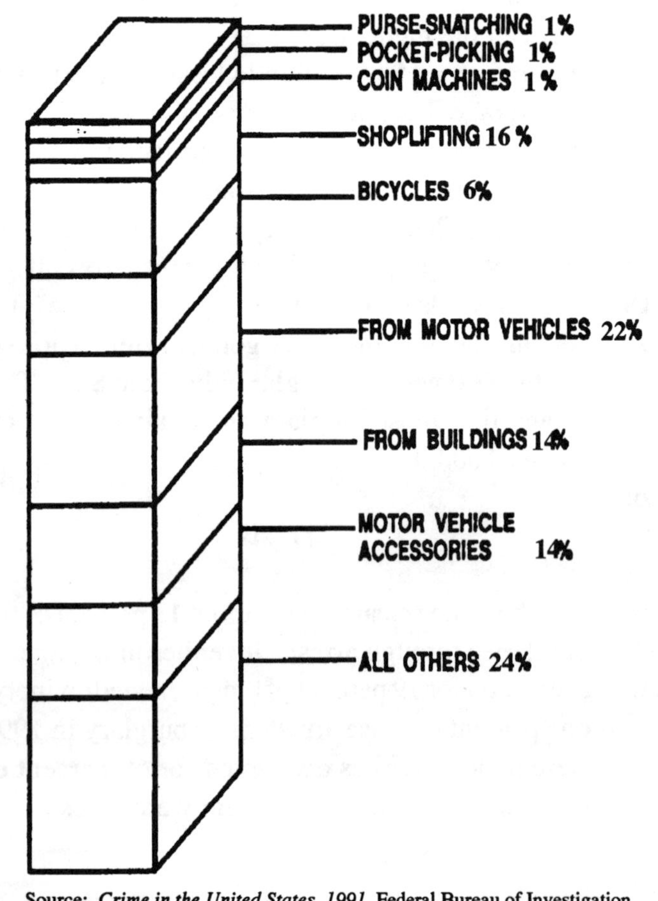

Source: *Crime in the United States, 1991*, Federal Bureau of Investigation, (WDC, 1992)

LARCENY-THEFT

The FBI defines larceny-theft as, "the unlawful taking, carrying, leading, or riding away of property from the possession...of another." This crime category includes shoplifting, pocket-picking, purse-snatching, thefts from motor vehicles, including motor vehicle parts and accessories, bicycle thefts, and so on, in which no use of force or fraud occurs. It does not include embezzlement, "con" games, forgery, and passing bad checks. In 1991, an estimated 8 million larceny-theft offenses were reported for a rate of 3,228 per 100,000. This is over half (55 percent) the Crime Index total, although the figures are well below the true rate of larceny-theft. The Bureau of Justice Statistics reports that only 26 percent of the people robbed without physical contact reported the theft, while 35 percent of those who had physical contact with the perpetrator reported the incident. The larceny-theft rate was 3,560 per 100,000 inhabitants of metropolitan areas; 3,647 per 100,000 in cities outside metropolitan areas; and 1,059 per 100,000 in rural counties. Larceny-theft was highest in the Western (3,522 per 100,000) and Southern states (3,518) and somewhat lower in the Midwestern (3,082) and Northeastern states (2,598). Larceny-theft occurred most frequently in July and August and least often in February (Table 2.14).

Losses

The average value of property stolen was $478 for an estimated total of about $3.9 billion. The estimated loss is considered conservative because many larceny-thefts of small amounts are never reported to authorities. The average amount taken differed depending on the specific crime. For example, the average pick-pocket made off with $366 and the average purse snatcher, $280. Shoplifting resulted in an average "take" of $104. Miscellaneous

TABLE 2.15

Relative Theft Claim Frequencies
1989-91 Model Year Passenger Cars With the Best and Worst Results

Best Results				Worst Results			
Make/Series	Body Style	Size	Result	Make/Series	Body Style	Size	Result
Ford Tempo 4WD	4Dr.	Midsize	11	Volkswagen GTI	2Dr.	Small	1204
Mercury Sable	S.W.	Midsize	24	Volkswagen Jetta	2Dr.	Small	725
Subaru Loyale 4WD**	S.W.	Small	28	Volkswagen Golf	2Dr.	Small	679
Chevrolet Cavalier	S.W.	Midsize	28	Volkswagen Jetta	4Dr.	Small	608
Oldsmobile Cutlass Supreme**	4Dr.	Midsize	28	Volkswagen Cabriolet	2Dr.	Small	602
Mercury Grand Marquis	S.W.	Large	29	Volkswagen Golf	4Dr.	Small	540
Toyota Corolla 4WD	S.W.	Small	29	Cadillac DeVille 2D	Lux.	Large	381
Subaru Legacy 4WD**	S.W.	Midsize	30	Volkswagen Fox	4Dr.	Small	355
Ford Crown Victoria	S.W.	Large	30	Cadillac Fleetwood 2D	Lux.	Large	348
Pontiac Grand Prix**	4Dr.	Midsize	32	Cadillac DeVille 4D	Lux.	Large	338
Pontiac Grand Prix	2Dr.	Midsize	32	Volkswagen Fox	2Dr.	Small	293
Mazda MPV Van 4WD	P.V.	Large	34	Cadillac Brougham	Lux.	Large	289
Oldsmobile Toronado	Lux.	Midsize	35	Cadillac Fleetwood 4D	Lux.	Large	285
Mercury Sable	4Dr.	Midsize	35	Honda Civic CRX	Sp.	Small	284
Toyota Corolla	S.W.	Small	37	Suzuki Swift	2Dr.	Small	275
Toyota Cressida	4Dr.	Midsize	37	Chevrolet Camaro Conv.	Sp.	Midsize	250
Mazda 929	4Dr.	Midsize	37	Hyundai Sonata	4Dr.	Midsize	239
Oldsmobile Cutlass Supreme	2Dr.	Midsize	38	Cadillac Eldorado	Lux.	Midsize	232
Chevrolet Cavalier	4Dr.	Midsize	38	Chevrolet Cavalier Conv.	2Dr.	Midsize	208
Ford Tempo	4Dr.	Midsize	38	Pontiac Firebird	Sp.	Midsize	206

Results are relative - 100 represents the average for all passenger cars.
S.W. = Station Wagon; P.V. = Passenger Van; Sp. = Sports; Lux = Luxury
** 1990-91 models only.

Source: *Insurance Theft Report, April 1992*, Highway Loss Data Institute, (Arlington, VA, 1992)

thefts from buildings and thefts from motor vehicles averaged $788 and $544, respectively, while thefts of motor vehicle accessories averaged $305. The average loss for bicycle theft was $233 per incident. The largest proportion of the larcenies was thefts of motor vehicle parts and contents (37 percent), while thefts from buildings and shoplifting accounted for 14 percent and 17 percent each, respectively, and bicycles accounted for 6 percent (Figure 2.4).

Arrests

Only 20 percent of the larceny-thefts that occurred in 1991 were cleared. Twenty-three percent of those arrested for larceny-theft were under 18 years of age, while 44 percent were under 21 years old. Females accounted for a significant proportion (32 percent) of all those arrested for this crime. Whites made up 67 percent of the total arrested for larceny-theft, while blacks accounted for 31 percent.

MOTOR VEHICLE THEFT

The FBI defines motor vehicle theft as, "the theft or attempted theft of a motor vehicle." In 1991, there were 1,661,738 reported cases of auto theft in the United States, a rate of 659 per 100,000 inhabitants, a 2 percent increase over 1990, and 29 percent above that of 1987. In metropolitan areas, the motor vehicle theft rate was 803 offenses per 100,000 people. Cities outside metropolitan areas had a much lower rate of 233 per 100,000, while in rural areas the theft rate was only 120, indicating that this offense is primarily a large-city problem. The most likely victims are also those who can least afford it. The Bureau of Justice Statistics found that black and Hispanic households headed by people under age 25 in center-city multiple or low-income housing were the most common victims. This is the only major crime that is most common in the Northeast at 795 per 100,000, followed by the West (791), the South (603), and the Midwest (507).

TABLE 2.16

Motor Vehicle Theft, 1991

[Percent distribution by region]

Region	Total[1]	Autos	Trucks and buses	Other vehicles
Total	100.0	79.7	14.7	5.6
Northeastern States	100.0	92.7	4.4	2.9
Midwestern States	100.0	83.0	10.5	6.5
Southern States	100.0	74.7	19.0	6.3
Western States	100.0	71.4	21.9	6.8

[1]Because of rounding, percentages may not add to totals.

Source: *Crime in the United States, 1991*, Federal Bureau of Investigation, (WDC, 1992)

Loss

The total estimated monetary loss from motor vehicle theft in 1991 exceeded $8 billion with an average value per stolen vehicle of $4,983. Many stolen cars are recovered, and insurance covers a portion of the loss for the victim. The Highway Loss Data Institute lists the cars for which the most theft claims are made. Of the 1989 to 1991 model years, seven of the ten cars most frequently reported stolen were Volkswagen models, which are believed to have been stolen because of a high quality radio mounted on a slide-out bracket. The top 10 also included three Cadillac models (Table 2.15).

Type of Theft

Eighty percent of stolen vehicles were cars, while 15 percent were trucks and buses. Lifestyle differences are evident in the accompanying chart which shows that nearly one quarter of the vehicles stolen in the West are trucks (buses probably play a small role in the numbers), closely followed by the South (nineteen percent). In the Northeast, 93 percent of stolen vehicles were cars (Table 2.16). Auto theft has created a multi-billion dollar-a-year industry in antitheft devices, including alarms and identification systems.

TABLE 2.17

Arson, Type of Property, 1991

[11,706 agencies; 1991 estimated population 195,914,000]

Property classification	Number of offenses	Percent distribution[1]
Total	86,147	100.0
Total structure	46,478	54.0
Single occupancy residential	20,233	23.5
Other residential	8,062	9.4
Storage	4,384	5.1
Industrial/manufacturing	750	.9
Other commercial	5,226	6.1
Community/public	4,701	5.5
Other structure	3,122	3.6
Total mobile	23,595	27.4
Motor vehicles	21,917	25.4
Other mobile	1,678	1.9
Other	16,074	18.7

[1]Because of rounding, percentages may not add to totals.

Source: *Crime in the United States, 1991*, Federal Bureau of Investigation, (WDC, 1992)

Arrests

Motor vehicle theft is a young, male crime. Ninety percent of those arrested were male, while 62 percent were under 21 and 43 percent were under 18. Whites were 59 percent of those arrested, and blacks were 38 percent of the arrestees.

ARSON

The FBI defines arson as, "any willful or malicious burning or attempt to burn, with or without intent to defraud, a dwelling house, public building, motor vehicle or aircraft, personal property of another, etc." Not included in the statistics are fires of suspicious or unknown origins. Arson statistics have been collected only since 1979, and only 70 percent of the United States population is represented by agencies that submitted statistics for all 12 months of the year; therefore, these figures do not represent the nation's total arson experience.

Rate

A total of 99,784 arson offenses were reported in 1991, a 1 percent increase from 1990. This is a

TABLE 2.18

Arson, Monetary Value of Property Damaged, 1991

[11,706 agencies; 1991 estimated population 195,914,000]

Property classification	Number of offenses	Average damage
Total	86,147	$11,980
Total structure	46,478	19,763
Single occupancy residential	20,233	13,602
Other residential	8,062	12,964
Storage	4,384	12,388
Industrial/manufacturing	750	84,942
Other commercial	5,226	43,730
Community/public	4,701	36,436
Other structure	3,122	6,712
Total mobile	23,595	4,202
Motor vehicles	21,917	3,920
Other mobile	1,678	7,884
Other	16,074	895

Source: *Crime in the United States, 1991*, Federal Bureau of Investigation, (WDC, 1992)

TABLE 2.19

Arson Offenses Cleared by Arrest,[1] 1991

[11,706 agencies[2]; 1991 estimated population 195,914,000]

Property classification	Number of offenses	Percent cleared by arrest
Total	86,147	18.0
Total structure	46,478	22.0
Single occupancy residential	20,233	22.1
Other residential	8,062	22.7
Storage	4,384	18.3
Industrial/manufacturing	750	14.0
Other commercial	5,226	14.9
Community/public	4,701	36.2
Other structure	3,122	17.0
Total mobile	23,595	9.2
Motor vehicles	21,917	8.8
Other mobile	1,678	14.6
Other	16,074	19.7

[1]Includes offenses cleared by exceptional means.
[2]To be included in this table, it was necessary that arson clearances be reported by property classification.

Source: *Crime in the United States, 1991*, Federal Bureau of Investigation, (WDC, 1992)

rate of 48 offenses per 100,000 people nationwide and 97 per 100,000 in cities versus 22 per 100,000 in rural areas. Arson occurred in the South at 67 per 100,000 inhabitants. The West had the next highest total of 56 per 100,000. The Northeast had a rate of 46, while the Midwest was the lowest at 44 per 100,000.

What is Being Burned

In 1991, structural arson accounted for more than half of the offenses, while mobile property (motor vehicles, trailers, airplanes, boats) accounted for more than one quarter. The remaining 19 percent were directed at other property such as crops, fences, signs, or timber. Of the structural arsons, 61 percent were of residential property, with 19 percent of that total uninhabited at the time of the fire. Ninety-three percent of the mobile property arson involved motor vehicles (Table 2.17). The average cost per incident was $11,980, for a total loss of more than one billion dollars. The overall average for all types of structures was $19,763 (Table 2.18). The lowest number of offenses (750) were against industrial/manufacturing structures, but they showed the highest average loss ($84, 942) per offense.

Arrests

Only 18 percent of all reported arson cases were cleared by arrest (Table 2.19). About 47 percent of those arrested for arson were under the age of 18, a higher percentage of juvenile involvement than for any other Index crime. About 87 percent of those arrested were men. Whites accounted for 77 percent of those arrested and blacks, 21 percent.

CHAPTER III

VICTIMIZATION

A GENERAL DOWNTURN IN CRIME

Despite the media spotlight on the high rate of crime in our cities, the findings from the 1990 survey of the *National Crime Victimization Survey* (NCVS) indicated that overall crime victimization dropped from the 1989 level and was 17 percent below the peak measured in 1981. Preliminary rates for 1991 show a slight increase from the preceding year, but they are still well below the rates of 1981. The National Crime Victimization Survey is a federal statistical study established in early 1972 by the now-defunct Law Enforcement Assistance Administration to measure the annual levels of victimization from criminal activity in the United States. Previously, the survey was known as the *National Crime Survey*, but it has been renamed to emphasize the measurement of victimizations experienced by citizens.

The *National Crime Victimization Survey* was created out of a concern raised by the President's Commission on Law Enforcement and Administration of Justice, commonly known as "The Crime Commission." The nation's primary source of crime information at that time, the FBI's system, provided (and still does) data on crimes reported to law enforcement authorities, but it

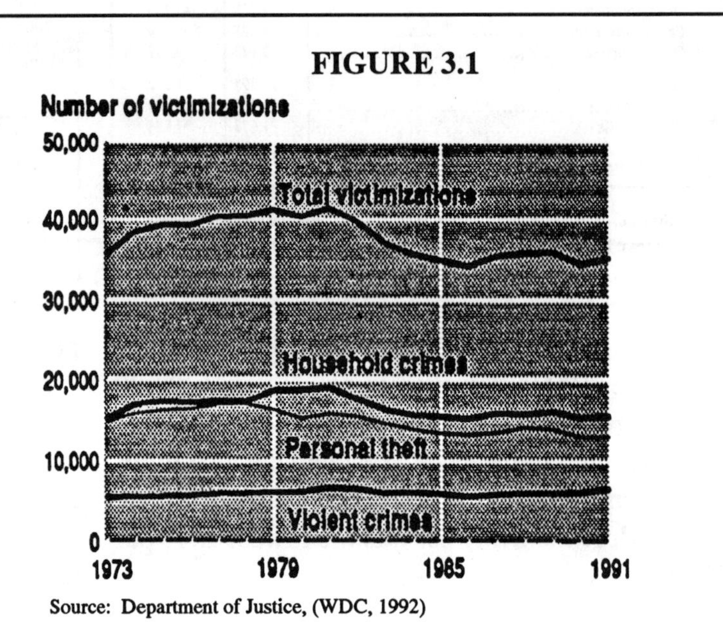

Source: Department of Justice, (WDC, 1992)

TABLE 3.1

Victimization levels, 1973–91

Year	Total	Number of victimizations (in 1,000s)		
		Violent crimes	Personal theft	Household crimes
1973	35,661	5,350	14,970	15,340
1974	38,411	5,510	15,889	17,012
1975	39,266	5,573	16,294	17,400
1976	39,318	5,599	16,519	17,199
1977	40,314	5,902	16,933	17,480
1978	40,412	5,941	17,050	17,421
1979	41,249	6,159	16,382	18,708
1980	40,252	6,130	15,300	18,821
1981	41,454	6,582	15,863	19,009
1982	39,756	6,459	15,553	17,744
1983	37,001	5,903	14,657	16,440
1984	35,544	6,021	13,789	15,733
1985	34,864	5,823	13,474	15,568
1986	34,118	5,515	13,235	15,368
1987	35,336	5,796	13,575	15,966
1988	35,796	5,910	14,056	15,830
1989	35,818	5,861	13,829	16,128
1990	34,404	6,009	12,975	15,419
1991 *	35,054	6,427	12,992	15,640

Source: Department of Justice, (WDC, 1992)

TABLE 3.2

Victimization rates, 1973–91

Year	Number of victimizations per 1,000 persons age 12 and older or per 1,000 households		
	Violent crimes	Personal theft	Household crimes
1973	32.6	91.1	217.8
1974	33.0	95.1	235.7
1975	32.8	96.0	236.5
1976	32.6	96.1	229.5
1977	33.9	97.3	228.8
1978	33.7	96.8	223.4
1979	34.5	91.9	235.3
1980	33.3	83.0	227.4
1981	35.3	85.1	226.0
1982	34.3	82.5	208.2
1983	31.0	76.9	189.8
1984	31.4	71.8	178.7
1985	30.0	69.4	174.4
1986	28.1	67.5	170.0
1987	29.3	68.7	173.9
1988	29.6	70.5	169.6
1989	29.1	68.7	169.9
1990	29.6	63.8	161.0
1991 *	31.3	63.3	161.5

*Figures for 1991 are preliminary.

Source: Department of Justice, (WDC, 1992)

made no attempt to calculate how many crimes go unreported. Consequently, The Crime Commission believed that the *Uniform Crime Reports* did not accurately portray (or underreported) the true volume of crime.

The NCVS is sponsored by the Bureau of Justice Statistics and has been gathering data since 1972. The survey is designed as a comparison to the FBI *Uniform Crime Reports* measure of the levels of criminal victimization of persons and households for the crimes of rape, robbery, assault, burglary, motor vehicle theft, and larceny. Murder is not included because the data is gathered through interviews with the victims. The definitions of these crimes are the same as those established in the FBI Crime Reports. (See Chapter II.)

The most recent *National Crime Victimization Survey*, the 18th in the series, measured criminal victimization in 1990 by interviewing approximately 95,000 people.* Many observers believe the NCVS is a better indicator of the volume and type of crime happening in the United States than the FBI statistics. It is, however, open to error for a number of reasons. The survey depends on people's memory of what happened to them up to six months before. Many times a victim is not sure what happened, even moments after the crime occurred. Victims who have been repeatedly victimized also tend to remember only the most recent event, and the NCVS has found that a disproportionately large number of incidents are reported to have occurred at the end of the time period that the Survey covered. Series incidents (repeated victimizations such as spousal abuse or threatened assault in the neighborhood or school) often cannot be remembered as discrete incidents and the details tend to blur together. In addition, the NCVS limits the collection of data to those over the age of 12, an admittedly arbitrary age selection. All surveys, however, run the risk of error, and the Bureau of Justice Statistics claims a 90 to 95 percent confidence level.

The FBI Uniform Crime Reporting System and the Bureau of Justice Statistics; in the *National Crime Victimization Survey,* are used as the primary sources of statistical information on crime in the United States. While each survey has drawbacks, and virtually all reporting systems do, they each provide valuable insights into the status of crime in the United States. At the same time, there have been some significant differences in their findings, probably the most notable of which have been that while the *Uniform Crime Reports* have reported a 15 percent increase in crime from 1982 to 1991, the NCVS has reported a levelling of crime and, in 1990, a decrease. This difference requires the reader to evaluate both sets of statistics carefully, not relying solely on one or the other.

The NCVS reported that an estimated 35 million victimizations occurred in 1991, 15.6 percent below the 41.5 million victimizations reported in

---

* In April 1992, the Department of Justice released some preliminary figures for 1991. These data will be presented in the chapter, although the detailed statistics come from the complete 1990 report.

TABLE 3.3

Victimization rates for personal and household crimes, 1973-90

	Victimizations per 1,000 persons age 12 or older or per 1,000 households																	
	1973	1974	1975	1976	1977	1978	1979	1980	1981	1982	1983	1984	1985	1986	1987	1988	1989	1990
Personal crimes	123.6	128.1	128.9	128.7	131.2	130.5	126.4	116.3	120.5	116.8	107.9	103.2	99.4	95.6	96.0	100.1	97.8	93.4
Crimes of violence	32.6	33.0	32.8	32.6	33.9	33.7	34.5	33.3	35.3	34.3	31.0	31.4	30.0	28.1	29.3	29.6	29.1	29.6
Rape	1.0	1.0	.9	.8	.9	1.0	1.1	.9	1.0	.8	.8	.9	.7	.7	.8	.8	.7	.6
Robbery	6.7	7.2	6.8	6.5	6.2	5.9	6.3	6.6	7.4	7.1	6.0	5.7	5.1	5.1	5.3	5.3	5.4	5.7
Assault	24.9	24.8	25.2	25.3	26.8	26.9	27.2	25.8	27.0	26.4	24.1	24.7	24.2	22.3	23.3	23.7	23.0	23.3
Aggravated	10.1	10.4	9.6	9.9	10.0	9.7	9.9	9.3	9.6	9.3	8.0	9.0	8.3	7.9	8.0	8.7	8.3	7.9
Simple	14.8	14.4	15.6	15.4	16.8	17.2	17.3	16.5	17.3	17.1	16.2	15.7	15.9	14.4	15.2	15.0	14.7	15.4
Crimes of theft	91.1	95.1	96.0	96.1	97.3	96.8	91.9	83.0	85.1	82.5	76.9	71.8	69.4	67.5	68.7	70.5	68.7	63.8
Personal larceny																		
With contact	3.1	3.1	3.1	2.9	2.7	3.1	2.9	3.0	3.3	3.1	3.0	2.8	2.7	2.7	2.6	2.5	2.7	3.1
Without contact	88.0	92.0	92.9	93.2	94.6	93.6	89.0	80.0	81.9	79.5	74.0	69.1	66.7	64.7	66.1	68.0	66.0	60.7
Household crimes	217.8	235.7	236.5	229.5	228.8	223.4	235.3	227.4	226.0	208.2	189.8	178.7	174.4	170.0	173.9	169.6	169.9	161.0
Household burglary	91.7	93.1	91.7	88.9	88.5	86.0	84.1	84.3	87.9	78.2	70.0	64.1	62.7	61.5	62.1	61.9	56.4	53.8
Household larceny	107.0	123.8	125.4	124.1	123.3	119.9	133.7	126.5	121.0	113.9	105.2	99.4	97.5	93.5	95.7	90.2	94.4	86.7
Motor vehicle theft	19.1	18.8	19.5	16.5	17.0	17.5	17.5	16.7	17.1	16.2	14.6	15.2	14.2	15.0	16.0	17.5	19.2	20.5

Note: Detail may not add to total shown because of rounding.

Source: *Criminal Victimization in the United States, 1990*, Bureau of Justice Statistics, (WDC, 1992)

the peak year of 1981. The rate of personal crime (rapes, robberies, assaults and personal thefts) per 1,000 people 12 years or older in 1990 was 94.6 per 1,000, well below the all-time high of 131 per 1,000 in 1977, and the rate of household crime (burglary, household theft, and motor vehicle theft) was 161.5 per 1,000, much lower than the 1975 high of 237 per 1,000.

TABLE 3.4

Victimization rates, 1973-91

	Number of victimizations per 1,000 persons age 12 and older				
	Rape	Robbery	Aggravated assault	Simple assault	Theft
1973	1.0	6.7	10.1	14.8	91.1
1974	1.0	7.2	10.4	14.4	95.1
1975	.9	6.8	9.6	15.6	96.0
1976	.8	6.5	9.9	15.4	96.1
1977	.9	6.2	10.0	16.8	97.3
1978	1.0	5.9	9.7	17.2	96.8
1979	1.1	6.3	9.9	17.3	91.9
1980	.9	6.6	9.3	16.5	83.0
1981	1.0	7.4	9.6	17.3	85.1
1982	.8	7.1	9.3	17.1	82.5
1983	.8	6.0	8.0	16.2	76.9
1984	.9	5.7	9.0	15.7	71.8
1985	.7	5.1	8.3	15.9	69.4
1986	.7	5.1	7.9	14.4	67.5
1987	.8	5.3	8.0	15.2	68.7
1988	.6	5.3	8.7	15.0	70.5
1989	.7	5.4	8.3	14.7	68.7
1990	.6	5.7	7.9	15.4	63.8
1991*	1.0	5.6	8.1	16.7	63.3

*Preliminary data

Source: Department of Justice, (WDC, 1992)

Decrease in Crime in a Dozen Years

NCVS findings indicate that crime victimization increased only about 8 percent from 1974 to 1981, a period during which the *Uniform Crime Reports* (UCR) and most newspapers and magazines reported crime soaring out of control. Both the UCR and the NCVS found that crime dropped from 1981 to 1984, but the *Uniform Crime Reports* indicated a huge jump in the crime rate in 1985 and 1986. (See Chapter I.) The NCVS, on the other hand, reported a slight increase in the late 1980s, a drop in 1990, and a slight upturn in 1991, representing a 17.7 percent drop in household crimes, and a 2.3 percent drop in violent crimes since 1981. (See Table 3.1 and Figure 3.1.)

The annual victimization rate indicates the estimated number of crimes per either 1,000 persons age 12 and over or 1,000 households. The rate of personal crime in 1990 was significantly lower than any year other than 1986. While crimes of violence rose slightly in 1990 and 1991, there was a drop in the personal theft rate from 68.7 per 1,000 in 1989 to 63.3 thefts per 1,000 persons in 1991. This is the lowest rate the

NCVS has ever recorded. Similarly, the rate of household crime (161.5 per 1,000 households) was virtually the same as the all time low of 161 crimes per 1,000 households in 1990. (See Tables 3.2 and 3.3.)

TYPES OF CRIME

About 56 percent of all crimes reported to the NCVS in 1990 were personal crimes in which the victim had some contact with his or her assailant. More than three out of 10 of these personal crimes were crimes of violence (31.6 percent), usually assault, where the victim, if not hurt, was usually at risk of being hurt. Almost all of the household victimization consisted of either burglary (33 percent) or larceny (54 percent).

In 1991, the victimization rate for crimes of violence was 31.3 per 1,000 people, and crimes of theft, 63.3 per 1,000 people. The rate of household victimization was 161.5 per 1,000 households with household burglary at 52.6, household larceny at 88.8, and car theft at 20.1 per 1,000 people. (See Table 3.4.)

The most likely victims of crime are male, under 25, poor, not well educated, residents of larger cities, and renters. With the obvious exception of rape and purse snatching, men were more likely to be victimized than women. When considering a violent offense, like aggravated assault, men were more than twice as likely to be victims. Men and women were equally likely to be victims of theft (Table 3.5). The highest victimization rates occurred among those between the ages of 12 and 24 for both crimes of violence and crimes of theft. Crime rates in both categories dropped considerably for each age group over 24 years of age, the steepest decline being for those over 65 years old, reflecting their sometimes severely restricted lifestyles. (Table 3.6).

TABLE 3.5

Victimization rates for persons age 12 and over, by type of crime and sex of victims

Type of crime	Rate per 1,000 persons age 12 or older		
	Both sexes	Male	Female
All personal crimes	93.4	105.1	82.6
Crimes of violence	29.6	37.5	22.2
Completed	11.9	14.1	9.9
Attempted	17.6	23.4	12.3
Rape	0.6	0.2	1.0
Completed	0.3	0.1 *	0.5
Attempted	0.3	0.1 *	0.5
Robbery	5.7	7.5	3.9
Completed	3.9	5.0	3.0
With injury	1.4	1.6	1.2
From serious assault	0.6	0.9	0.4
From minor assault	0.8	0.8	0.8
Without injury	2.5	3.4	1.7
Attempted	1.7	2.5	1.0
With injury	0.5	0.8	0.3
From serious assault	0.2	0.4	0.0 *
From minor assault	0.3	0.3	0.3
Without injury	1.2	1.8	0.6
Assault	23.3	29.8	17.2
Aggravated	7.9	11.5	4.5
Completed with injury	3.1	4.2	2.1
Attempted with weapon	4.8	7.3	2.4
Simple	15.4	18.3	12.7
Completed with injury	4.6	4.8	4.4
Attempted without weapon	10.8	13.5	8.4
Crimes of theft	63.8	67.5	60.4
Completed	59.8	63.3	56.6
Attempted	4.0	4.3	3.8
Personal larceny with contact	3.1	2.6	3.7
Purse snatching	0.8	0.0 *	1.6
Pocket picking	2.3	2.6	2.1
Personal larceny without contact	60.7	65.0	56.7
Completed	56.9	60.7	53.3
Less than $50	22.6	22.0	23.1
$50 or more	31.7	36.5	27.3
Amount not available	2.5	2.1	2.9
Attempted	3.8	4.3	3.4
Population age 12 and over	203,273,870	97,836,860	105,437,010

Note: Detail may not add to total shown because of rounding.
* Estimate is based on about 10 or fewer sample cases.

Source: *Criminal Victimization in the United States, 1990,* Bureau of Justice Statistics, (WDC, 1992)

Black Victimization

During 1990, the violent crime victimization rate for blacks over 12 years old was 39.7 per 1,000 blacks compared to 28.2 per 1,000 whites. Black men were more often victims of violent crimes, especially robbery and aggravated assault with injury, than black females or either male or female whites. Both blacks and whites were equally victimized by crimes of theft. In fact, black women were the least victimized at 55.9 per 1,000 black females compared to a rate of 60.9 for white females. In the case of robberies, black males (18.1 per 1,000) and black females (8.8 per 1,000) suffered more than twice as much victimization as white males (6.0 per 1,000) and white females, the least often robbed at 3.2 per 1,000. (See Table 3.7.)

TABLE 3.6

Victimization rates for persons age 12 and over, by sex and age of victims and type of crime

Sex and age	Total population	Crimes of violence	Completed violent crimes	Attempted violent crimes	Rape	Robbery Total	Robbery With injury	Robbery Without injury	Assault Total	Assault Aggravated
Male										
12–15	6,899,480	92.2	37.5	54.7	0.3 *	20.6	4.5	16.1	71.3	20.6
16–19	6,930,150	94.7	34.3	60.3	0.4 *	12.5	2.0 *	10.5	81.8	39.6
20–24	8,815,790	78.4	30.4	47.9	0.2 *	17.1	4.7	12.5	61.0	23.5
25–34	21,437,380	44.3	16.7	27.7	0.4 *	9.7	3.7	6.0	34.2	13.8
35–49	25,580,960	21.6	7.8	13.8	0.3 *	3.7	1.6	2.2	17.6	6.2
50–64	15,689,980	8.9	2.4	6.5	0.0 *	2.0	0.6 *	1.3 *	6.9	2.0
65 and over	12,483,090	3.7	1.6 *	2.1	0.0 *	1.7	1.1 *	0.6 *	2.0	1.4 *
Female										
12–15	6,569,620	44.1	16.5	27.6	3.4	6.3	2.3 *	4.0	34.4	6.9
16–19	6,808,710	53.8	22.7	31.1	2.5 *	6.5	2.1 *	4.4	44.8	12.6
20–24	9,201,300	48.5	26.6	22.0	3.5	7.8	2.5	5.2	37.3	10.5
25–34	21,740,780	28.6	12.9	15.8	0.9 *	5.6	2.3	3.2	22.2	6.0
35–49	26,481,020	16.8	6.7	10.1	0.5 *	2.8	1.4	1.4	13.6	3.2
50–64	17,196,280	6.3	2.8	3.5	0.1 *	2.3	0.9 *	1.4	3.9	0.8 *
65 and over	17,437,250	3.3	1.6	1.7	0.1 *	1.3	0.5 *	0.8 *	1.9	0.9 *

Note: Detail may not add to total shown because of rounding.

* Estimate is based on about 10 or fewer sample cases.

Source: *Criminal Victimization in the United States, 1990,* Bureau of Justice Statistics, (WDC, 1992)

TABLE 3.7

Victimization rates for persons age 12 and over, by type of crime and sex and race of victims

Type of crime	Rate per 1,000 persons age 12 and over Male White	Male Black	Female White	Female Black
All personal crimes	102.1	127.1	82.2	84.0
Crimes of violence	35.5	53.3	21.3	26.2
Completed	13.0	23.3	9.0	16.2
Attempted	22.6	30.0	12.3	12.0
Rape	0.3	0.2 *	1.0	1.0 *
Robbery	6.0	18.1	3.2	8.8
Completed	3.9	12.2	2.2	6.1
With injury	1.3	3.2	1.0	2.6
Without injury	2.6	8.9	1.2	5.5
Attempted	2.1	5.9	1.0	0.7 *
With injury	0.7	1.5 *	0.3	0.4 *
Without injury	1.4	4.4	0.7	0.3 *
Assault	29.3	35.1	17.1	18.4
Aggravated	10.6	20.2	4.4	5.4
Completed with injury	3.7	8.7	1.9	3.0
Attempted with weapon	6.8	11.5	2.5	2.5
Simple	18.7	14.9	12.8	13.0
Completed with injury	5.2	2.5	4.4	4.5
Attempted without weapon	13.5	12.4	8.3	8.5
Crimes of theft	66.5	73.7	60.9	55.9
Completed	62.1	70.2	56.9	53.1
Attempted	4.4	3.5	4.0	2.8
Personal larceny with contact	2.1	6.0	3.5	4.7
Personal larceny without contact	64.4	67.7	57.4	51.2
Completed	60.0	64.2	53.8	48.9
Attempted	4.4	3.5	3.6	2.3
Population age 12 and over	83,895,500	10,847,420	89,213,650	12,881,300

Note: Detail may not add to total shown because of rounding.

* Estimate is based on about 10 or fewer sample cases.

Source: *Criminal Victimization in the United States, 1990,* Bureau of Justice Statistics, (WDC, 1992)

subject. When Hispanics are selected as a separate, ethnic category, the NCVS found that, overall, they have a higher victimization rate than non-Hispanics, although this is mainly due to much higher rates of robbery (13.9 per 1,000 Hispanics versus 5.0 per 1,000 non-Hispanics). As shown in Table 3.8, the rate of rape (there were fewer than 10 cases on which to base the rate), simple assault without a weapon, and the overall rate of crimes of theft, especially larceny, were higher for white victims. Like the black population, Hispanics were much more likely to be members of the high risk group of high crime characteristics. They are, on average, younger, poorer, less well educated, and more likely to live in central cities than the rest of the population. Although they suffer a higher rate of violent crime, they appear to be subjected to fewer crimes of theft than are white victims.

Blacks are more likely than whites to be members of the higher risk categories for victimization.

Hispanic Victimization

Hispanic data are usually incorporated into white/black statistics depending on the color of the

VIOLENCE BREEDS VIOLENCE

Being a victim of violence can lead to becoming an offender as an act of retaliation. Juveniles may join a gang or start carrying a weapon as support and protection from the gangs around

TABLE 3.8

Victimization rates for persons age 12 and over, by type of crime and ethnicity of victims

Type of crime	Rate per 1,000 persons age 12 and over		
	Total	Hispanic	Non–Hispanic
All personal crimes	93.4	97.2	92.9
Crimes of violence	29.6	37.3	28.8
Completed	11.9	18.8	11.3
Attempted	17.6	18.5	17.5
Rape	0.6	0.4 *	0.7
Robbery	5.7	13.9	5.0
Completed	3.9	9.7	3.4
With injury	1.4	3.9	1.2
From serious assault	0.6	1.4	0.5
From minor assault	0.8	2.5	0.7
Without injury	2.5	5.8	2.3
Attempted	1.7	4.2	1.5
With injury	0.5	1.2 *	0.5
From serious assault	0.2	0.4 *	0.2
From minor assault	0.3	0.8 *	0.3
Without injury	1.2	3.0	1.0
Assault	23.3	23.1	23.2
Aggravated	7.9	10.1	7.6
Completed with injury	3.1	3.0	3.1
Attempted with weapon	4.8	7.1	4.6
Simple	15.4	13.0	15.6
Completed with injury	4.6	5.9	4.4
Attempted without weapon	10.8	7.1	11.1
Crimes of theft	63.8	59.9	64.0
Completed	59.8	55.5	60.0
Attempted	4.0	4.4	4.0
Personal larceny with contact	3.1	5.7	2.9
Purse snatching	0.8	1.8	0.7
Pocket picking	2.3	3.8	2.2
Personal larceny without contact	60.7	54.2	61.1
Completed	56.9	49.9	57.3
Less than $50	22.6	16.3	23.1
$50 or more	31.7	30.9	31.8
Amount not available	2.5	2.7	2.5
Attempted	3.8	4.3	3.8
Population age 12 and over	203,273,870	16,261,040	186,605,780

Note: Detail may not add to total shown because of rounding.

* Estimate is based on about 10 or fewer sample cases.

being victims of serious crime, while 32 percent of whites did. More than two-thirds (68 percent) who reported being victims also claimed to have committed serious, violent offenses.

Income and Victimization

The very poor experience violent crime at a higher rate (51.2 per 1,000 persons) than those earning $30,000 and above (a rate of 23 to 21 per 1,000). On the other hand, those earning $50,000 or more suffer more crimes of theft (73.6 per 1,000) than any other income group. Theft rates were next highest for the very poor at 67.1 per 1,000 of those earning under $7,500. Those in the $7,500 to $9,999 bracket reported the least number of thefts at a rate of 52.2 per 1,000. (See Table 3.9.) Well-to-do blacks generally remained subject to higher levels of violent crimes than comparable whites; in cases of theft, assault, and larceny, wealthy whites were equal to or greater than blacks in rates of victimization (Table 3.10). In 1990, for those earning more than $10,000 per year, blacks were subjected to more than twice as much motor vehicle theft than were whites. Blacks who earned $30,000 to $49,999 or over $50,000 reported a rate of 60.8 and 74.1 per 1,000 persons, respectively. The comparable white rates were 18.7 and 20.1 per 1,000 (Table 3.11).

Relationship to the Victim

In 61 percent of the crimes of violence, the victims did not know the offenders. Nearly 82 percent of the robberies were committed by strangers, while in 64.6 percent of the aggravated assaults and 52.3 percent of the simple assaults, the victims did not know their attackers (Figure 3.2). As shown in Table 3.12, of the 43 percent who were victimized by someone they knew, those persons (in single-offender victimizations) were, in most cases, well-known to the victims (66.4 percent). In 19.6 percent of the cases, the offender and the

them. Youths who have been abused at home or perceive abuse from the system can turn to violence as an act of power against a situation in which they have felt powerless. Simon I. Singer, in "Victims of Subcultural Violence and Their Criminal Behavior: Subcultural Theory and Beyond" (1986, *Violence and Victims*, N.Y: Springer Publishing), looked at the records of 975 males originally studied in a survey of all males born in 1945 in Philadelphia ("Delinquency in a Birth Cohort"). Singer found that offenders who had been victims of a serious assault or theft with injury had a 64 percent rate of official arrests compared to 21 percent of nonvictims. Blacks were also far more likely than whites to experience an adult arrest — 48 percent versus 18 percent, while gang members had an official arrest record in 46 percent of the cases compared to only 20 percent of non-gang members. Forty-six percent of blacks also reported

TABLE 3.9

Victimization rates for persons age 12 and over, by type of crime and annual family income of victims

Type of crime	Less than $7,500	$7,500–$9,999	$10,000–$14,999	$15,000–$24,999	$25,000–$29,999	$30,000–$49,999	$50,000 or more
				Rate per 1,000 persons age 12 and over			
All personal crimes	118.3	89.2	96.6	91.2	85.4	85.2	94.5
Crimes of violence	51.2	37.0	37.7	29.8	25.0	23.1	20.9
Completed	25.2	18.0	14.9	11.4	9.4	8.4	7.3
Attempted	26.0	19.0	22.8	18.4	15.6	14.7	13.6
Rape	1.2	0.2 *	1.2	0.8	0.4 *	0.4 *	0.5 *
Robbery	11.4	8.8	7.9	5.6	3.4	3.4	3.2
Completed	8.7	7.0	5.5	3.9	2.2	2.3	1.9
With injury	3.1	3.8	1.7	1.6	0.8 *	0.7	0.4 *
From serious assault	1.5	1.0 *	0.8 *	0.7	0.1 *	0.4 *	0.3 *
From minor assault	1.5	2.8	0.9 *	1.0	0.7 *	0.3 *	0.1 *
Without injury	5.6	3.2	3.8	2.2	1.4	1.6	1.5
Attempted	2.7	1.9 *	2.3	1.8	1.2 *	1.1	1.3
With injury	1.1	0.4 *	0.8 *	0.7	0.2 *	0.3 *	0.2 *
From serious assault	0.5 *	0.0 *	0.3 *	0.2 *	0.2 *	0.0 *	0.1 *
From minor assault	0.6 *	0.4 *	0.4 *	0.5 *	0.0 *	0.3 *	0.1 *
Without injury	1.6	1.5 *	1.6	1.1	0.9 *	0.8	1.1
Assault	38.5	27.9	28.7	23.4	21.2	19.3	17.2
Aggravated	13.9	10.2	12.4	7.8	6.3	5.9	4.2
Completed with injury	6.4	5.3	4.4	2.9	1.7	2.2	1.7
Attempted with weapon	7.5	4.9	8.0	4.9	4.6	3.6	2.5
Simple	24.7	17.7	16.2	15.6	14.8	13.4	13.0
Completed with injury	9.7	5.8	4.4	4.3	5.1	3.7	3.5
Attempted without weapon	15.0	12.0	11.9	11.3	9.8	9.7	9.6
Crimes of theft	67.1	52.2	58.9	61.4	60.4	62.0	73.6
Completed	63.3	48.1	54.5	57.7	57.0	58.2	68.8
Attempted	3.8	4.2	4.3	3.7	3.4	3.8	4.7
Personal larceny with contact	5.8	3.6	2.5	3.3	3.1	1.9	3.2
Purse snatching	1.4	0.9 *	0.8 *	0.6	0.6 *	0.7	0.5 *
Pocket picking	4.3	2.6	1.8	2.7	2.5	1.3	2.7
Personal larceny without contact	61.3	48.6	56.3	58.0	57.3	60.1	70.3
Completed	57.6	44.5	52.3	54.6	54.0	56.4	65.9
Less than $50	21.9	19.1	21.5	22.6	21.0	24.7	22.8
$50 or more	32.5	22.9	29.2	30.3	31.2	29.5	40.2
Amount not available	3.2	2.6	1.6	1.7	1.8	2.2	2.8
Attempted	3.7	4.2	4.0	3.4	3.3	3.7	4.4
Population age 12 and over	18,952,170	8,109,400	19,087,540	35,152,180	14,368,140	45,852,880	32,486,220

Note: Detail may not add to total shown because of rounding.
Excludes data on persons whose family income level was not ascertained.
* Estimate is based on about 10 or fewer sample cases.

Source: *Criminal Victimization in the United States, 1990*, Bureau of Justice Statistics, (WDC, 1992)

TABLE 3.10

Victimization rates for persons age 12 and over, by race and annual family income of victims and type of crime

Race and income	Total population	Crimes of violence	Completed violent crimes	Attempted violent crimes	Rape	Robbery Total	Robbery With injury	Robbery Without injury	Assault Total	Assault Aggravated	Assault Simple	Crimes of theft	Completed theft	Attempted theft	Personal larceny With contact	Personal larceny Without contact
												Rate per 1,000 persons age 12 and over				
White																
Less than $7,500	13,460,520	49.5	22.7	26.8	1.3 *	7.9	3.2	4.7	40.3	13.5	26.8	70.9	66.1	4.8	4.3	66.6
$7,500–$9,999	6,310,100	36.6	18.6	18.0	0.3 *	8.1	3.9	4.2	28.2	10.1	18.0	55.0	50.1	4.8	3.6	51.3
$10,000–$14,999	15,745,200	35.0	13.3	21.7	1.4	6.8	2.1	4.7	26.8	11.2	15.6	56.1	51.7	4.4	2.6	53.6
$15,000–$24,999	29,894,930	29.5	11.0	18.5	0.7	5.0	2.2	2.7	23.8	7.4	16.4	60.9	57.1	3.8	3.2	57.7
$25,000–$29,999	12,695,160	24.3	9.1	15.2	0.3 *	2.8	0.9 *	1.8	21.2	6.4	14.8	58.0	54.4	3.5	2.9	55.1
$30,000–$49,999	41,067,010	23.1	8.4	14.7	0.5 *	2.8	0.9	1.9	19.8	5.8	14.0	61.7	57.8	4.1	1.7	60.1
$50,000 or more	29,782,020	20.7	6.9	13.8	0.4 *	2.8	0.5 *	2.2	17.5	3.9	13.6	73.6	68.9	4.7	3.2	70.4
Black																
Less than $7,500	4,852,550	54.9	31.7	23.2	1.3 *	19.5	5.9	13.6	34.1	15.6	18.5	50.8	48.7	1.3 *	8.0	41.9
$7,500–$9,999	1,526,540	38.1	16.3	21.8	0.0 *	11.0 *	3.7 *	7.3	27.1	11.0 *	16.1	41.7	38.7	2.1 *	3.9 *	37.8
$10,000–$14,999	2,818,840	51.5	26.4	25.1	0.0 *	14.1	4.5 *	9.6	37.4	18.9	17.5	73.5	68.0	4.5 *	2.7 *	70.8
$15,000–$24,999	4,332,130	30.7	14.1	16.7	0.5 *	10.4	2.8 *	7.6	18.9	10.3	8.6	58.5	54.5	2.9 *	3.3 *	55.2
$25,000–$29,999	1,390,170	33.5	12.4 *	21.1	0.0 *	9.1 *	2.8 *	6.3	24.4	7.0 *	17.4	75.0	71.7	3.3 *	3.2 *	71.8
$30,000–$49,999	3,322,850	23.1	7.9	15.3	0.0 *	9.5	1.5 *	8.0	13.6	5.5 *	8.2	72.5	71.2	1.3 *	6.2	66.3
$50,000 or more	1,521,220	29.1	18.7	10.4 *	2.7 *	9.4 *	1.8 *	7.6	17.0	10.1 *	6.9 *	70.9	67.2	3.7 *	3.5 *	67.5

Note: Detail may not add to total shown because of rounding.
* Estimate is based on about 10 or fewer sample cases.

Source: *Criminal Victimization in the United States, 1990*, Bureau of Justice Statistics, (WDC, 1992)

TABLE 3.11

Victimization rates by race of head of household, annual family income, and type of theft

| | | Rate per 1,000 households | | |
Race and income	Total households	All vehicle thefts	Completed theft	Attempted theft
White				
Less than $7,500	8,575,920	13.2	7.0	6.2
$7,500–$9,999	3,627,370	14.9	9.3	5.6
$10,000–$14,999	8,313,950	17.8	13.2	4.6
$15,000–$24,999	14,688,700	15.8	9.9	5.9
$25,000–$29,999	5,870,100	18.3	11.9	6.4
$30,000–$49,999	17,540,100	18.7	12.4	6.4
$50,000 or more	11,897,250	20.1	12.9	7.2
Black				
Less than $7,500	2,816,600	12.7	8.9	3.8 *
$7,500–$9,999	711,840	10.7 *	10.7 *	0.0 *
$10,000–$14,999	1,316,710	41.2	28.5	12.6 *
$15,000–$24,999	1,852,320	43.0	30.0	13.1
$25,000–$29,999	542,360	53.2	29.6 *	23.6 *
$30,000–$49,999	1,341,420	60.8	30.0	30.8
$50,000 or more	552,540	74.1	35.3 *	38.8

Note: Detail may not add to total shown because of rounding.
Excludes data on families whose income level was not ascertained.
* Estimate is based on about 10 or fewer sample cases.

Source: *Criminal Victimization in the United States, 1990*, Bureau of Justice Statistics, (WDC, 1992)

FIGURE 3.2

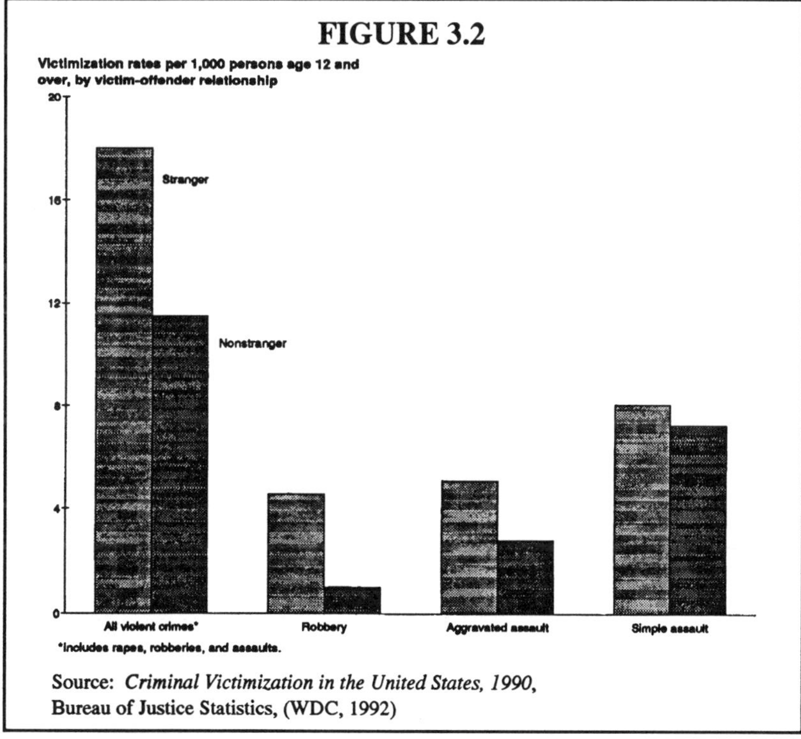

Source: *Criminal Victimization in the United States, 1990*, Bureau of Justice Statistics, (WDC, 1992)

CHARACTERISTICS OF THE CRIME

What Time Does It Happen?

Crime happens at all times of the day or night. When it happens, however, can be affected by whether the offender is armed or not and whether or not the victim is a stranger. Armed robberies (63.7 percent) and assaults (59.1 percent) are more likely to happen at night. Crimes involving nonstrangers happen more frequently in the day, except for rape, which is reported to have occurred at night in three-quarters of the cases. Far more violent crimes were committed from 6 p.m. to midnight than from midnight to 6 a.m., regardless of whether or not they were committed by armed offenders or whether or not the offenders were strangers. (See Tables 3.13 and 3.14.)

Where Does It Happen?

Just as a crime may happen at any time, it may also occur in any place. Most violent crimes happened on the street (24.2 percent). The next most frequent occurrence is on a person's own property or in a friend's, relative's, or neighbor's home (20.7 percent). Nearly one in 10 violent crimes occurred on school property (9.8 percent). A high percentage of rapes took place in the home (35 percent) or on the street,

victim were related, most often a spouse (7.5 percent) or ex-spouse (3.6 percent). In instances where the victim was attacked by more than one person (multiple-offender attacks), the offenders were almost always casual acquaintances (56.4 percent) or well-known, but not related to the victim (39.1 percent).

not near one's own or a friend's home (17.9 percent). Most robberies took place on the street (47 percent), with an additional 12.7 percent occurring in a parking lot or garage. The home, which generally represents safety and security in the American mind, is the second most common crime site, after the street. This is logical, however, since

TABLE 3.12

Percent distribution of single—offender victimizations, by type of crime and detailed victim—offender relationship

| Type of crime | Number of single—offender victimizations | Total | Percent of single—offender victimizations | | | | | | | Well known, not related[1] | Casual acquaintance |
| | | | Related | | | | | | | | |
			Total	Spouse	Ex-spouse	Parent	Own child	Brother or sister	Other relative		
Crimes of violence	1,931,760	100 %	19.6 %	7.5 %	3.6 %	2.1 %	1.1 %	2.5 %	2.7 %	46.8 %	33.7 %
Completed	803,040	100 %	27.3	13.2	4.4	2.4 *	0.9 *	3.3	3.1	48.0	24.7
Attempted	1,128,720	100 %	14.1	3.5	3.0	2.0	1.2 *	1.9	2.5	45.9	40.0
Rape	73,960	100 %	4.8 *	0.0 *	0.0 *	0.0 *	0.0 *	0.0 *	4.8 *	53.6	41.5
Robbery	152,290	100 %	25.5	7.6 *	2.5 *	3.7 *	2.3 *	4.6 *	4.8 *	51.2	23.4
Completed	116,840	100 %	20.7	6.4 *	3.2 *	0.0 *	1.4 *	3.5 *	6.3 *	52.0	27.3
Attempted	35,450	100 %	41.2 *	11.6 *	0.0 *	16.0 *	5.3 *	8.3 *	0.0 *	48.4 *	10.4 *
Assault	1,705,490	100 %	19.7	7.8	3.8	2.1	1.0 *	2.4	2.5	46.1	34.3
Aggravated	449,720	100 %	25.6	9.3	4.1 *	2.4 *	2.3 *	4.5	2.9 *	39.2	35.2
Simple	1,255,770	100 %	17.6	7.3	3.7	2.0	0.6 *	1.7	2.3	48.5	33.9

Note: Detail may not add to total shown because of rounding.
* Estimate is based on about 10 or fewer sample cases.
[1] Includes data on offenders well known to the victim whose relationship could not be ascertained.

TABLE 3.13

Percent distribution of incidents by type of crime, type of offender, and time of occurrence

| Type of crime and offender | Number of incidents | Total | Percent of incidents | | | | | |
| | | | Daytime 6 a.m. — 6 p.m. | Nighttime | | | Not known | Not known and not available |
				Total	6 p.m.— midnight	Midnight — 6 a.m.		
Robbery								
By armed offenders	514,480	100 %	35.2 %	63.7 %	45.7 %	18.0 %	0.0 %*	1.1 %*
By unarmed offenders	394,540	100 %	56.3	43.7	35.9	7.8	0.0 *	0.0 *
Assault								
By armed offenders	1,177,100	100 %	40.4	59.1	40.7	18.4	0.1 *	0.5 *
By unarmed offenders	2,566,320	100 %	52.8	46.7	35.5	11.0	0.3 *	0.4 *

Note: Excludes data in which the presence of a weapon was not ascertained.
Detail may not add to total shown because of rounding.
* Estimate is based on about 10 or fewer sample cases.

TABLE 3.14

Percent distribution of incidents by victim—offender relationship, type of crime, and time of occurrence

| Relationship and type of crime | Number of incidents | Total | Percent of incidents | | | | | |
| | | | Daytime 6 a.m. — 6 p.m. | Nighttime | | | Not known | Not known and not available |
				Total	6 p.m. — midnight	Midnight — 6 a.m.		
Involving strangers								
Crimes of violence	3,105,710	100 %	43.5 %	56.3 %	40.7 %	15.4 %	0.2 %*	0.2 %*
Rape	48,440	100 %	30.2 *	69.8	50.0	19.8 *	0.0 *	0.0 *
Robbery	844,270	100 %	42.4	57.1	43.1	14.0	0.0 *	0.5 *
Assault	2,212,990	100 %	44.2	55.7	39.6	15.8	0.3 *	0.1 *
Involving nonstrangers								
Crimes of violence	2,145,280	100 %	52.5	46.8	35.6	10.9	0.3 *	0.7 *
Rape	76,030	100 %	25.0 *	75.0	38.2	34.4	2.4 *	0.0 *
Robbery	192,570	100 %	50.8	48.2	35.0	13.2	0.0 *	1.0 *
Assault	1,876,670	100 %	53.8	45.5	35.6	9.7	0.2 *	0.7 *

Note: Detail may not add to total shown because of rounding.
* Estimate is based on about 10 or fewer sample cases.

Source of above tables: *Criminal Victimization in the United States, 1990*, Bureau of Justice Statistics, (WDC, 1992)

TABLE 3.15

Percent distribution of incidents, by type of crime and place of occurrence

Type of crime	Number of incidents	Percent of incidents						
		Total	At or in respondent's home	Near home	On the street near home	At, in, or near a friend's relative's or neighbor's home	On street near a friend's relative's or neighbor's home	Inside a restaurant, bar, or nightclub
Crimes of violence	5,251,000	100 %	13.1 %	7.1 %	4.0 %	7.6 %	1.6 %	5.2 %
Completed	2,137,840	100 %	16.9	4.7	3.2	9.1	1.5	4.8
Attempted	3,113,150	100 %	10.5	8.7	4.5	6.5	1.6	5.5
Rape	124,480	100 %	35.0	10.3 *	2.0 *	10.5 *	0.0 *	1.5 *
Robbery	1,036,840	100 %	9.4	3.6	3.8	4.8	2.0	1.8 *
Completed	724,950	100 %	10.8	2.6 *	3.9	4.3	1.7 *	2.0 *
With injury	265,630	100 %	11.6	2.7 *	6.5 *	8.0	0.0 *	0.9 *
Without injury	459,310	100 %	10.3	2.6 *	2.4 *	2.1 *	2.6 *	2.6 *
Attempted	311,890	100 %	6.3 *	5.8 *	3.6 *	6.1 *	2.9 *	1.3 *
With injury	103,890	100 %	8.4 *	8.1 *	1.8 *	5.5 *	2.0 *	1.0 *
Without injury	208,000	100 %	5.2 *	4.7 *	4.6 *	6.3 *	3.3 *	1.4 *
Assault	4,089,660	100 %	13.4	7.8	4.1	8.2	1.5	6.2
Aggravated	1,282,850	100 %	11.8	7.7	4.5	10.1	2.0	5.3
Simple	2,806,810	100 %	14.1	7.9	3.9	7.3	1.2	6.6
Personal larceny with contact	632,010	100 %	1.8 *	3.4	3.0 *	1.7 *	0.7 *	5.6
Motor vehicle theft	1,967,540	100 %	1.0 *	21.4	18.2	4.5	4.0	...
Completed	1,226,990	100 %	1.6 *	20.3	17.3	6.1	4.4	...
Attempted	740,550	100 %	0.0 *	23.3	19.9	2.0 *	3.4	...

Type of crime	Percent of incidents						
	Other commercial building	Parking lot or garage	Inside school building	On school property	In apartment yard, park, field, or playground	On the street not near own or friend's home	On public trans-portation or inside station	Other
Crimes of violence	6.6 %	8.7 %	5.3 %	4.5 %	3.7 %	24.2 %	1.8 %	6.6 %
Completed	5.1	9.0	3.5	3.6	3.7	26.7	2.6	5.6
Attempted	7.7	8.5	6.5	5.2	3.7	22.4	1.3	7.4
Rape	7.9 *	3.4 *	0.0 *	0.0 *	0.5 *	17.9	1.6 *	9.4 *
Robbery	3.1	12.7	3.1	1.7 *	3.0	41.2	4.3	5.4
Completed	4.4	11.4	2.8	1.2 *	3.3	42.8	4.7	4.2
With injury	2.2 *	6.5 *	0.8 *	0.3 *	4.8 *	43.3	6.7 *	5.7 *
Without injury	5.6	14.3	4.0 *	1.7 *	2.4 *	42.6	3.6 *	3.4 *
Attempted	0.2 *	15.8	3.9 *	2.8 *	2.5 *	37.3	3.4 *	8.2
With injury	0.0 *	21.0	2.5 *	2.0 *	1.8 *	40.0	3.1 *	2.8 *
Without injury	0.3 *	13.2	4.6 *	3.2 *	2.9 *	35.9	3.5 *	11.0
Assault	7.5	7.9	6.0	5.4	4.0	20.0	1.2	6.9
Aggravated	6.6	9.6	2.3	3.9	4.8	22.1	1.5 *	7.7
Simple	7.9	7.1	7.7	6.1	3.6	19.1	1.0	6.5
Personal larceny with contact	20.9	6.5	3.8	1.6 *	0.8 *	23.0	18.5	8.6
Motor vehicle theft	0.4 *	33.6	...	2.0	1.2	11.5	0.0 *	2.0
Completed	0.7 *	32.8	...	2.3	1.4 *	11.4	0.0 *	1.8
Attempted	0.0 *	34.9	...	1.6 *	1.1 *	11.8	0.0 *	2.2 *

Note: Detail may not add to total shown because of rounding.
* Estimate is based on about 10 or fewer sample cases.
... Not applicable

Source: *Criminal Victimization in the United States, 1990*, Bureau of Justice Statistics, (WDC, 1992)

people spend the majority of their time either in the streets near their houses or in their homes. (See Table 3.15.)

The Use of Weapons

In 1990, less than a third of violent crimes (32.6 percent) involved the use of a weapon. Weapons were used less frequently in rapes (17.2 percent) and more frequently in robberies (49.6 percent). Weapons were used more frequently when strangers were the offenders (39.3 percent) than when nonstrangers were the offenders (22.9 percent). (See Table 3.16.) When a weapon was used in a crime, 25.7 percent involved knives, 32.9 percent involved firearms of different kinds including the 27.4 percent which were handguns, and 41.4 percent involved weapons other than knives or guns such as rocks, sticks, brass knuckles, fists, and feet (Table 3.17).

Did the Victim Resist?

In 1990, slightly more women (73.5 percent) than men (70.5 percent) took some kind of self-protective measure in cases of violent crime. These measures included trying to reason with the offender, fleeing, screaming for help, hitting, kick-

35

TABLE 3.16

Percent of incidents in which offenders used weapons by type of crime and victim–offender relationship

| | Percent of all incidents involving weapons | | |
Type of crime	All incidents	Involving strangers	Involving nonstrangers
Crimes of violence	**32.6 %**	**39.3 %**	**22.9 %**
Completed	36.8	45.7	24.6
Attempted	29.8	35.1	21.7
Rape	17.2	34.6 *	6.1 *
Robbery	49.6	53.4	32.9
Completed	50.5	55.2	32.4
With injury	34.9	37.7	27.4 *
Without injury	59.6	64.0	37.2
Attempted	47.5	49.6	34.6 *
With injury	38.6	37.7	41.7 *
Without injury	52.0	54.9	27.4 *
Assault[1]	28.8	34.0	22.6
Aggravated	91.8	94.1	87.9

* Estimate is based on about 10 or fewer sample cases.
[1] Includes data on simple assault, which by definition does not involve the use of a weapon.

Source: *Criminal Victimization in the United States, 1990*, Bureau of Justice Statistics, (WDC, 1992)

3.18.) Of those victims who thought their self-protective measures were helpful, nearly half thought they avoided injury, and almost a fifth scared off their offender (Table 3.19). The majority (64.8 percent) of those who did not think their self-protective measures were helpful, however, thought they had made the attacker more aggressive and angrier and 15.6 percent estimated that this had lead to greater injury (Table 3.20).

Was the Victim Injured?

As shown in Table 3.21, in a third of the cases of robbery and assault, the victim was injured. Females were somewhat more likely than males to be injured. Elderly robbery victims were more likely to be hurt than younger ones. Those crimes involving strangers were less likely to result in injuries than those crimes involving nonstrangers. Poorer victims were more likely to be injured than wealthier ones. An estimated 10.4 percent of all crimes of violence incurred medical expenses. Of the violent crime victims, nearly half (47.7 percent) received hospital care, 33.6 percent of them in the emergency room without requiring a hospital stay.

ing, or scratching, and using a weapon. It is always hard to know what to do in the midst of a violent crime. Often a victim's reaction is not a conscious one, but an unthinking, instinctive act. Nearly a quarter of the men and one-fifth of the women in 1990 resisted or captured the offender. (See Table

TABLE 3.17

Percent distribution of types of weapons used in incidents by armed offenders, by victim–offender relationship, type of crime, and type of weapon

| | | | Percent of weapon types used | | | | | | | | |
| | | | Firearm | | | | | | | | |
Relationship and type of crime	Total number of weapons used	Total	Total	Hand-gun	Other gun	Gun type unknown	Knife	Sharp object	Blunt object	Other weapon	Type unknown
All incidents											
Crimes of violence	1,830,840	100 %	32.9 %	27.4 %	5.4 %	0.1 %*	25.7 %	2.6 %	18.7 %	15.2 %	4.9 %
Completed	864,640	100 %	29.6	27.0	2.5	0.0 *	27.1	2.3 *	20.8	15.1	5.2
Attempted	966,200	100 %	36.0	27.7	8.0	0.2 *	24.4	2.9	16.9	15.2	4.6
Rape	24,570	100 %	48.3 *	48.3 *	0.0 *	0.0 *	31.7 *	8.1 *	11.9 *	0.0 *	0.0 *
Robbery	537,750	100 %	40.6	38.4	2.3 *	0.0 *	32.0	2.8 *	11.3	10.1	3.2 *
Completed	387,700	100 %	45.8	43.1	2.6 *	0.0 *	32.6	0.7 *	9.7	8.6	2.6 *
With injury	98,540	100 %	36.4	34.9	1.5 *	0.0 *	20.6	0.9 *	24.3	12.6 *	5.1 *
Without injury	289,150	100 %	49.0	46.0	3.0 *	0.0 *	36.7	0.6 *	4.8 *	7.2	1.8 *
Attempted	150,050	100 %	27.3	26.0	1.3 *	0.0 *	30.5	8.2 *	15.2	14.1	4.7 *
With injury	40,050	100 %	4.8 *	4.8 *	0.0 *	0.0 *	31.5 *	10.7 *	25.5 *	27.4 *	0.0 *
Without injury	109,990	100 %	35.4	33.7	1.8 *	0.0 *	30.1	7.3 *	11.4 *	9.3 *	6.4 *
Aggravated assault	1,268,510	100 %	29.4	22.3	6.9	0.2 *	22.9	2.5	22.0	17.6	5.7
Completed with injury	461,530	100 %	15.0	12.5	2.5 *	0.0 *	22.2	3.8 *	30.5	21.1	7.5
Attempted with weapon	806,970	100 %	37.6	28.0	9.3	0.3 *	23.3	1.7 *	17.1	15.6	4.7
Involving strangers											
Crimes of violence	1,319,720	100 %	36.5	31.6	4.7	0.2 *	24.9	2.5	17.6	14.0	4.6
Rape	19,930	100 %*	46.9 *	46.9 *	0.0 *	0.0 *	28.4 *	10.0 *	14.7 *	0.0 *	0.0 *
Robbery	473,960	100 %	44.3	41.7	2.6 *	0.0 *	32.1	3.1 *	9.8	7.8	2.8 *
Aggravated assault	825,810	100 %	31.7	25.5	6.0	0.3 *	20.7	1.9 *	22.2	17.8	5.7
Involving nonstrangers											
Crimes of violence	511,120	100 %	23.9	16.5	7.4	0.0 *	27.6	3.1 *	21.5	18.3	5.8
Rape	4,640	100 %*	54.3 *	54.3 *	0.0 *	0.0 *	45.7 *	0.0 *	0.0 *	0.0 *	0.0 *
Robbery	63,780	100 %	13.3 *	13.3 *	0.0 *	0.0 *	31.4 *	0.0 *	22.3 *	27.1 *	5.9 *
Aggravated assault	442,690	100 %	25.1	16.5	8.6	0.0 *	26.8	3.5 *	21.6	17.2	5.8

Note: Detail may not add to total shown because of rounding.
Some respondents may have cited more than one weapon present.
* Estimate is based on about 10 or fewer sample cases.

Source: *Criminal Victimization in the United States, 1990*, Bureau of Justice Statistics, (WDC, 1992)

TABLE 3.18

Percent distribution of self-protective measures employed by victims, by selected characteristics of victims

Self-protective measure	Percent of self-protective measures				
	Sex			Race	
	Both sexes	Male	Female	White	Black
Total	100.0 %	100.0 %	100.0 %	100.0 %	100.0 %
Attacked offender with weapon	1.3	1.4	1.1	1.3	1.7 *
Attacked offender without weapon	11.1	13.6	7.8	10.8	12.3
Threatened offender with weapon	1.4	1.8	0.9	1.6	1.0 *
Threatened offender without weapon	2.0	2.6	1.2	2.1	2.0
Resisted or captured offender	21.9	24.8	18.1	21.4	24.2
Scared or warned offender	9.5	7.1	12.7	9.7	8.8
Persuaded or appeased offender	13.7	13.6	13.9	14.3	10.4
Ran away or hid	16.6	16.3	16.9	16.1	19.5
Got help or gave alarm	10.9	7.8	15.0	11.3	8.7
Screamed from pain or fear	2.6	1.2	4.5	2.6	2.7
Took another method	8.9	9.7	7.9	9.0	8.6
Total number of self-protective measures	6,635,420	3,772,790	2,862,620	5,429,180	1,051,340

Note: Detail may not add to total shown because of rounding.

Some respondents may have cited more than one self-protective measure employed.

* Estimate is based on about 10 or fewer sample cases.

TABLE 3.19

Percent distribution of victimizations in which self-protective measures taken by victim were helpful

Type of crime	Number of victimizations	Percent of victimizations							
		Total	Avoided injury or greater injury	Scared off offender	Enabled victim to escape	Actions protected property	Actions protected other people	Some other way	Not available
Crimes of violence	3,699,900	100 %	49.0 %	19.0 %	14.6 %	5.4 %	5.3 %	6.5 %	0.1 %*
Rape	89,690	100 %	38.8	21.5 *	37.4	2.2 *	0.0 *	0.0 *	0.0 *
Robbery	624,740	100 %	36.3	23.7	11.1	17.7	4.5	6.6	0.3 *
Assault	2,985,450	100 %	52.0	18.0	14.7	3.0	5.6	6.6	0.1 *
Aggravated	1,095,720	100 %	55.4	13.9	14.8	2.8	7.7	5.4	0.0 *
Simple	1,889,730	100 %	50.0	20.3	14.6	3.1	4.4	7.3	0.2 *

Note: Detail may not add to total shown because of rounding.

* Estimate is based on about 10 or fewer sample cases.

TABLE 3.20

Percent distribution of victimizations in which self-protective measures taken by the victim were harmful

Type of crime	Number of victimizations	Percent of victimizations							
		Total	Made offender angrier, more aggressive	Led to injury or greater injury	Caused greater property damage	Caused others to get hurt	Let offender get away	Made situation worse in other ways	Not available
Crimes of violence[1]	638,280	100 %	64.8 %	15.6 %	2.6 %*	4.1 %	0.3 %*	12.6 %	0.0 %*
Robbery	115,140	100 %	51.8	24.5	7.7 *	0.0 *	0.0 *	16.0 *	0.0 *
Assault	495,210	100 %	68.4	13.0	1.5 *	4.6	0.4 *	12.1	0.0 *
Aggravated	180,310	100 %	61.3	15.4	0.0 *	8.0 *	0.0 *	15.3	0.0 *
Simple	314,890	100 %	72.5	11.5	2.4 *	2.7 *	0.6 *	10.2	0.0 *

Note: Detail may not add to total shown because of rounding.

* Estimate is based on about 10 or fewer sample cases.

[1] Includes data on rape, not shown separately.

Source of above tables: *Criminal Victimization in the United States, 1990*, Bureau of Justice Statistics, (WDC, 1992)

37

TABLE 3.21

Percent of victimizations in which victims sustained physical injury, by selected characteristics of victims and type of crime

Characteristic	Percent of all victims who sustained physical injury		
	Robbery and assault	Robbery	Assault
Sex			
Both sexes	33.2 %	34.5 %	33.0 %
Male	30.5	31.5	30.2
Female	37.8	39.8	37.3
Age			
12–15	30.9	25.0	32.3
16–19	31.8	21.4	33.4
20–24	35.5	28.9	37.2
25–34	34.8	39.7	33.5
35–49	33.1	45.5	30.5
50–64	26.8	38.7	22.0
65 and over	37.6	52.8	26.3 *
Race			
White	33.5	36.0	33.0
Black	33.1	29.0	35.2
Victim–offender relationship			
Strangers	29.7	31.5	29.0
Nonstrangers	38.9	47.8	38.0
Income			
Less than $7,500	40.6	36.8	41.8
$7,500–$9,999	41.4	47.5	39.5
$10,000–$14,999	30.8	31.4	30.6
$15,000–$24,999	32.9	41.3	30.9
$25,000–$29,999	32.2	31.9	32.2
$30,000–$49,999	30.7	29.2	31.0
$50,000 or more	28.3	19.2	29.9

Note: Excludes data on persons whose income level was not ascertained.

* Estimate is based on about 10 or fewer sample cases.

How Much Was Lost?

There are several different ways for a crime victim to consider his or her loss. There are direct costs to the victim that are easy to pinpoint, as well as indirect costs that must be shared by the entire society (the expenses of the criminal justice system or higher insurance premiums). Also to be considered are the differences between material costs (actual loss of property and medical expenses) versus emotional costs which can affect the victim the rest of his or her life, sometimes producing radical and permanent changes in one's lifestyle.

Almost 40 percent of all losses from personal crimes were valued at less than $50. Over 70 percent of all crimes involved a loss of less than $250, although household burglary often ran higher, and 90 percent of completed motor vehicle theft victims listed their losses at more than $500 (Table 3.22). Almost no one recovered their lost goods in cases of personal crime (89.4 percent), an increase over the nearly 75 percent who reported not recov-

TABLE 3.22

Percent distribution of victimizations resulting in economic loss, by race of victims, type of crime, and value of loss

Race and type of crime	Number of victimizations	Total	Percent of victimizations						
			No monetary value	Less than $50	$50–$99	$100–$249	$250–$499	$500 or more	Not known and not available
All races[1]									
All personal crimes	13,941,790	100 %	2.2 %	34.7 %	15.5 %	18.4 %	10.3 %	11.6 %	7.3 %
Crimes of violence[2]	1,412,580	100 %	6.4	29.9	11.2	16.3	8.2	15.3	12.7
Completed	1,090,070	100 %	3.8	32.4	11.9	15.8	8.2	17.8	10.1
Attempted	322,510	100 %	15.4	21.4	8.5	17.8	8.4	7.0	21.5
Robbery	851,090	100 %	1.6 *	31.1	12.0	16.7	9.4	20.1	9.0
Completed	800,510	100 %	0.8 *	32.4	12.1	16.1	9.8	20.3	8.6
With injury	286,020	100 %	0.7 *	29.8	7.5	21.4	12.2	23.1	5.3 *
Without injury	514,480	100 %	0.9 *	33.9	14.6	13.1	8.4	18.7	10.4
Attempted	50,580	100 %	14.6 *	10.8 *	11.3 *	26.1 *	3.6 *	17.0 *	16.6 *
With injury	23,520	100 %	0.0 *	15.0 *	0.0 *	32.9 *	0.0 *	16.5 *	35.6 *
Without injury	27,050	100 %	27.4 *	7.1 *	21.2 *	20.1 *	6.7 *	17.5 *	0.0 *
Assault	542,500	100 %	14.1	28.6	9.5	15.5	6.7	7.7	17.9
Aggravated	242,970	100 %	12.6	27.1	7.9 *	11.7	7.5 *	6.5 *	26.6
Simple	299,520	100 %	15.3	29.9	10.8	18.5	5.9 *	8.7	10.8
Crimes of theft	12,529,200	100 %	1.7	35.2	15.9	18.6	10.6	11.2	6.7
Completed	12,154,550	100 %	1.5	35.8	16.0	18.3	10.6	11.4	6.3
Attempted	374,640	100 %	8.7	15.9	13.8	27.0	9.6	6.0	19.1
Personal larceny with contact	597,640	100 %	0.0 *	29.4	25.5	20.3	10.5	4.1	10.2
Personal larceny without contact	11,931,550	100 %	1.8	35.5	15.5	18.5	10.6	11.6	6.5
All household crimes	14,158,740	100 %	2.9	26.1	11.8	16.8	9.1	23.4	9.9
Completed	12,687,320	100 %	2.0	26.7	11.8	16.8	9.5	25.4	7.8
Attempted	1,471,410	100 %	10.1	21.5	11.7	16.8	5.5	5.9	28.5
Burglary	4,415,740	100 %	4.5	16.8	7.5	14.6	11.0	30.4	15.2
Completed	3,691,040	100 %	2.5	13.8	7.9	15.8	12.7	36.0	11.3
Forcible entry	1,719,580	100 %	2.5	7.2	3.5	9.5	11.2	49.4	16.7
Unlawful entry without force	1,971,460	100 %	2.6	19.6	11.7	21.2	14.0	24.3	6.6
Attempted forcible entry	724,700	100 %	14.8	32.0	5.7	8.6	2.0 *	2.0 *	34.8
Household larceny	7,998,580	100 %	2.3	36.4	15.5	19.7	9.1	10.1	7.0
Completed	7,769,280	100 %	1.9	37.0	15.6	19.6	9.2	10.1	6.6
Attempted	229,290	100 %	13.4	16.4	13.6	21.4	5.4 *	11.0	18.9
Motor vehicle theft	1,744,410	100 %	1.3	2.8	5.8	9.2	4.5	66.2	10.2
Completed	1,226,990	100 %	1.0 *	0.1 *	0.2 *	1.9	2.1	90.3	4.4
Attempted	517,410	100 %	2.0 *	8.9	19.1	26.4	10.4	9.1	24.0

Source of both tables: *Criminal Victimization in the United States, 1990*, Bureau of Justice Statistics, (WDC, 1992)

TABLE 3.23

Percent of victimizations reported to the police, by type of crime, victim–offender relationship, and sex of victims

| | Percent of all victimizations reported to the police | | | | | | | | |
| | All victimizations | | | Involving strangers | | | Involving nonstrangers | | |
Type of crime	Both sexes	Male	Female	Both sexes	Male	Female	Both sexes	Male	Female
Crimes of violence	48.0 %	42.7 %	56.5 %	47.9 %	43.3 %	58.7 %	48.3 %	41.2 %	54.6 %
Completed	60.6	55.4	67.4	60.7	54.5	75.2	60.4	57.7	62.0
Attempted	39.6	35.0	47.7	39.6	36.0	48.1	39.5	32.8	47.4
Rape	53.9	49.3 *	54.9	49.2	54.4 *	45.8 *	57.2	0.0 *	59.0
Robbery	50.1	42.3	64.0	49.8	41.8	66.3	51.3	45.1	57.3
Completed	57.1	49.1	69.7	58.5	49.4	75.4	51.2	47.1	54.7
With injury	67.7	65.5	70.5	67.2	67.1	67.5	69.1	58.8 *	75.6
From serious assault	78.5	84.0	67.2	78.7	86.2	53.1 *	78.0	72.2 *	81.9 *
From minor assault	59.5	44.9	72.0	58.4	43.8	72.4	62.4	48.4 *	71.1 *
Without injury	51.1	41.2	69.1	54.3	41.5	79.9	34.6	39.0 *	29.7 *
Attempted	34.1	28.8	46.8	31.3	27.2	41.8	51.3	40.0 *	68.9 *
With injury	53.6	45.0	71.0	49.4	42.6	63.4 *	69.8 *	54.6 *	100.0 *
From serious assault	46.5	43.5 *	100.0 *	44.0 *	40.0 *	100.0 *	55.7 *	55.7 *	0.0 *
From minor assault	58.3	46.9 *	69.1	53.0	45.7 *	60.3 *	79.9 *	52.7 *	100.0 *
Without injury	25.1	21.8	33.5	23.8	21.5	30.4 *	35.5 *	25.3 *	48.5 *
Assault	47.4	42.7	54.9	47.2	43.6	56.2	47.6	40.9	54.0
Aggravated	58.7	55.1	67.4	56.4	53.9	65.6	62.9	58.0	68.9
Completed with injury	71.1	68.1	76.7	70.7	68.7	77.6	71.6	66.8	76.2
Attempted with weapon	50.7	47.6	59.5	48.7	46.0	58.6	55.3	52.1	60.5
Simple	41.6	34.9	50.5	41.4	36.1	52.3	41.9	33.0	49.3
Completed with injury	56.3	51.0	61.7	55.0	48.4	72.5	57.4	55.5	58.3
Attempted without weapon	35.4	29.2	44.6	36.8	31.5	46.9	33.5	25.5	42.5
Crimes of theft	28.6	27.3	29.9	...	...	...	...	...	...
Completed	28.9	27.7	30.2	...	...	...	...	...	...
Attempted	23.1	20.6	25.7	...	...	...	...	...	...
Personal larceny with contact	37.2	30.3	41.7	38.3	31.1	42.8	12.9 *	20.3 *	0.0 *
Purse snatching	52.1	0.0 *	52.1	52.8	0.0 *	52.8	0.0 *	0.0 *	0.0 *
Completed	59.5	0.0 *	59.5	60.5	0.0 *	60.5	0.0 *	0.0 *	0.0 *
Attempted	30.2 *	0.0 *	30.2 *	30.2 *	0.0 *	30.2 *	0.0 *	0.0 *	0.0 *
Pocket picking	32.0	30.3	33.9	33.0	31.1	35.2	14.0 *	20.3 *	0.0 *
Personal larceny without contact	28.1	27.1	29.2	...	...	...	...	...	...
Completed	28.5	27.6	29.4	...	...	...	...	...	...
Less than $50	13.3	11.6	14.8	...	...	...	...	...	...
$50 or more	39.5	37.2	42.4	...	...	...	...	...	...
Amount not available	25.3	26.3	23.2	...	...	...	...	...	...
Attempted	22.7	20.6	25.2	...	...	...	...	...	...

Note: Detail may not add to total shown because of rounding.

* Estimate is based on about 10 or fewer sample cases.

... Not available. The distinction between stranger and nonstranger is not made for the noncontact larcenies because the victim rarely sees the offender.

Source: *Criminal Victimization in the United States, 1990*, Bureau of Justice Statistics, (WDC, 1992)

ering lost goods in 1987. Auto theft is the only crime where the stolen property is frequently recovered. About 28.6 percent of some portion of the theft was recovered, and in 45 percent of the cases, the entire car was recovered. The figures do not reveal the condition of the car once it was found.

HOW MANY CRIMES ARE REPORTED TO THE POLICE

In 1990, 37.7 percent of all crimes, 48 percent of violent victimizations, 28.6 percent of thefts, and 41.3 percent of all household crimes were reported to the police. Generally, the more serious or costly the crime, the more likely it was to be reported to police; 60.6 completed crimes of violence were reported to the police, while 53.9 percent of rapes, up from 44 percent in 1989, were reported. Crimes resulting in an injury and those that were completed were more likely to be reported than those where no injury took place or those that were attempted, but never completed. The crime most frequently reported was completed motor vehicle theft (94.8 percent), followed by completed robbery with injury from a serious assault (78.5 percent), and aggravated assault result-

TABLE 3.24

Percent distribution of reasons for reporting victimizations to the police, by type of crime

Type of crime	Number of reasons for reporting	Total	Stop or prevent this incident	Needed help due to injury	To recover property	To collect insurance	Prevent further crimes by offender against victim
All personal crimes	5,999,020	100 %	7.6 %	0.8 %	19.3 %	7.5 %	10.6 %
Crimes of violence	2,310,120	100 %	14.8	2.0	4.8	0.5 *	20.1
Completed	1,135,590	100 %	11.6	3.2	8.3	0.7 *	18.5
Attempted	1,174,520	100 %	18.0 *	0.8 *	1.3 *	0.3 *	21.7
Rape	106,760	100 %	8.1	7.0 *	1.8 *	0.0 *	25.2
Robbery	531,890	100 %	8.2	1.4 *	17.9	0.7 *	10.2
Completed	436,610	100 %	6.9	0.8 *	20.4	0.8 *	11.5
With injury	144,590	100 %	5.3 *	2.4 *	23.3	0.0 *	16.6
From serious assault	68,640	100 %	5.5 *	5.0 *	26.7 *	0.0 *	15.2 *
From minor assault	75,940	100 %	5.1 *.	0.0 *	20.2 *	0.0 *	17.8 *
Without injury	294,020	100 %	7.7	0.0 *	18.9	1.3 *	9.0
Attempted	93,270	100 %	14.3 *	4.0 *	6.3 *	0.0 *	4.2 *
With injury	43,560	100 %	8.2 *	4.1 *	8.9 *	0.0 *	0.0 *
From serious assault	14,890 *	100 %*	0.0 *	11.9 *	0.0 *	0.0 *	0.0 *
From minor assault	28,670	100 %	12.5 *	.0.0 *	13.6 *	0.0 *	0.0 *
Without injury	49,710	100 %	19.6 *	4.0 *	3.9 *	0.0 *	7.9 *
Assault	1,671,460	100 %	17.4	1.8	0.8 *	0.5 *	22.9
Aggravated	610,340	100 %	13.0	3.1 *	1.2 *	0.3 *	17.8
Simple	1,061,110	100 %	19.9	1.1 *	0.5 *	0.6 *	25.9
Crimes of theft	3,688,900	100 %	3.0	0.1 *	28.3	11.9	4.6
Completed	3,508,370	100 %	2.9	0.1 *	29.7	11.7	4.4
Attempted	180,520	100 %	6.8 *	1.1 *	1.0 *	15.7	8.2 *
Personal larceny with contact	253,680	100 %	6.3 *	0.0 *	26.2	1.3 *	2.5 *
Personal larceny without contact	3,435,210	100 %	2.8	0.1 *	28.5	12.7	4.8
All household crimes	7,000,960	100 %	4.7	0.1 *	26.8	7.6	10.4
Completed	6,237,730	100 %	4.0	0.1 *	30.0	7.9	9.8
Attempted	763,230	100 %	11.1	0.2 *	1.3 *	5.6	15.2
Burglary	3,006,850	100 %	6.1	0.2 *	21.0	6.1	14.0
Completed	2,668,850	100 %	5.3	0.2 *	23.6	6.6	13.0
Forcible entry	1,647,280	100 %	4.9	0.3 *	23.1	7.0	13.4
Unlawful entry without force	1,021,570	100 %	5.9	0.2 *	24.5	5.9	12.3
Attempted forcible entry	337,990	100 %	12.7	0.0 *	0.5 *	1.7 *	22.1
Household larceny	2,486,180	100 %	3.9	0.0 *	25.7	8.3	9.9
Completed	2,303,180	100 %	3.3	0.0 *	27.6	8.5	9.4
Attempted	182,990	100 %	10.7 *	0.0 *	2.4 *	5.9 *	15.5
Motor vehicle theft	1,507,920	100 %	3.4	0.1 *	40.3	9.5	3.9
Completed	1,265,680	100 %	2.3	0.0 *	47.7	9.3	3.6
Attempted	242,230	100 %	9.0	0.8 *	1.5 *	10.8	5.3 *

Note: Detail may not add to total shown because of rounding.   * Estimate is based on about 10 or fewer sample cases.

Source: *Criminal Victimization in the United States, 1990*, Bureau of Justice Statistics, (WDC, 1992)

ing in injury (71.1 percent). The least reported personal crimes were attempted robbery without injury (25.1 percent), attempted theft (23.1 percent), and larceny without contact (13.3 percent) (Table 3.23).

Females reported crimes slightly more often than males, while blacks and whites reported crimes in almost equal numbers, except for theft in which slightly more whites (29.1 percent) reported the crime to the police than did blacks (25.1 percent). A similar relationship existed in reporting between Hispanic and non-Hispanic victims. Crimes of violence committed by a family member or acquaintance were reported as often (48.3 percent) as crimes committed by a stranger (47.9 percent). Teenagers were the least likely group to report a crime (38.2 percent) compared to over half of those older than 35 years old (56 to 63.5 percent).

The leading reasons victims gave for reporting the crime to police was that they wanted to recover the property (19.3 percent for personal crimes and 26.8 percent for household crimes) or simply because it was a crime (13.4 percent of violent crimes and 13.8 percent of household crimes). The per-

TABLE 3.25

Percent distribution of reasons for not reporting victimizations to the police, by type of crime

Type of crime	Number of reasons for not reporting	Total	Reported to another official	Private or personal matter	Object recovered; offender unsuccessful	Not important enough	Insurance would not cover
All personal crimes	14,852,980	100 %	14.7 %	8.8 %	24.2 %	3.6 %	1.7 %
Crimes of violence	3,674,490	100 %	10.8	20.0	17.3	6.2	0.1 *
Completed	1,099,250	100 %	10.8	17.3	12.5	3.8	0.2 *
Attempted	2,575,230	100 %	10.8	21.1	19.3	7.2	0.0 *
Rape	71,910	100 %	5.3 *	26.9 *	2.6 *	0.0 *	0.0 *
Robbery	714,460	100 %	7.2	8.7	19.4	0.9 *	0.3 *
Completed	423,140	100 %	6.4	9.3	14.7	1.0 *	0.5 *
With injury	132,560	100 %	2.1 *	12.1 *	9.8 *	1.5 *	1.6 *
From serious assault	37,950	100 %	7.2 *	9.8 *	8.5 *	5.2 *	5.5 *
From minor assault	94,600	100 %	0.0 *	13.1 *	10.4 *	0.0 *	0.0 *
Without injury	290,580	100 %	8.4	7.9	16.9	0.7 *	0.0 *
Attempted	291,310	100 %	8.3	7.8	26.2	0.7 *	0.0 *
With injury	71,740	100 %	6.5 *	2.9 *	31.4	0.0 *	0.0 *
From serious assault	37,070	100 %	0.0 *	0.0 *	31.1 *	0.0 *	0.0 *
From minor assault	34,670	100 %	13.5 *	6.0 *	31.7 *	0.0 *	0.0 *
Without injury	219,560	100 %	8.9 *	9.5	24.6	0.9 *	0.0 *
Assault	2,888,110	100 %	11.8	22.6	17.1	7.7	0.0 *
Aggravated	758,690	100 %	9.7	18.4	13.4	5.8	0.0 *
Simple	2,129,410	100 %	12.6	24.1	18.5	8.3	0.0 *
Crimes of theft	11,178,490	100 %	16.0	2.5	26.5	2.7	2.2
Completed	10,440,950	100 %	16.6	2.5	25.1	2.7	2.2
Attempted	737,540	100 %	8.4	2.6 *	46.2	3.1	1.6 *
Personal larceny with contact	464,480	100 %	14.1	1.4 *	18.9	1.8 *	0.0 *
Purse snatching	87,080	100 %	10.8 *	0.0 *	33.1	0.0 *	0.0 *
Pocket picking	377,390	100 %	14.8	1.7 *	15.6	2.2 *	0.0 *
Personal larceny without contact	10,714,010	100 %	16.1	2.5	26.8	2.7	2.3
Completed	10,005,430	100 %	16.7	2.5	25.5	2.7	2.3
Less than $50	4,661,380	100 %	20.3	2.1	37.9	3.5	1.1
$50 or more	4,887,940	100 %	13.7	3.0	13.2	1.5	3.5
Amount not available	456,100	100 %	11.2	2.7 *	30.6	7.0	2.1 *
Attempted	708,570	100 %	8.5	2.7 *	45.4	3.2	1.6 *
All household crimes	11,061,260	100 %	3.5	5.0	30.5	3.9	1.9
Completed	9,290,890	100 %	3.1	5.3	28.2	3.8	2.1
Attempted	1,770,360	100 %	5.6	3.4	42.2	4.9	1.2
Burglary	3,048,790	100 %	5.9	4.2	25.4	5.2	1.3
Completed	2,202,240	100 %	4.8	4.7	19.3	4.8	1.6
Forcible entry	558,390	100 %	6.8	4.6	18.2	4.4	2.9 *
Unlawful entry without force	1,643,850	100 %	4.1	4.7	19.6	4.9	1.1 *
Attempted forcible entry	846,540	100 %	9.0	3.0	41.5	6.4	0.6 *
Household larceny	7,435,160	100 %	2.5	5.3	32.3	3.5	2.2
Completed	7,019,590	100 %	2.6	5.3	31.2	3.4	2.2
Less than $50	3,311,020	100 %	2.1	4.2	47.8	4.9	1.0
$50 or more	3,373,950	100 %	2.9	6.0	14.8	1.7	3.5
Amount not available	334,620	100 %	4.2	9.2	32.0	8.4	1.6 *
Attempted	415,580	100 %	0.8 *	5.2	51.0	4.8 *	0.8 *
Motor vehicle theft	577,280	100 %	3.8	5.6	33.2	2.7 *	2.2 *
Completed	69,050	100 %	2.6 *	28.5 *	10.4 *	5.3 *	0.0 *
Attempted	508,230	100 %	3.9	2.5 *	36.3	2.4 *	2.5 *

Note: Detail may not add to total shown because of rounding.

Some respondents may have cited more than one reason for not reporting victimizations to the police.

* Estimate is based on about 10 or fewer sample cases.

(Continued)

centages of those who did it to do their duty, improve police surveillance, or in hopes of punishing the offender were small. (See Table 3.24.) The main reasons for not reporting crimes to the police were that the object was recovered or the offender was unsuccessful (24.2 percent of personal crimes and 30.5 percent of household crimes), the victim reported it to someone else (14.7 percent of personal crimes), and a lack of proof (10.5 percent and 12.4 percent) (Table 3.25). In 29.1 percent of all violent crimes involving nonstrangers, as compared with 14.5 percent of all violent crimes involving strangers, the victims regarded the matter as personal and did not inform the authorities.

HOUSEHOLDS TOUCHED BY CRIME

Almost one-fourth of the nation's households were victimized by crime in 1991, the same proportion as in the previous year and slightly less than in the four years before that. This is well below the one-third of all households touched by crime in

Not aware crime occurred until later	Unable to recover property; no ID no.	Lack of proof	Police would not want to be bothered	Police inefficient, ineffective, or biased	Fear of reprisal	Too inconvenient or time consuming	Other reasons
			Percent of reasons for not reporting				
4.3 %	6.8 %	10.5 %	8.0 %	3.3 %	1.3 %	4.1 %	10.7 %
0.4 *	0.6	6.0	8.1	5.5	4.4	4.4	16.2
0.7 *	2.1	8.8	7.2	8.5	6.8	4.1	17.2
0.2 *	0.0 *	4.8	8.5	4.3	3.4	4.5	15.8
0.0 *	0.0 *	2.6 *	11.2 *	10.4 *	7.6 *	0.0 *	33.4
1.4 *	3.3	10.4	8.3	11.3	7.1	6.8	15.1
1.8 *	5.5	13.8	8.5	15.5	6.0	4.9	12.3
5.7 *	4.6 *	18.5	8.8 *	25.5	0.0 *	2.8 *	7.0 *
10.0 *	10.2 *	29.4 *	0.0 *	5.1 *	0.0 *	10.0 *	9.2 *
4.0 *	2.3 *	14.1 *	12.4 *	33.7	0.0 *	4.0 *	6.1 *
0.0 *	5.9 *	11.6	8.3	10.9	8.7	5.8 *	14.7
0.7 *	0.0 *	5.4 *	8.0	5.3 *	8.7	9.5	19.3
3.0 *	0.0 *	2.8 *	8.1 *	13.5 *	5.8 *	12.8 *	13.4 *
0.0 *	0.0 *	0.0 *	15.7 *	26.1 *	10.9 *	16.2 *	0.0 *
6.2 *	0.0 *	5.8 *	0.0 *	0.0 *	0.0 *	9.1 *	27.8 *
0.0 *	0.0 *	6.3 *	8.0 *	2.6 *	9.7	8.5 *	21.2
0.1 *	0.0 *	5.1	7.9	4.0	3.7	3.9	16.1
0.5 *	0.0 *	7.6	7.9	7.4	4.5	6.6	18.3
0.0 *	0.0 *	4.1	8.0	2.8	3.4	3.0	15.2
5.6	8.8	12.0	8.0	2.6	0.3	3.9	8.9
5.8	9.4	11.9	8.1	2.7	0.3	3.9	8.9
4.1	0.0 *	12.9	5.4	1.5 *	0.0 *	5.1	9.1
6.9	15.0	17.4	6.8	5.3	1.5 *	3.0 *	8.1
2.4 *	17.6 *	10.1 *	3.6 *	6.6 *	4.3 *	2.2 *	9.3 *
7.9	14.3	19.0	7.5	5.0 *	0.9 *	3.2 *	7.8
5.6	8.5	11.8	8.0	2.5	0.2	4.0	9.0
5.7	9.1	11.7	8.2	2.6	0.2	3.9	9.0
3.3	5.8	8.4	6.5	1.3	0.1 *	2.7	6.9
7.7	12.4	15.0	9.9	4.0	0.3 *	5.0	10.9
8.6	7.3	9.2	7.2	0.7 *	0.8 *	3.8 *	8.8
4.2	0.0 *	13.2	5.6	1.3 *	0.0 *	5.3	8.9
7.4	7.9	12.4	9.7	4.0	0.6	2.6	10.5
7.6	9.4	12.6	9.5	3.8	0.6	2.8	11.1
6.1	0.2 *	11.3	11.0	5.2	0.1 *	1.7	7.0
9.5	6.0	12.6	8.9	5.5	0.8	2.2	12.4
10.6	8.2	13.8	8.9	5.7	1.1	2.6	14.2
9.0	6.3	12.9	9.5	8.5	0.3 *	2.4 *	14.3
11.0	8.9	14.1	8.7	4.7	1.3	2.7	14.2
6.9	0.2 *	9.4	9.0	5.0	0.2 *	1.1 *	7.6
6.6	9.3	12.2	9.8	3.2	0.5	2.7	9.9
6.8	9.8	12.3	9.7	3.2	0.5	2.8	10.0
5.2	6.7	9.7	8.3	1.1	0.1 *	2.5	6.5
8.5	13.5	15.1	11.0	5.2	1.0	3.1	13.6
6.3	3.9 *	9.6	11.6	3.2 *	0.5 *	3.4 *	8.2
3.0 *	0.0 *	10.8	11.1	3.6 *	0.0 *	0.9 *	8.0
6.7	0.6 *	13.2	12.6	7.3	0.0 *	4.0	8.0
2.6 *	2.7 *	0.0 *	0.0 *	12.8 *	0.0 *	7.6 *	27.6 *
7.3	0.4 *	15.0	14.3	6.6	0.0 *	3.5 *	5.3

Source: *Criminal Victimization in the United States, 1990*, Bureau of Justice Statistics, (WDC, 1992)

1975, the first year for which this information was available. A little less than 5 percent of the households in the United States had a member who was the victim of a violent crime in 1991. Five percent of all households suffered a completed or attempted burglary during the year, 16.7 percent were victimized by a completed or attempted theft, and 7.2 percent suffered a crime of high concern (rape, robbery, assault by a stranger, or a burglary) (Table 3.26). Households with high incomes, in urban areas, and Hispanic households were more vulnerable to crime than others.

During 1991, 26.7 percent of black households, 23.2 percent of white households, and 30.4 percent of Hispanic households suffered crime. The rate for crimes of high concern for blacks and Hispanics was especially high, 9.5 percent and 10.9 percent, respectively (Table 3.27). Households with incomes of $50,000 or more (26.7 percent — because of high theft rates) and 29.1 percent of urban households were touched by crime. Households in the Northeast were hit least (19.3 percent), while those in the West (28.8 percent) suffered more often. About 23 percent of the

TABLE 3.26

Households experiencing crime in 1991,
and relative percent change since 1990

	1990		1991		Relative percent change, 1990-91
Households	Number of house-holds	Percent	Number of house-holds	Percent	
Total	95,461,000	100.0%	96,561,000	100.0%	
Victimized by:					
Any NCVS crime	22,652,000	23.7%	22,855,000	23.7%	-.3%
Violent crime	4,478,000	4.7	4,711,000	4.9	4.0
Rape	104,000	.1	161,000	.2	53.2[b]
Robbery	967,000	1.0	951,000	1.0	-2.9
Assault	3,591,000	3.8	3,852,000	4.0	6.1
Aggravated	1,287,000	1.3	1,367,000	1.4	5.0
Simple	2,527,000	2.6	2,752,000	2.9	7.7
Total theft	15,905,000	16.7%	16,069,000	16.6%	-.1%
Personal	10,042,000	10.5	10,029,000	10.4	-1.3
With contact	548,000	.6	463,000	.5	-16.6
Without contact	9,592,000	10.0	9,655,000	10.0	-.5
Household	7,199,000	7.5	7,421,000	7.7	1.9
Burglary	4,557,000	4.8	4,554,000	4.7	-1.2
Motor vehicle theft	1,825,000	1.9	1,755,000	1.8	-5.0
Crimes of high concern (a rape, robbery, or assault by a stranger or a burglary)	6,854,000	7.2%	6,964,000	7.2%	.4%

Note: Detail does not add to total or crime subtotals because of overlap in households experiencing various crimes. Relative percent change is based on unrounded figures.

[a]Change was statistically significant at the 95% confidence level.

[b]Change was statistically significant at the 90% confidence level.

Source: *Crime in the Nation's Households, 1991,*
Bureau of Justice Statistics, (WDC, 1992)

TABLE 3.27

Percent of households experiencing crime,
by race and ethnicity of household head, 1991

Percent of households experiencing:	Race of household head			Ethnicity of household head	
	White	Black	Other	Non-Hispanic	Hispanic
Any NCVS crime	23.2%	26.7%	24.3%	23.2%	30.4%
Violent crime	4.7%	5.7%	5.3%	4.8%	6.1%
Rape	.2	.2	.2	.2	.2
Robbery	.8	2.1	1.5	.9	2.0
Assault	4.0	3.8	3.7	4.0	4.3
Aggravated	1.4	1.7	1.2	1.4	2.0
Simple	2.9	2.3	2.8	2.9	2.5
Total theft	16.6%	16.7%	17.0%	16.4%	19.8%
Personal	10.5	9.5	11.3	10.3	11.4
Household	7.6	8.8	7.6	7.5	10.4
Burglary	4.4	6.8	4.8	4.6	6.8
Motor vehicle theft	1.6	3.3	2.4	1.7	3.5
Serious violent crime[a]	2.3%	3.8%	2.9%	2.3%	4.1%
Crimes of high concern[b]	6.9%	9.5%	8.2%	6.9%	10.9%

Note: Detail does not add to total or crime subtotals because of overlap in households experiencing various crimes.

[a]Rape, robbery, or aggravated assault.

[b]A rape, robbery, or assault by a stranger or a burglary.

Source: *Crime in the Nation's Households, 1991,*
Bureau of Justice Statistics, (WDC, 1992)

households in the Midwest and South were victimized in 1991. (See Table 3.28.)

SCHOOL CRIME

The National Crime Victimization Survey (NCVS) made a special study of crime in the nation's schools during the first half of 1989. The report (Bastian and Taylor, 1991, "School Crime," WDC: Bureau of Justice Statistics) found that 9 percent of students ages 12 to 19 were crime victims in or around their schools. Two percent reported one or more violent crimes, mainly simple assault, and 7 percent reported property crime.

A nearly equal number of male and female, black and white, and city and suburban students reported being victimized. Hispanic students, however, were less likely than non-Hispanics to experience a property crime. Income did not seriously influence the rate of violent crime — slightly more students with household incomes of $10,000 to $14,999 were victims of violent crime, while those in the income range of $7,500 to $9,999 were victimized less often. Wealthier students suffered more property crimes than poorer students. (See Table 3.29.)

Hispanics and blacks were more fearful of being victimized going to and from school although equal percentages of all races were afraid of attack while in school (22 percent). Younger students and central city students were more afraid in school and out. (Table 3.30.) Table 3.31 shows that 3 percent of males report having brought a weapon to school for protection compared to 1 percent of females. Equal percentages of black, white, and Hispanic students carried

TABLE 3.28

Percent of households experiencing crime, by selected characteristics, 1991

Percent of households experiencing:	Annual household income					Place of residence[a]			Region			
	Under $7,500	$7,500-$14,999	$15,000-$24,999	$25,000-$49,999	$50,000 or more	Urban	Suburban	Rural	North-east	Mid-west	South	West
Any NCVS crime	22.4%	22.4%	23.4%	24.8%	26.7%	29.1%	22.8%	17.4%	19.3%	23.5%	23.8%	26.8%
Violent crime	6.3%	5.7%	4.9%	4.7%	3.9%	6.2%	4.4%	3.8%	3.9%	5.1%	4.7%	6.0%
Rape	.2	.2	.2	.1	.2	.2	.1	.1	.1	.2	.2	.2
Robbery	1.3	1.3	.9	.8	.6	1.8	.7	.3	1.2	.8	.9	1.0
Assault	5.2	4.4	4.1	4.0	3.3	4.6	3.8	3.5	2.8	4.3	3.9	5.1
Aggravated	2.3	1.6	1.5	1.3	1.0	1.8	1.3	1.1	.9	1.4	1.6	1.7
Simple	3.3	3.2	2.8	3.0	2.6	3.1	2.8	2.7	2.1	3.2	2.6	3.7
Total theft	14.1%	14.7%	16.5%	17.9%	20.4%	20.0%	16.5%	11.9%	13.3%	16.5%	16.6%	20.6%
Personal	7.9	8.5	9.8	11.5	14.3	11.7	10.9	7.2	8.2	10.3	10.2	13.1
Household	7.6	7.8	7.9	7.8	7.9	10.1	7.0	5.4	6.1	7.5	7.7	9.8
Burglary	6.7	5.5	4.5	4.2	3.9	6.3	4.0	3.8	3.4	4.7	5.1	5.5
Motor vehicle theft	.9	1.7	1.7	1.9	2.3	2.9	1.6	.5	2.0	1.5	1.6	2.3
Serious violent crime[b]	3.7%	3.0%	2.4%	2.1%	1.8%	3.6%	2.1%	1.5%	2.1%	2.3%	2.6%	2.8%
Crimes of high concern[c]	9.8%	7.9%	7.0%	6.8%	6.1%	9.8%	6.3%	5.3%	5.5%	7.1%	7.4%	8.8%

Source: *Crime in the Nation's Households, 1991*, Bureau of Justice Statistics, (WDC, 1992)

TABLE 3.29

Students reporting at least one victimization at school, by personal and family characteristics

Student characteristic	Total number of students	Percent of students reporting victimization at school		
		Total	Violent	Property
Sex				
Male	11,166,316	9%	2%	7%
Female	10,387,776	9	2	8
Race				
White	17,306,626	9%	2%	7%
Black	3,449,488	8	2	7
Other	797,978	10	2*	8
Hispanic origin				
Yes	2,026,968	7%	3%	5%
No	19,452,697	9	2	8
Not ascertained	74,428	3*	--	3*
Age				
12	3,220,891	9%	2%	7%
13	3,318,714	10	2	8
14	3,264,574	11	2	9
15	3,214,109	9	3	7
16	3,275,002	9	2	7
17	3,273,628	8	1	7
18	1,755,635	5	1*	4
19	231,348	2*	--	2*
Number of times family moved in last 5 years				
None	18,905,538	8%	2%	7%
Once	845,345	9	2*	7
Twice	610,312	13	3*	11
3 or more	1,141,555	15	6	9
Not ascertained	51,343	5*	5*	--
Family income				
Less than $7,500	2,041,418	8%	2%	6%
$7,500 - $9,999	791,086	4	1*	3
$10,000 - $14,999	1,823,150	9	3	7
$15,000 - $24,999	3,772,445	8	1	8
$25,000 - $29,999	1,845,313	8	2	7
$30,000 - $49,999	5,798,448	10	2	8
$50,000 and over	3,498,382	11	2	9
Not ascertained	1,983,849	7	3	5
Place of residence				
Central city	5,816,321	10%	2%	8%
Suburbs	10,089,207	9	2	7
Nonmetropolitan area	5,648,564	8	1	7

*Estimate is based on 10 or fewer sample cases
--Less than .5%.

Source: *School Crime*, Bureau of Justice Statistics, (WDC, 1992)

weapons and they did so more frequently in the center city than in the suburbs or nonmetropolitan areas.

While overall victimization has decreased in the NCVS surveys, it has increased for teenagers. In 1981, the peak year for violent crime, the rate of victimization for people 20 years or older was 33.1 compared to 74.6 for older teens (16 to 19 years old) and 64.8 for younger teens (12 to 15 years old). In 1988 when the adult rate had dropped to 26.1, the older teen rate had risen to 78.9 and younger teens had increased to 63.3. Crimes of theft have decreased for all age groups since 1979. (See Table 3.32.)

LIFETIME LIKELIHOOD OF VICTIMIZATION

What is the individual's likelihood of suffering a crime during his or her lifetime? In "Lifetime Likelihood of Victimization" (1987, WDC), based on 1975-84 annual victimization rates (except for rape in which 1973-82 rates are used), the Bureau of Justice Statistics (BJS) calcu-

TABLE 3.30

Students avoiding places at school out of fear, or ever fearing an attack, by selected student characteristics

Student characteristic	Total number of students	Percent of students		
		Avoiding places at school	Ever fearing an attack	
			At school	Going to and from school
Sex				
Male	11,166,316	6%	22%	14%
Female	10,387,776	6	21	16
Race				
White	17,306,626	6%	22%	13%
Black	3,449,488	7	22	21
Other	797,978	6	22	18
Hispanic origin				
Yes	2,026,968	8%	26%	22%
No	19,452,697	6	21	14
Not ascertained	74,428	14*	23*	19*
Age				
12	3,220,891	8%	27%	18%
13	3,318,714	7	27	17
14	3,264,574	7	24	15
15	3,214,109	6	21	13
16	3,275,002	5	20	14
17	3,273,628	4	17	12
18	1,755,825	4	13	10
19	231,348	8*	20	15
Number of times family moved in last 5 years				
None	18,905,538	6%	21%	15%
Once	845,345	5	18	11
Twice	610,312	8	27	16
3 or more	1,141,555	6	26	16
Not ascertained	51,343	7	24*	14*
Family income				
Less than $7,500	2,041,418	8%	24%	18%
$7,500-$9,999	791,086	9	25	18
$10,000-$14,999	1,823,150	8	25	19
$15,000-$24,999	3,772,445	6	23	15
$25,000-$29,999	1,845,313	6	21	15
$30,000-$49,999	5,798,448	5	21	13
$50,000 or more	3,498,382	4	19	11
Not ascertained	1,983,849	5	18	16
Place of residence				
Central city	5,816,321	8%	24%	19%
Suburbs	10,089,207	5	20	12
Nonmetroplitan area	5,648,564	6	22	13

*Estimate is based on 10 or fewer sample cases

Source: *School Crime*, Bureau of Justice Statistics, (WDC, 1992)

TABLE 3.31

Students reporting that they had taken something to school to protect themselves

Student characteristic	Total number of students	Percent of students who had taken a weapon or object to school for protection
Sex		
Male	11,166,316	3%
Female	10,387,776	1
Race		
White	17,306,626	2%
Black	3,449,488	2
Other	797,978	2
Hispanic origin		
Yes	2,026,968	2%
No	19,452,697	2
Not ascertained	74,428	—
Place of residence		
Central city	5,816,321	3%
Suburbs	10,089,207	2
Nonmetroplitan area	5,648,564	1

Source: *School Crime*, Bureau of Justice Statistics, (WDC, 1992)

TABLE 3.32

Trends in annual victimization rates, by age of victim, 1979-88

Year	Type of crime and age of victim					
	Crimes of violence			Crimes of theft		
	12-15	16-19	20 or older	12-15	16-19	20 or older
1979	59.2	77.4	32.2	147.4	148.3	82.5
1980	53.5	73.9	31.1	122.8	126.9	76.7
1981	64.8	74.6	33.1	133.5	135.3	77.7
1982	56.2	76.2	32.8	132.9	130.2	75.1
1983	55.9	70.9	29.3	130.8	121.1	69.9
1984	57.4	71.4	28.6	124.3	122.4	64.2
1985	59.3	71.3	26.6	112.7	123.9	62.5
1986	59.7	65.7	25.8	112.4	119.4	60.8
1987	64.4	73.8	25.6	112.1	123.9	61.9
1988	63.3	78.9	26.1	117.5	123.0	64.2

Note: The victimization rate is the number of victimizations per 1,000 persons in each age group.

Source: *Teenage Victims*, Bureau of Justice Statistics, (WDC, 1991)

TABLE 3.33

Lifetime likelihood of victimization

| | Percent of persons who will be victimized by crime starting at 12 years of age | | | |
| | Total One or more victimizations | Number of victimizations | | |
		One	Two	Three or more
Violent crimes, total*				
Total population	83%	30%	27%	25%
Male	89	24	27	38
Female	73	35	23	14
White	82	31	26	24
Male	88	25	27	37
Female	71	36	22	13
Black	87	26	27	34
Male	92	21	26	45
Female	81	31	26	24
Violent crimes, completed*				
Total population	42%	32%	9%	2%
Male	48	34	11	3
Female	36	28	6	1
White	41	31	8	2
Black	53	35	13	4
Rape				
Total female	8%	8%	—	—
White	8	7	—	—
Black	11	10	1	—
Robbery				
Total population	30%	25%	5%	1%
Male	37	29	7	1
Female	22	19	2	—
White	27	23	4	—
Black	51	35	12	4
Assault				
Total population	74%	35%	24%	15%
Male	82	31	26	25
Female	62	37	18	7
White	74	35	24	16
Black	73	35	25	12
Robbery or assault resulting in injury				
Total population	40%	30%	7%	2%
Personal theft				
Total population	99%	4%	8%	87%
Male	99	3	8	88
Female	99	4	10	84
White	99	4	9	87
Male	99	3	8	88
Female	99	4	10	86
Black	99	5	12	81
Male	99	5	10	84
Female	98	7	15	76

Note: Data are based on average victimization rates measured by the National Crime Survey for 1975–84, except for rape data, which are based on victimization rates for 1973–82. All crimes include attempts except where noted.
— Less than 0.5%.
* Includes rape, robbery, and assault.

Source: *Lifetime Likelihood of Victimization*, Bureau of Justice Statistics, (WDC, 1987)

lated the likelihood of becoming a victim, assuming that the current crime rates remain steady and that past victimization reports are accurate. While neither of these factors are necessarily true, this offers a useful probability of the chances of being victimized during a lifetime. The BJS has calculated that about five out of six people will become victims of violent crimes (rape, robbery, and assault), either completed or attempted at least once during their lives. About half the population will be victimized by violent crime more than once. Males are somewhat more likely to become victims than females (Table 3.33).

The younger a person is, the more likely he or she will be victimized during a lifetime. This is because young people have more years to live and so have more time to become victims. This is balanced by the fact, however, that those who are older are more likely to have already been victimized (Table 3.34).

Over the next 20 years, the average household has about a three in four (72 percent) chance of being burglarized, a nine out-of-10 chance of suffering household larceny, and a one-in-five chance of having a car stolen. Households in urban areas are the most likely to be victimized and those in rural areas, the least likely. This is most apparent in the case of motor vehicle theft, a more urban crime. (See Table 3.35)

The Fear of Becoming a Victim

The fear of becoming a victim is often much greater than the likelihood of being one and has permeated our society so completely that it plays a daily role in our lives. For more information on being a victim of Crime see Chapter IV.

TABLE 3.34

Lifetime likelihood of victimization, by age

| | Percent of persons who will be victimized by crime starting at various ages | | | |
| | Total | Number of victimizations | | |
	One or more victimizations	One	Two	Three or more
Violent crimes*				
Current age				
12 years old	83%	30%	27%	25%
20	72	36	23	14
30	53	35	13	4
40	36	29	6	1
50	22	19	2	—
60	14	13	1	—
70	8	7	—	—
Robbery or assault				
resulting in injury				
Current age				
12 years old	40%	30%	7%	2%
20	30	25	4	1
30	19	17	2	—
40	11	11	1	—
50	7	6	—	—
60	4	4	—	—
70	2	2	—	—
Personal theft				
Current age				
12 years old	99%	4%	8%	87%
20	98	9	16	73
30	93	19	25	48
40	82	31	19	33
50	64	37	19	8
60	43	32	9	2
70	24	21	3	—

Note: Data are based on average victimization rates measured by the National Crime Survey for 1975–84. All crimes include attempts.
— Less than 0.5 percent.
* Includes rape, robbery, and assault.

TABLE 3.35

Long-term likelihood of household victimization

| | Percent of households that will be victimized by crime over a 20-year period | | | |
| | Total | Number of victimizations | | |
	One or more victimizations	One	Two	Three or more
Burglary				
All households	72%	36%	23%	14%
Urban	80	32	26	22
Suburban	70	36	22	12
Rural	64	37	19	8
Household larceny				
All households	89%	24%	27%	38%
Urban	93	19	25	49
Suburban	90	23	26	41
Rural	82	31	27	25
Motor vehicle theft				
All households	19%	17%	2%	—
Urban	27	23	4	—
Suburban	20	18	2	—
Rural	11	10	1	—

Note: Data are based on average victimization rates measured by the National Crime Survey for 1975–84. Only completed crimes are included.
— Less than 0.5%.

Source o both table: *Lifetime Likelihood of Victimization*, Bureau of Justice Statistics, (WDC, 1987)

CHAPTER IV

VICTIMS OF CRIME

*When I wanted to talk about my son, I soon found that murder is a
taboo subject in our society. I found, to my surprise, that nice people
apparently just don't get killed. — a victim's mother*

*I'm a senior citizen but I never considered myself old. I was active,
independent. Now I live in a nursing home and sit in a wheelchair.
The day I was mugged was the day I began to die. — a victim*

*The general feeling of being a living victim or victim-survivor is
one of an outcast. Ostracized from society, forgotten by family,
friends, fellow workers. No one, or very few, bring
the subject up. — a victim*

Witnesses testifying at *The President's Task Force on Victims of Crime*

THE IMPACT

Becoming a crime victim can have grave consequences — consequences the victim neither asked for nor deserves. The victim rarely expects to be victimized, is not prepared for it, and seldom knows to whom or where to turn. The victim may lose his or her life, the ultimate result of a crime for which the victim can never be repaid. The victim may end up in the hospital to be treated and released or be admitted and confined to a bed for days, weeks, or longer. The injuries may be temporary or they may be permanent and forever change the way the victim lives. The victim may lose money or property - for some, the money or item may be impossible to replace.

The effects of crime are not limited to the victim. The family is frequently devastated, and the psychological trauma spreads to everyone connected to the victim. In the most serious cases a parent may have lost a child, or a child may have lost a parent. A spouse or friend may be gone forever.

Lasting Trauma

Often the monetary damage of a crime is small but the trauma continues long after the end of the criminal event. Some of the emotional scars include feelings of fear, anger, shame, self-blame, helplessness, and depression. These are emotions that can scar a victim's life for years after the event.

In the aftermath of a crime when a victim most needs support and understanding, there is rarely anyone to talk to. Friends who do not understand what has happened may withdraw. A victim's whole concept of right and wrong may be turned upside-down. If the victims are attacked in the home, or the home was entered, they may feel as if they or their homes were violated. They may no longer feel secure anywhere. Their self-esteem may suffer terribly — surely they could have handled themselves better, they think, as if they were responsible for their victimization. A parent or spouse may feel guilty that he or she had not done more to protect their loved one. They may no longer trust other people. Someone who has lost a loved one or who has suffered physical violence is considered vengeful when they want to see the perpetrator put in prison, as if this were somehow an unreasonable response.

The criminal often feels no remorse for the crime and carries no emotional burden. The victims, who asked for none of it, may carry a terrible, painful weight around with them for the rest of their lives. They may move, they may try to start their lives all over again, but for some, the burden of their victimization will never leave them. Adding insult to injury, the pain doesn't end here however — the victim may be victimized again by the very system to which he or she turns to for help. In the "Statement of the Chairman" in the *President's Task Force on Victims of Crime* (1982, WDC), Lois Haight observes, "Somewhere along the way, the system began to serve lawyers and judges and defendants, treating the victim with institutionalized disinterest."

AN UNCARING SYSTEM

It may begin with an unfeeling police officer who questions whether a victim was really raped or whether she had enticed the rapist. The rape victim may then wait alone in a hospital waiting room to be treated. She may have to pay for the rape examination herself. The assault victim may find out that the hospital is concerned only with whether he or she can pay for their services. The victim seems to have little role in the judicial process, and nobody seems to care. The victim may never know when the trial takes place. He or she may sit all day in a bare hall outside the courtroom, waiting to testify as a witness, never to be called. The victim may meet the person accused of the crime against them in the court and be threatened with hostile gestures or overt threats. The victim may have to show up repeatedly, only to find out that the case has been continued or delayed for some unexplained reason. Everybody may seem more concerned with the accused than the victim. The accused may be out on bail and may even threaten the victim and his or her family. Most cases are plea-bargained without concern for the victim's

opinion. Rarely is the victim even informed. Terrible crimes often result in seemingly short criminal sentences for the perpetrator.

A New Approach

A change in attitude has developed over the last decade, however. The *Figgie Report on Crime Part III: A Fourteen-City Profile* (1982, N.Y.: Figgie International) was part of an extensive study on crime and its effects. Part III polled community leaders to get a local perspective on the fear of crime. Detroit Judge George Deneweth, "expressed the views of many when he said: 'The liberals in the Correction Department and the high court have lost sight of the fact that prisoners are supposed to be punished. The public is demanding that they be put away. People feel there are too many rights for the criminal and not enough for society.'" In response to this change in attitude, the judicial system has been trying to do something to help the victim.

VICTIMIZATION PROGRAMS

Background

Interest in assisting victims in the United States first developed as a concern for restitution to be paid to a victim. Restitution for criminal acts has a long history dating back to biblical times. Money payments for injuries are often cited in the Bible and this practice continued well into the Middle Ages. Around 1100, England's Henry I began to take a part of the compensation as a charge for holding a trial and for the injury done to the state because the criminal act had disturbed the peace of the kingdom. Eventually, the king took the entire payment, and the assault upon an individual became an assault upon the society. All compensation and penalties were assessed for the state and nothing was given to the individuals harmed by the crime.

Ms. Margery Fry, a British magistrate and legal reformer, began advocating a victim compensation program during the 1950s. "Have we not neglected overmuch the customs of our earlier ancestors in the matter of restitution," she asked in her book, *Arms of the Law* (1951, London). "We have seen that in primitive societies this idea of 'making up' for a wrong done has wide currency. Let us once more look into the ways of earlier men, which may still hold some wisdom for us." Her book and articles advocating compensation programs aroused considerable discussion in the United Kingdom and New Zealand. As a result, New Zealand's parliament passed a law permitting the government to award compensation to victims. After several years of debate, the British Parliament created an experimental program in 1964.

Compensation Programs in the United States

In the United States, interest in victim compensation grew rapidly in the mid-1960s. In 1964, Senator Ralph Yarborough (D-TX) proposed federal legislation, and, in 1965, California became the first state to develop a victim compensation program. The idea began to spread over the country with New York (1966), Hawaii (1967), Maryland (1968), Massachusetts (1968), and New Jersey (1971) soon adopting compensation programs. Today, they are common across the country.

Increasing Concern for Victims
and Witnesses

During the 1970s, many individuals in the criminal justice system became concerned about the harmful effects of the mistreatment of victims and witnesses by police, prosecutors, and judges. Studies had shown an increasing tendency of victims who did not want to "get involved." This made pursuing a case more difficult because most of the evidence to solve and prosecute a case comes from victims. Furthermore, many witnesses were so inconvenienced or upset by their involvement with the courts, or so afraid they would suffer injury from the defendant if they appeared, that they failed to testify. Consequently, many cases were dropped because the prosecutor had no witnesses. Another problem was that failing to consider the victim's personal problems resulting from the crime could have a deleterious effect on the

quality of the evidence he or she was able to provide — a serious consideration when the single most important factor in whether a case will be solved hinges on the evidence provided by witnesses.

Consequences

Researchers began to recognize and document the psychological and emotional consequences of crime, which was often more serious than the actual property loss or physical injury. In 1975, researchers at Marquette University interviewed 4,600 crime victims. They found mental or emotional suffering to be the most frequent problem expressed by victims in general, while time and income loss posed the greatest difficulties for victims involved in the court process. The fear and emotional distress experienced by victims often extended to the victims' families and friends.

At the same time that the criminal justice system began to recognize the consequences of victim and witness mistreatment by the system, several special interest groups were troubled by the psychological and financial burdens that crime imposes on its victims. Women's groups, in particular, were concerned about the double trauma of rape victims, who were first assaulted by the rapist and then often handled insensitively by the criminal justice system. Other organizations began looking into the special problems of battered women and elderly victims. In 1975 and 1976, social service and criminal justice personnel met in Fresno, California, to create a National Organization for Victim Assistance to promote a victim-oriented perspective in the administration of justice.

The American Psychiatric Association responded to the political and professional focus on victims by codifying (naming) the victim's condition. Post-Traumatic Stress Disorder (PTSD) is the term for the sometimes delayed psychological reaction to having been a victim of a crime or a natural disaster. Rape victims, Vietnam veterans, and hurricane survivors can all suffer PTSD as a result of their experiences.

TABLE 4.1
Legislation should be proposed and enacted to accomplish the following:
a. Require victim impact statements at sentencing;
b. Provide for the protection of victims and witnesses from intimidation;
c. Require restitution in all cases, unless the court provides specific reasons for failing to require it;
d. Develop and implement guidelines for the fair treatment of crime victims and witnesses; and
e. Prohibit a criminal from making any profit from the sale of the story of his crime. Any proceeds should be used to provide full restitution to his victims, pay the expenses of his prosecution, and finally, assist the crime victim compensation fund.
Legislation should be proposed and enacted to establish or expand employee assistance programs for victims of crime employed by government.
Legislation should be proposed and enacted to ensure that sexual assault victims are not required to assume the cost of physical examinations and materials used to obtain evidence.
Source: *President's Task Force on Victims of Crime, Final Report*, (WDC, December 1982)

In 1974, the Law Enforcement Assistance Administration (LEAA) funded eight victim assistance programs. LEAA contributed $50 million to victim witness programs nationwide before LEAA went out of existence. During the 1980s, federal funding for victim programs declined. As a result, many programs switched from federal to local government funding which was simultaneously experiencing its own declining budgets. With reduced funding, many programs had to curtail or discontinue some services (e.g., child care, security repair) and restrict others to only the most needy victims such as the elderly.

THE FEDERAL VICTIM AND WITNESS PROTECTION ACT OF 1982

In 1982, Congress enacted the Federal Victim and Witness Protection Act (PL 97-291), a bill designed to protect and assist victims and witnesses of federal crimes. The law permits victim impact statements in sentencing hearings to provide judges with information concerning financial, psychological, or physical harm suffered by victims; provides for restitution for victims; prevents victims and/or witnesses from being intimidated by forbidding verbal harassment of witnesses; and penalizes acts of retaliation by defendants against those who testify against them.

The legislation also called for the Attorney General to prepare guidelines to guarantee that victims and witnesses are treated fairly and with understanding by federal officials. In 1983, the Attorney General published guidelines calling for federal law enforcement personnel to provide victims and witnesses with information concerning available services, including medical and social services, compensation programs, and private counseling and support programs. Witnesses should also be advised of laws and procedures that protect them from intimidation by those they are testifying against. Victims who provided addresses and telephone numbers are to be notified of major events in the criminal proceedings, including the arrest of the accused, the times of any court appearances at which the victim may appear, the release or detention of the accused, and the victim's opportunities to address the sentencing court. The guidelines also recommend that federal officials consult victims and witnesses to obtain their views on such procedures as proposed dismissals and plea negotiations. Officials are to try not to disclose the names and addresses of victims and witnesses.

THE PRESIDENT'S TASK FORCE ON CRIME VICTIMS

One dramatic reflection of the growing concern with the rights of the victims of crime was the creation in 1982 of the Presidential Task Force on the Victims of Crime. The Task Force's final report (1982, WDC) called for more understanding treatment of victims by all parts of the criminal justice system and greater protection for victims and witnesses. They further recommended fundamental changes in the American judicial system including the abolition of the exclusionary rule (which throws out any evidence gained as a result of improper police conduct); the abolition of parole so that the offender would be forced to serve the full sentence, reduced only by the good-time credits which the prisoner earned; change the bail laws to permit courts to deny bail to persons found by clear and convincing evidence to present a danger to the community; to forbid the release of those convicted and awaiting sentencing or appeal; and that laws be passed forbidding a criminal to make money from his or her crime through the sale of the story or movie rights about the crime. The recommendations for federal and state action that pertain specifically to crime victims are listed in Table 4.1.

FEDERAL VICTIMS OF CRIME ACT (VOCA)

In 1984, Congress passed the Federal Victims of Crime Act (VOCA, PL 98-473) which committed the federal government to promote state and local victim support and compensation programs. The act established a Crime Victims Fund which has a budget of $150 million annually for 1992 through 1994. The money comes from criminal fines collected from convicted federal offenders, new penalty assessments (e.g. fees paid by parolees during their supervision), forfeited bail bonds, and criminals' literary profits. The money is to be distributed to compensation programs, assistance programs, and Child Abuse Prevention and Treat-

TABLE 4.2

The NOVA Victim Rights System[1]

VICTIM RIGHTS			VICTIM AND WITNESS RIGHTS				
Stage 1: Emergency Response	**Stage 2:** Victim Stabilization	**Stage 3:** Resource Mobilization	**Stage 4:** After Arrest	**Stage 5:** Pre-Court Appearance	**Stage 6:** Court Appearance	**Stage 7:** Pre-Sentence	**Stage 8:** Post-Sentence
When: First contact after crime	**When:** At scene or within 48 hours	**When:** Until resolution of victimization experience	**When:** First contact after arrest	**When:** Prior to hearing/trial	**When:** Day of hearing or trial	**When:** After conviction or entry of guilty plea	**When:** After sentencing
What: Trauma assessment; First aid; Other emergency aid; Crisis intervention	**What:** Safety measures; Crisis counseling; Conflict mediation; Shelter and other emergency aid; Orientation; Referrals	**What:** Outreach; Follow-up counseling and referrals; Monitor referrals; Assistance with financial claims; Assistance with creditors, employers; Property return; Crime prevention; Advocacy	**What:** Start or continue with Stages II and III	**What:** Criminal justice orientation; Scheduling and hearing notification; Case status information; Witness preparation; Employer intervention; Consultation on plea bargaining; Counseling; Advocacy	**What:** Transportation; Reception; Escort; Counseling; Child care; Witness fees; Preparation for outcomes; Advocacy	**What:** Victim impact statement; Restitution plan; Counseling; Information on civil entitlements	**What:** Victim impact statement for parole hearing; Victim input to revocation hearings; Notice on hearing outcomes

[1]Adapted from *Campaign for Victim Rights* (Washington, D.C.: National Organization for Victim Assistance, n.d.), pp. 12-13.

Source: *Serving Crime Victims and Witnesses*, National Institute of Justice, (WDC, 1987)

ment Grants. Two significant changes were made in the VOCA in 1988. In order to be eligible for federal funds, state programs must include compensation for survivors of victims of drunk driving and domestic violence. These two groups had previously been excluded from compensation. The potential for unjust financial gain is perhaps highest for cases of domestic violence and, therefore, they had been excluded in order to avoid compensating the very family that was causing the victimization.

Programs administered by the states provide financial assistance to victims and the survivors of victims of criminal violence. Payments are made for medical expenses, including expenses for mental health counseling and care; loss of wages attributable to a physical injury; and funeral expenses attributable to a death resulting from a compensable crime. Some other compensable expenses are eyeglasses or other corrective lenses, dental services, and prosthetic devices.

THE COMPREHENSIVE CRIME CONTROL ACT OF 1990

In 1990, President George Bush signed the Comprehensive Crime Control Act which covered many aspects of crime control including protections for victims of child abuse, penalties for savings and loan fraud, and mandatory death penalties. Included in the bill is the Victims' Rights and Restitution Act of 1990, which secures for victims of federal crimes the rights to be treated with fairness and respect, reasonably protected from the accused, notified of court procedings, provided an opportunity to meet with a federal prosecutor, and be provided restitution. The act also bars criminals and convicted drunken drivers from declaring bankruptcy to avoid paying restitution.

What do Victim Witness Programs Do?

Victimization programs have to meet the most urgent needs of victims and witnesses, providing the maximum benefit for both the recipient and the criminal justice system while staying within an often inadequate budget. The programs give highest priority to crisis intervention, follow-up counseling, helping victims secure their rights, and court-related services.

Victim witness assistance programs provide a wide range of services to clients, from babysitting to crisis intervention. The National Organization for Victim Rights (NOVA) has divided the services that victims and witnesses may need into eight stages of the criminal justice process, from crime scene assistance to post-sentencing help. Table 4.2 shows this process and the services that may be needed at each stage. Table 4.3 shows the services in functional groupings rather than chronological ones.

Assistance Programs

There are two groups of assistance programs: programs administered by criminal justice agencies (prosecutors, police, and sheriffs) and independently operated multi-service agencies. Programs provided by law enforcement agencies focus on giving out printed information, referrals to other services, notification of the status of investigations, short-term or next day counseling, notification of court dates, and accompaniment of victims to court. The services of the independent agencies focus on informing victims of their rights and the criminal justice processes, providing short-term counseling, making referrals to mental health and social service agencies, and serving as advocates for victims when dealing with employers.

VICTIMS' APPEARANCE AT SENTENCING

Because a victim has a right does not necessarily mean that he or she will exercise that right, nor does it mean that the person has to exercise the right to benefit from it — sometimes it is enough just to have the right. California's Proposition 8, the state's "Victim's Bill of Rights," includes Penal Code Section 1191.1, which states,

TABLE 4.3

Range and Definitions of Victim Witness Services[1]

1. **EMERGENCY SERVICES**
1a. **Medical care:** first aid at the scene of the crime.
1b. **Shelter/food:** finding housing for victims who cannot safely remain in their current lodgings or have no place to stay, and providing food to tide them over the initial crisis period.
1c. **Security repair:** repairing locks, boarding up windows, and similar security measures designed to prevent immediate reburglarization of a home or apartment.
1d. **Financial assistance:** providing petty cash for meeting immediate needs related to transportation, food, shelter, and other necessities.
1e. **On-scene comfort:** providing reassurance and support at the scene of the crime and shortly thereafter.
2. **COUNSELING**
2a. **24-Hour hotline:** round-the-clock availability for providing counseling or referrals to victims who telephone with troubles.
2b. **Crisis Intervention:** meeting urgent emotional or physicial needs of victims as they arise regardless of when they occur.
2c. **Follow-up counseling:** counseling by telephone, in person, or in the home after the initial victimization and for other than crisis reactions; includes providing reassurance and sympathetic listening, and advice for resolving practical problems created by the victimization experience.
2d. **Mediation:** assistance in resolving family disputes and neighborhood or friend disputes without resort to the criminal justice system.
3. **ADVOCACY AND SUPPORT SERVICES**
3a. **Personal advocacy:** acting on behalf of victims or witnesses to secure their rights vis-a-vis other social service agencies and the criminal justice system. Includes the individual services 3b through 3g.
3b. **Employer intervention:** documenting legitimacy of clients' absences or tardinesses to employers and facilitating payment of wages or salary when client must come to court to testify.
3c. **Landlord intervention:** facilitation of postponements in payment of rent, mortgages, utility bills, and similar financial obligations.
3d. **Property return:** facilitating swift return of victims' property being kept by police as evidence.
3e. **Intimidation intervention:** providing reassurance or protection for victims and witnesses experiencing fear of reprisal.
3f. **Victim impact reports:** providing prosecutors and judges with descriptions of the impact of the crime on victims to assist in imposing sentencing and restitution.

ADVOCACY AND SUPPORT SERVICES (continued)
3g. **Legal/paralegal counsel:** providing legal advice, for example, in civil areas related to having been victimized.
3h. **Referral:** recommending or obtaining other sources of assistance not provided directly by the program.
4. **CLAIMS ASSISTANCE**
4a. **Insurance claims aid:** help in securing financial reimbursement for medical expenses, life insurance, and lost wages.
4b. **Restitution assistance:** assistance in urging prosecutors to recommend judges to impose, or probation authorities to collect, restitution.
4c. **Compensation assistance:** help in filling out application forms for victims of violent crime compensation in states that have this program.
4d. **Witness fee assistance:** help in securing any available fee for appearing in court.
5. **COURT-RELATED SERVICES**
5a. **Witness reception:** stationing and staffing a reception area in the courthouse to greet and orient victims and witnesses.
5b. **Court orientation:** providing information on the criminal justice system and the victim's or witness' responsibilities in court.
5c. **Notification:** informing witnesses by mail or phone of required upcoming court appearances.
5d. **Witness alert:** placing witnesses on stand-by to come into court, usually on an hour's notice by telephone if needed to testify.
5e. **Transportation:** transporting witnesses to and from court (and, less often, to shelters or social service agencies).
5f. **Child care:** providing baby-sitting services for witnesses testifying in court.
5g. **Escort to court:** accompanying witnesses to the courtroom and sitting with them during the proceedings.
6. **SYSTEM-WIDE SERVICES**
6a. **Public education:** informing the public at large through the media, brochures, or speeches of what they can do to minimize their risks of victimization and availability of the program.
6b. **Legislative advocacy:** lobbying or providing assistance (e.g., drafting legislation, providing testimony from victims and witnesses) to secure state legislation that provides or funds additional services to victims.
6c. **Training:** training police, prosecutors, or other human service provider groups on how to improve their handling of victims and witnesses and how to avail themselves of the program's services.

[1]These categories (but not the definitions) were originally suggested, in somewhat different form, in the National Evaluation Program Phase I Assessment of Victim/Witness Assistance Projects conducted for the Law Enforcement Assistance Administration by the American Institutes for Research.

Source: *Serving Crime Victims and Witnesses*, National Institute of Justice, (WDC, 1987)

The victim or next of kin has the right to appear, personally or by counsel, at the sentencing proceeding and to reasonably express his or her views concerning the crime, the person responsible, and the need for restitution. The court, in imposing sentence, shall consider the statements of victims and next of kin . . . and shall state on the record its conclusion concerning whether the person would pose a threat to public safety if granted probation . . .

Edwin Villmoare and Virginia V. Neto, in *Victim Appearances at Sentencing Under California's Victims' Bill of Rights* (1987, WDC: NIJ), found that, "in California, victim appearances seem to have had little effect on the criminal justice system or on sentencing." The victims, rather than wanting to participate in their cases, were generally more concerned with what was going on with their case. About 80 percent of the victims interviewed indicated that the existence of the right was the important thing, not whether they actually made use of that right. "Victim impact statements included in the presentence reports prepared by the local probation departments provide many victims with a satisfactory opportunity to express their views. An informal interview with a sympathetic probation officer is often preferable to a recitation in open court." Most victims seemed only to want somebody to understand their situation, and recognize their rights as victims.

Only 44 percent of those interviewed were aware of the right to appear at sentencing, and victims showed up in fewer than 3 percent of the cases. Of those who knew of their right and indicated why they did not use it, 37 percent were satisfied with the criminal justice system's handling of the case, while 30 percent believed their appearance before the judge would make no difference. Another 28 percent were too upset, afraid of retaliation, or confused.

Of the 3 percent who did show up, 34 percent wanted to express their feelings to the judge, 32

percent, to perform their "duty," and 26 percent, to achieve a sense of justice or to influence the sentence. Over half (54 percent) of these appearing victims reported that they felt different after making their statement to the judge. Of these, 59 percent expressed positive feelings of satisfaction or relief, 25 percent felt angry, fearful, or helpless, and 10 percent felt dissatisfied. Fewer than half (45 percent) believed their participation affected the sentence. Four out of five (82 percent) thought the sentence was too light.

Two-thirds of the judges saw no need for the victim to appear, but an equally large majority of district attorneys thought it was needed. When asked whether the right was "effective," 81 percent of probation officers answered "minimally or not at all" compared with 69 percent of judges and 48 percent of prosecutors. Sixty-six percent of district attorneys, compared with 40 percent of judges, thought that victim appearances increased the amount of restitution awarded.

KEEPING THE VICTIM INFORMED

Brian E. Forst and Jolene C. Hernon, in *The Criminal Response to Victim Harm* (1985, WDC), found that victims were more likely to be satisfied — both with the way their cases turned out and with the criminal justice system generally — when they knew the outcome of the case, when they perceived that they had influenced that outcome, when they had contact with a victim assistance program, and when the defendant was convicted and sent to jail or prison. Forty-eight percent of the victims also said they would have been more satisfied had they been better informed about case progress. Not surprisingly, when all groups in the system — victim, police, prosecutor, and judge — were asked how to improve the system, only one recommendation was offered by more than 20 percent of each of the four groups — keep victims better informed. Forst and Hernon concluded that, "the primary opportunity for improved dealings with victims lies in keeping them better informed."

In June 1991, the United States Supreme Court ruled, in *Payne v. Tennessee* (59 LW 4818), that the family of a murder victim could provide victim impact evidence (the effect the murder had on the rest of the victim's family) during the sentencing portion of the trial.

Pervis Payne was convicted of two counts of first-degree murder and one count of assault with intent to commit murder for killing Charisse Christopher, her 2-year-old daughter, and attempting to kill her 3-year-old son. In arguing for the death penalty the prosecutor had presented statements from the victims' family. "There is obviously nothing you can do for Charisse and Lacie Jo. But there is something you can do for Nicholas."

The Supreme Court majority in an opinion written by Chief Justice Rehnquist, overturned two other similar cases, (*Booth v. Maryland*, 482 LW 496, and *South Carolina v. Gathers*, 490 LW 805). In these two cases the court had held that under the Eighth Amendment (cruel and unusual punishment shall not be inflicted), a jury could not consider a victim impact statement in a capital (punishable by death) case.

Rehnquist cited the Supreme Court in *Booth* which had found that, "the capital defendant must be treated as a 'uniquely individual human being,' and therefore the Constitution requires the jury to make an individualized determination as to whether the defendant should be executed based on the 'character of the individual and the circumstances of the crime.'" In *Payne*, the majority found that a victim impact statement in no way limited the defendant's right to plead his case, and the addition of the "victim's impact evidence is simply another form or method of informing the sentencing authority about the specific harm caused by the crime in question, evidence of a general type long considered by sentencing authorities." The High court concluded that by prohibiting victim impact statements, the case was unfairly weighted in favor of the defendant.

. . . while virtually no limits are placed on the relevant mitigating evidence a capital defendant may introduce concerning his own circumstances, the state is barred from either offering "a glimpse of the life" which a defendant "chose to extinguish," or demonstrating the loss to the victim's family and to society. . . . Victim impact evidence is simply another form or method of informing the sentencing authority about the specific harm caused by the crime in question. . . .

Justice Stevens and Justice Marshall, with Justice Blackmun joining, dissented, fearing that the present court was overturning constitutional liberties and that if this decision could reinterpret Supreme Court precedent, then scores of other Court decisions depended on nothing more than the inclination of the majority of the Court. Justice Stevens wrote,

Until today our capital punishment jurisprudence has required that any decision to impose the death penalty be based solely on evidence that tends to inform the jury about the character of the offense and the character of the defendant. Evidence that serves no purpose other than to appeal to the sympathies or emotions of the juror has never been considered admissible. . . .

Today's majority has obviously been moved by an argument that has strong political appeal but no proper place in a reasoned judicial argument.

THE FEAR OF BEING A VICTIM

The fear of being a victim can affect anyone, whether he or she has been victimized or not. In fact, research has found that fear of crime is only weakly related to having been a victim. A stronger predictor of fear is vulnerability, that is a lack of defense or protection (loss of control), exposure to risk, and the perceived seriousness of the consequences. For this reason, the elderly, who often feel unable to defend themselves and for whom an attack could lead to injury from which they could have a hard time recovering, and women, who fear rape, a crime with higher levels of injury and longer lasting trauma than any other crime, report the greatest fear of victimization.

In "Vulnerability: Towards a Better Understanding of a Key Variable in the Genesis of Fear of Crime," Martin Killias examined international crime research and factors of fear (1990, vol. 5, no. 2, *Violence and Victims*, New York: Springer Publishing). He found that the availability of help influenced how seriously respondents perceived the consequences of a crime. Elderly people who lived alone were not more fearful than those who did not unless they saw themselves as socially isolated and financially limited. Those who lived in center cities were fearful of places where they saw a high rate of crime (parks, parking lots, deserted commercial areas), while rural people feared areas where the risk might be very low, but the chance of getting help was minimal and the consequences could therefore be very serious. For example, Swiss villagers reported being afraid of walking in the forest at night.

Nighttime provokes more fear than daytime. Humans orient themselves with their eyes, and the loss of control and sense of isolation contribute to the fear of being out at night. The National Crime Victimization Survey reports higher rates of armed offenses at night, although the overall rates of crime are not significantly different between night and day. (See Chapter III.)

Killias concluded that fear of crime was a combination of how people perceived the three factors of exposure to risk, the seriousness of the possible consequences, and the loss of control — not the actual rates of crime. By dealing with these issues, Killias proposes more progress could be made against the fear of crime than by sticking to statistics or dismissing the fear felt by women and the elderly as "irrational."

CHAPTER V

JUVENILE DELINQUENCY

In 1991, the FBI *Uniform Crime Reports* (UCR) reported 1,749,343 juveniles were arrested. A juvenile is defined by each state and, although most states put the upper age limit at 17 years old, some states set it as low as 15 years of age. The UCR, however, breaks down arrest records by age, using under 18 years as one category. Five percent of the arrests were for violent crimes (see Chapter II for definitions), 32 percent for property crime, and the rest for a wide variety of offenses including fraud, vandalism, prostitution, offenses against family and children, vagrancy, etc. About 11 percent of arrests involved a drug or liquor law offense (Table 5.1). As in all types of crimes, men were arrested far more frequently than women; 77 percent of arrests were males (Table 5.2) while 23 percent

TABLE 5.1

Total Arrests of Persons under 15, 18, 21, and 25 Years of Age, 1991

[10,148 agencies; 1991 estimated population 189,961,000]

Offense charged	Total all ages	Number of persons arrested				Percent of total all ages			
		Under 15	Under 18	Under 21	Under 25	Under 15	Under 18	Under 21	Under 25
TOTAL	10,743,755	614,863	1,749,343	3,244,997	4,908,560	5.7	16.3	30.2	45.7
Murder and nonnegligent manslaughter	18,654	302	2,626	6,722	10,192	1.6	14.1	36.0	54.6
Forcible rape	30,350	1,742	4,766	8,745	13,468	5.7	15.7	28.8	44.4
Robbery	139,182	9,979	35,632	61,981	86,098	7.2	25.6	44.5	61.9
Aggravated assault	368,483	16,029	52,653	100,001	158,203	4.3	14.3	27.1	42.9
Burglary	328,790	44,320	109,965	168,084	213,484	13.5	33.4	51.1	64.9
Larceny–theft	1,215,303	168,007	369,227	533,450	677,244	13.8	30.4	43.9	55.7
Motor vehicle theft	161,628	20,076	70,659	100,181	120,607	12.4	43.7	62.0	74.6
Arson	14,916	4,756	6,940	8,391	9,699	31.9	46.5	56.3	65.0
Violent crime[1]	556,669	28,052	95,677	177,449	267,961	5.0	17.2	31.9	48.1
Property crime[2]	1,720,637	237,159	556,791	810,106	1,021,034	13.8	32.4	47.1	59.3
Crime Index total[3]	2,277,306	265,211	652,468	987,555	1,288,995	11.6	28.7	43.4	56.6
Other assaults	789,144	50,026	122,624	211,150	335,600	6.3	15.5	26.8	42.5
Forgery and counterfeiting	77,066	1,221	6,866	19,272	33,297	1.6	8.9	25.0	43.2
Fraud	292,597	2,870	10,943	40,627	93,629	1.0	3.7	13.9	32.0
Embezzlement	10,602	158	784	2,505	4,441	1.5	7.4	23.6	41.9
Stolen property; buying, receiving, possessing	130,579	10,107	35,220	61,822	82,201	7.7	27.0	47.3	63.0
Vandalism	252,469	53,730	107,890	144,351	175,427	21.3	42.7	57.2	69.5
Weapons; carrying, possessing, etc.	178,955	10,693	37,575	70,785	102,070	6.0	21.0	39.6	57.0
Prostitution and commercialized vice	81,536	148	1,075	7,875	24,250	.2	1.3	9.7	29.7
Sex offenses (except forcible rape and prostitution)	82,228	7,406	14,417	21,565	31,052	9.0	17.5	26.2	37.8
Drug abuse violations	781,250	8,582	60,428	174,608	317,541	1.1	7.7	22.3	40.6
Gambling	12,913	143	912	2,243	3,550	1.1	7.1	17.4	27.5
Offenses against family and children	72,527	996	2,944	9,185	20,007	1.4	4.1	12.7	27.6
Driving under the influence	1,288,876	402	13,437	112,991	329,755	[4]	1.0	8.8	25.6
Liquor laws	453,807	9,320	104,210	311,161	357,216	2.1	23.0	68.6	78.7
Drunkenness	657,119	1,994	16,372	74,446	169,357	.3	2.5	11.3	25.8
Disorderly conduct	569,314	32,346	99,322	187,133	289,980	5.7	17.4	32.9	50.9
Vagrancy	31,262	596	2,257	5,186	8,276	1.9	7.2	16.6	26.5
All other offenses (except traffic)	2,480,902	74,706	247,853	586,947	1,026,278	3.0	10.0	23.7	41.4
Suspicion	14,707	1,253	3,150	4,994	7,042	8.5	21.4	34.0	47.9
Curfew and loitering law violations	73,125	21,859	73,125	73,125	73,125	29.9	100.0	100.0	100.0
Runaways	135,471	60,296	135,471	135,471	135,471	44.5	100.0	100.0	100.0

[1]Violent crimes are offenses of murder, forcible rape, robbery, and aggravated assault.
[2]Property crimes are offenses of burglary, larceny–theft, motor vehicle theft, and arson.
[3]Includes arson.
[4]Less than one-tenth of 1 percent.

Source: *Crime in the United States, 1990*, Federal Bureau of Investigation, (WDC, 1992)

TABLE 5.2

Male Arrests, Distribution by Age, 1991

[10,148 agencies; 1991 estimated population 189,961,000]

Offense charged	Total all ages	Ages under 15	Ages under 18	Ages 18 and over
TOTAL	8,729,684	458,371	1,351,758	7,377,926
Percent distribution[1]	100.0	5.3	15.5	84.5
Murder and nonnegligent manslaughter	16,733	283	2,504	14,229
Forcible rape	29,964	1,706	4,679	25,285
Robbery	127,280	8,786	32,525	94,755
Aggravated assault	318,180	13,104	44,678	273,502
Burglary	299,541	39,841	100,688	198,853
Larceny-theft	825,976	121,094	263,323	562,653
Motor vehicle theft	145,446	16,992	62,669	82,777
Arson	12,965	4,306	6,319	6,646
Violent crime[2]	492,157	23,879	84,386	407,771
Percent distribution[1]	100.0	4.9	17.1	82.9
Property crime[3]	1,283,928	182,233	432,999	850,929
Percent distribution[1]	100.0	14.2	33.7	66.3
Crime Index total[4]	1,776,085	206,112	517,385	1,258,700
Percent distribution[1]	100.0	11.6	29.1	70.9
Other assaults	659,120	37,087	93,778	565,342
Forgery and counterfeiting	50,116	820	4,567	45,549
Fraud	167,066	1,961	7,933	159,133
Embezzlement	6,474	113	508	5,966
Stolen property; buying, receiving, possessing	114,964	8,915	31,645	83,319
Vandalism	224,934	49,093	98,890	126,044
Weapons; carrying, possessing, etc.	166,133	9,744	35,193	130,940
Prostitution and commercialized vice	27,786	80	510	27,276
Sex offenses (except forcible rape and prostitution)	76,440	6,793	13,407	63,033
Drug abuse violations	652,168	7,200	53,899	598,269
Gambling	11,270	139	888	10,382
Offenses against family and children	59,406	591	1,932	57,474
Driving under the influence	1,117,678	318	11,591	1,106,087
Liquor laws	366,496	5,189	75,189	291,307
Drunkenness	588,569	1,414	13,837	574,732
Disorderly conduct	455,189	24,552	78,531	376,658
Vagrancy	27,898	501	1,956	25,942
All other offenses (except traffic)	2,057,464	56,206	195,497	1,861,967
Suspicion	12,287	980	2,481	9,806
Curfew and loitering law violations	53,511	15,122	53,511	....
Runaways	58,630	25,441	58,630	....

Source: *Crime in the United States, 1990,*
Federal Bureau of Investigation, (WDC, 1992)

TABLE 5.3

Female Arrests, Distribution by Age, 1991

[10,148 agencies; 1991 estimated population 189,961,000]

Offense charged	Total all ages	Ages under 15	Ages under 18	Ages 18 and over
TOTAL	2,014,871	155,692	397,585	1,616,486
Percent distribution[1]	100.0	7.7	19.7	80.3
Murder and nonnegligent manslaughter	1,921	19	122	1,799
Forcible rape	386	36	87	299
Robbery	11,902	1,193	3,107	8,795
Aggravated assault	50,303	2,925	7,975	42,328
Burglary	29,249	4,479	9,277	19,972
Larceny-theft	389,327	46,913	105,904	283,423
Motor vehicle theft	16,182	3,084	7,990	8,192
Arson	1,951	450	621	1,330
Violent crime[2]	64,512	4,173	11,291	53,221
Percent distribution[1]	100.0	6.5	17.5	82.5
Property crime[3]	436,709	54,926	123,792	312,917
Percent distribution[1]	100.0	12.6	28.3	71.7
Crime Index total[4]	501,221	59,099	135,083	366,138
Percent distribution[1]	100.0	11.8	27.0	73.0
Other assaults	130,024	12,939	28,846	101,178
Forgery and counterfeiting	26,950	401	2,299	24,651
Fraud	125,531	909	3,010	122,521
Embezzlement	4,128	45	276	3,852
Stolen property; buying, receiving, possessing	15,615	1,192	3,575	12,040
Vandalism	27,535	4,637	9,000	18,535
Weapons; carrying, possessing, etc.	12,822	949	2,382	10,440
Prostitution and commercialized vice	53,750	68	565	53,185
Sex offenses (except forcible rape and prostitution)	5,788	613	1,010	4,778
Drug abuse violations	129,082	1,382	6,529	122,553
Gambling	1,643	4	24	1,619
Offenses against family and children	13,121	405	1,012	12,109
Driving under the influence	171,198	84	1,846	169,352
Liquor laws	87,311	4,131	29,021	58,290
Drunkenness	68,550	580	2,535	66,015
Disorderly conduct	114,125	7,794	20,791	93,334
Vagrancy	3,364	95	301	3,063
All other offenses (except traffic)	423,438	18,500	52,356	371,082
Suspicion	2,420	273	669	1,751
Curfew and loitering law violations	19,614	6,737	19,614	....
Runaways	76,841	34,855	76,841	....

Source: *Crime in the United States, 1990,*
Federal Bureau of Investigation, (WDC, 1992)

were women (Table 5.3). Men were arrested three times more often for the more serious crimes listed by the FBI Crime Index. Female juveniles were arrested more often than male juveniles only for running away and prostitution. Between 1990 and 1991 arrests for persons under 18 years of age increased 3.2 percent (Table 5.4). Despite yearly increases in juvenile arrests, it is important to remember that the juvenile population has declined by 14 percent during the past decade.

THE CRIMES

The Office of Juvenile Justice and Delinquency Prevention (OJJDP), a branch of the United States Department of Justice, keeps two sets of statistics on juvenile crime — juveniles who go to court and juveniles who are put in custody (1991,"Children in Custody" WDC: *Juvenile Justice Bulletin*). The OJJDP has divided juvenile crimes into general categories for statistical purposes. The two main

TABLE 5.4

Total Arrest Trends, 1990–1991

[8,757 agencies; 1991 estimated population 173,791,000; 1990 population 171,641,000]

Offense charged	Total all ages			Under 15 years of age			Under 18 years of age			18 years of age and over		
	1990	1991	Percent change	1990	1991	Percent change	1990	1991	Percent change	1990	1991	Percent change
TOTAL	10,034,629	9,885,040	−1.5	539,533	578,112	+7.2	1,593,302	1,643,815	+3.2	8,441,327	8,241,225	−2.4
Murder and nonnegligent manslaughter	16,971	17,397	+2.5	263	288	+9.5	2,384	2,485	+4.2	14,587	14,912	+2.2
Forcible rape	27,806	28,000	+.7	1,496	1,642	+9.8	4,249	4,476	+5.3	23,557	23,524	−.1
Robbery	126,814	130,323	+2.8	8,452	9,648	+14.2	30,905	34,136	+10.5	95,909	96,187	+.3
Aggravated assault	329,692	333,427	+1.1	13,122	14,875	+13.4	45,254	48,621	+7.4	284,438	284,806	+.1
Burglary	299,817	304,312	+1.5	39,098	41,637	+6.5	98,876	103,237	+4.4	200,941	201,075	+.1
Larceny—theft	1,098,004	1,122,142	+2.2	150,102	158,014	+5.3	331,382	346,481	+4.6	766,622	775,661	+1.2
Motor vehicle theft	156,611	152,704	−2.5	18,668	19,202	+2.9	67,690	67,430	−.4	88,921	85,274	−4.1
Arson	13,467	13,777	+2.3	3,882	4,490	+15.7	5,905	6,533	+10.6	7,562	7,244	−4.2
Violent crime[1]	501,283	509,147	+1.6	23,333	26,453	+13.4	82,792	89,718	+8.4	418,491	419,429	+.2
Property crime[2]	1,567,899	1,592,935	+1.6	211,750	223,343	+5.5	503,853	523,681	+3.9	1,064,046	1,069,254	+.5
Crime Index total[3]	2,069,182	2,102,082	+1.6	235,083	249,796	+6.3	586,645	613,399	+4.6	1,482,537	1,488,683	+.4
Other assaults	706,932	733,221	+3.7	41,681	47,597	+14.2	106,013	116,233	+9.6	600,919	616,988	+2.7
Forgery and counterfeiting	65,134	68,856	+5.7	1,102	1,133	+2.8	5,931	6,369	+7.4	59,203	62,487	+5.5
Fraud	236,498	261,741	+10.7	2,310	2,759	+19.4	8,606	10,433	+21.2	227,892	251,308	+10.3
Embezzlement	10,101	9,607	−4.9	114	153	+34.2	791	746	−5.7	9,310	8,861	−4.8
Stolen property; buying, receiving, possessing	118,548	117,957	−.5	8,430	9,484	+12.5	30,756	32,564	+5.9	87,792	85,393	−2.7
Vandalism	233,682	237,434	+1.6	46,113	51,158	+10.9	94,813	102,803	+8.4	138,869	134,631	−3.1
Weapons; carrying, possessing, etc.	159,884	165,565	+3.6	7,884	10,073	+27.8	29,797	35,266	+18.4	130,087	130,299	+.2
Prostitution and commercialized vice	79,342	76,549	−3.5	127	135	+6.3	1,138	995	−12.6	78,204	75,554	−3.4
Sex offenses (except forcible rape and prostitution)	75,744	75,450	−.4	6,300	7,041	+11.8	12,467	13,670	+9.6	63,277	61,780	−2.4
Drug abuse violations	782,758	722,077	−7.8	8,102	8,021	−1.0	59,156	56,182	−5.0	723,602	665,895	−8.0
Gambling	13,733	11,876	−13.5	142	139	−2.1	741	821	+10.8	12,992	11,055	−14.9
Offenses against family and children	59,674	65,582	+9.9	779	892	+14.5	2,419	2,683	+10.9	57,255	62,899	+9.9
Driving under the influence	1,273,054	1,173,704	−7.8	313	354	+13.1	14,445	12,157	−15.8	1,258,609	1,161,547	−7.7
Liquor laws	476,523	421,542	−11.5	9,565	8,796	−8.0	111,159	97,938	−11.9	365,364	323,604	−11.4
Drunkenness	666,448	611,906	−8.2	2,146	1,876	−12.6	17,861	15,384	−13.9	648,587	596,522	−8.0
Disorderly conduct	537,125	509,372	−5.2	28,043	30,423	+8.5	90,254	92,670	+2.7	446,871	416,702	−6.8
Vagrancy	28,670	30,465	+6.3	746	568	−23.9	2,413	2,139	−11.4	26,257	28,326	+7.9
All other offenses (except traffic)	2,245,542	2,290,839	+2.0	64,375	69,195	+7.5	221,842	232,148	+4.6	2,023,700	2,058,691	+1.7
Suspicion (not included in totals)	16,896	14,392	−14.8	1,048	1,222	+16.6	2,953	3,060	+3.6	13,943	11,332	−18.7
Curfew and loitering law violations	66,446	69,414	+4.5	19,355	20,743	+7.2	66,446	69,414	+4.5	....	....	....
Runaways	129,609	129,801	+.1	56,823	57,776	+1.7	129,609	129,801	+.1	....	....	....

[1]Violent crimes are offenses of murder, forcible rape, robbery, and aggravated assault.
[2]Property crimes are offenses of burglary, larceny–theft, motor vehicle theft, and arson.
[3]Includes arson.

Source: *Crime in the United States, 1990*, Federal Bureau of Investigation, (WDC, 1992)

categories are delinquency offenses (acts which are illegal regardless of the age of the perpetrator) and status offenses (acts which are illegal only for minors such as truancy or underage drinking). These categories are subdivided into types of crimes — crimes against persons (murder, forcible rape, robbery, and assault are defined as violent, while manslaughter, simple assault and sexual assault are defined as "other"); crimes against property (burglary, larceny/theft, automobile theft, and arson are labelled serious, and vandalism, forgery, counter- feiting, fraud, possessing stolen property and unauthorized use of a motor vehicle are "other"); drug/alcohol law violations (manufacture, sale or use); public order offenses; probation offenses; sex offenses, excluding forcible rape, but including statutory rape, prostitution, indecent exposure; disorderly conduct, probation and parole violations. Status offenses include running away, truancy, curfew violations, ungovernability, and liquor law violations.

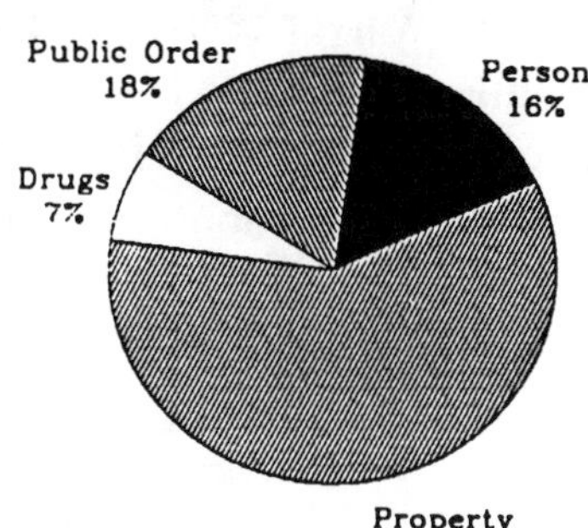

FIGURE 5.1

Offense Characteristics of
Delinquency Cases, 1988

Source: Juvenile *Court Statistics, 1988*, National Center for Juvenile Justice (WDC, December 1990)

COURT STATISTICS

Juvenile courts disposed of an estimated 559,000 delinquency cases in 1988 (the most recent year for which statistics are available). A case can include more than one charge, i.e. a youth that is brought in on three different robbery charges at the same time is counted as one case. Disposed refers to the court taking some definite action (a petitioned case), thereby excluding all the cases that are informally dismissed (nonpetitioned) by releasing the youth or referring him/her to another agency. The reason that the Department of Justice only includes the petitioned cases in their analysis is that there is no standard procedure among different agencies on how they handle nonpetitioned cases, making statistical evaluation impossible.

Processing

There is no uniform procedure for processing juvenile cases, but cases do follow a similar path. Cases are first screened by an intake department. The intake department can be the court itself, a state department of social services or a prosecutor's office. The intake officer may decide that the case will be dismissed for lack of evidence or be resolved informally by referring it to a social services agency, by imposing a fine or some form of restitution, or through informal probation. A petition is filed with the court requesting an adjudicatory (meaning that it will be judged) or waiver hearing when a case is to be handled formally. At an adjudication hearing, the case can be dismissed or recommendations can be made for sentencing, but in the cases where a youth is judged to be delinquent or a status offender, the case then goes on to a disposition hearing where the judge decides the

TABLE 5.5

Delinquency Case Trends, 1987-1988

	Number of Cases (in thousands)				Number of Cases (in thousands)		
	1987	1988	Percent Change		1987	1988	Percent Change
Delinquency	1,150	1,156	0.5	Race			
Person	184	190	3.0	White	810	790	-2.4
Property	683	681	-0.3	Person	106	107	0.5
Drugs	73	81	10.1	Property	499	487	-2.4
Public Order	209	204	-2.5	Drugs	49	50	0.6
				Public Order	156	147	-5.5
Age				Nonwhite	340	366	7.5
15 or Less	644	652	1.3	Person	78	83	6.5
Person	107	113	5.3	Property	184	194	5.4
Property	412	413	0.2	Drugs	24	31	29.8
Drugs	25	29	14.7	Public Order	54	57	6.3
Public Order	99	98	-1.7				
16 or More	506	503	-0.5	Secure Detention	229	237	3.7
Person	77	77	0.0	Person	43	46	7.5
Property	27	27	-1.1	Property	112	113	0.9
Drugs	48	52	7.6	Drugs	22	26	22.3
Public Order	110	107	-3.1	Public Order	53	52	-1.0
Sex				White	139	136	-2.2
Male	932	941	0.9	Person	20	21	5.0
Person	148	152	2.7	Property	72	69	-4.1
Property	557	557	0.1	Drugs	10	11	4.5
Drugs	62	69	11.6	Public Order	37	35	-4.1
Public Order	166	163	-1.7				
Female	218	215	-1.4	Nonwhite	89	101	12.8
Person	37	38	4.3	Person	22	24	9.9
Property	126	124	-1.9	Property	40	43	9.9
Drugs	12	12	1.8	Drugs	11	16	38.3
Public Order	43	41	-5.4	Public Order	16	17	6.0

Note: Detail may not add to total because of rounding

Source: Juvenile *Court Statistics, 1988*, National Center for Juvenile Justice (WDC, December 1990)

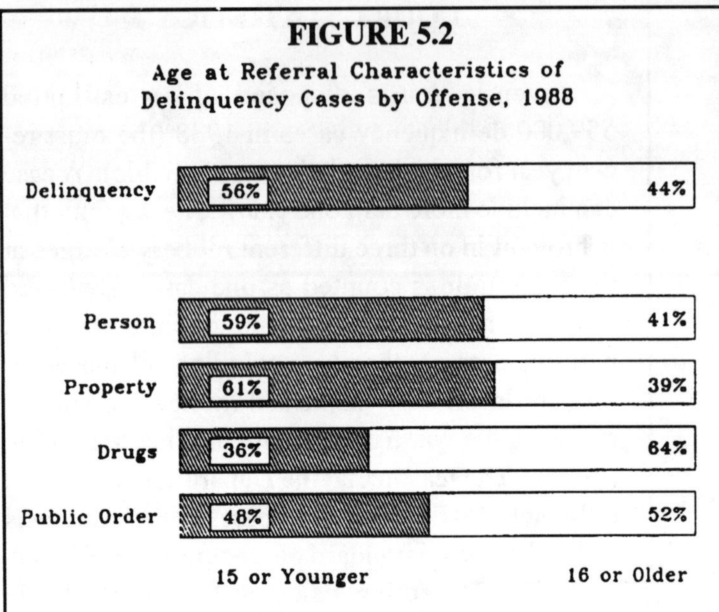

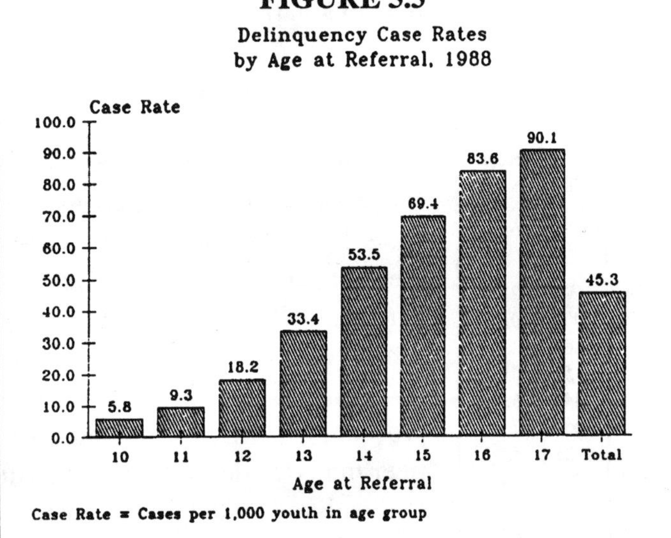

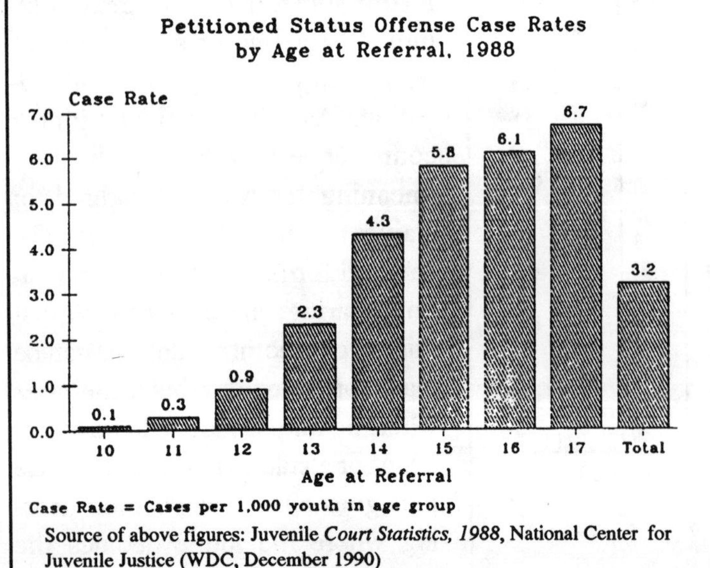

Source of above figures: Juvenile *Court Statistics, 1988*, National Center for Juvenile Justice (WDC, December 1990)

most appropriate sentence. Options vary, but sentences can include commitment to an institution for delinquents, referral to an agency, community service, or restitution. If a waiver hearing is requested, the juvenile court judge is asked to decide if the case should be waived to a criminal court for prosecution where the youth will be tried as an adult.

The Offenses

The number of juvenile delinquency cases increased 0.5 percent from 1987 to 1988. Property offenses made up 59 percent of the cases, 16 percent involved an offense against persons, and 7 percent were drug law violations. Between 1987 and 1988, drug cases increased 10 percent, person offense cases increased 13 percent, and property offense cases declined 0.3 percent (Figure 5.1 and Table 5.5).

The delinquency rate per 1,000 youth at risk increases with age. Fifty-six percent of petitioned delinquency cases involved youth who were 15 years or younger (Figure 5.2). Delinquency case rates averaged 70 cases per 1,000 youth for 15 year olds; 83 per 1,000 for 16 year olds; and for 17 year olds, 90 per 1,000 (Figure 5.3). The rate of status offenses declined sharply after 17 years (Figure 5.4) except for liquor law violations. Offenses such as truancy and ungovernability dropped between 15 and 17 years of age, while liquor law violations continued to increase with age (Figure 5.5).

Half of the delinquent crimes were nonindex crimes (crimes not counted by the FBI statistics), while 6 percent were violent crimes, and 44 percent were index property crimes (Table 5.6). Between 1987 and 1988, the number of male delinquency crimes increased .9 percent, while

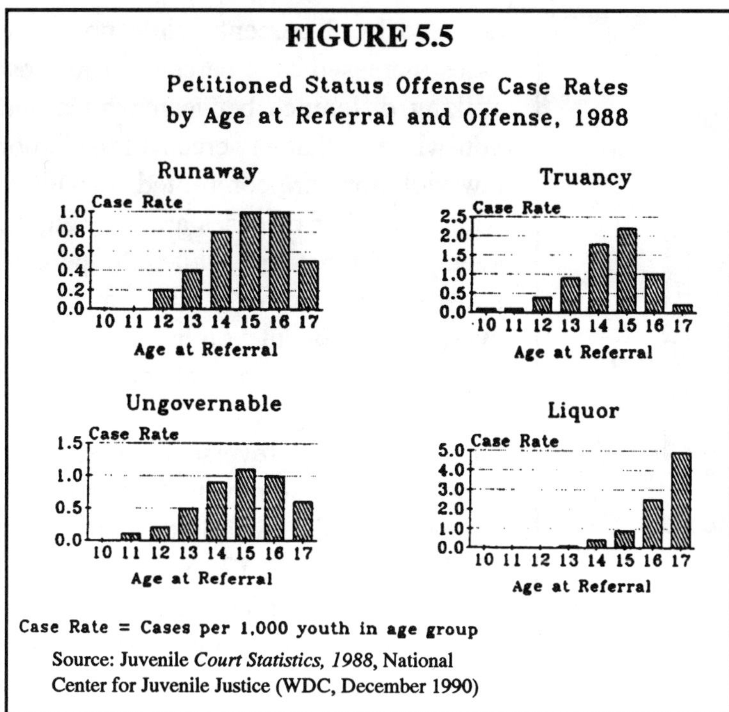

Source: Juvenile *Court Statistics, 1988*, National
Center for Juvenile Justice (WDC, December 1990)

TABLE 5.6
Reasons for Referral of Delinquency Cases, 1988

Reason for Referral	Number of Cases	Percent
Index Violent	68,400	5.9
Criminal Homicide	1,700	0.1
Forcible Rape	4,000	0.3
Robbery	21,300	1.8
Aggravated Assault	41,400	3.6
Index Property	503,000	43.5
Burglary	130,500	11.3
Larceny-Theft	311,100	26.9
Motor Vehicle Theft	54,700	4.7
Arson	6,700	0.6
Nonindex Delinquency	584,500	50.6
Simple Assault	102,300	8.9
Stolen Property Offenses	30,000	2.6
Trespassing	48,100	4.2
Vandalism	82,300	7.1
Weapons Offenses	22,000	1.9
Other Sex Offenses	17,000	1.5
Drug Law Violations	80,200	6.9
Obstruction of Justice	78,500	6.8
Liquor Law Violations	14,000	1.2
Disorderly Conduct	46,300	4.0
Other Delinquent Acts	63,800	5.5
Total Delinquency	1,156,000	100.0

Note: Detail may not add to total because of rounding.

Source: Juvenile *Court Statistics, 1988*, National
Center for Juvenile Justice (WDC, December 1990)

17 years of age was 82 per 1,000 to 148 per 1,000, and for females, 23 per 1,000 at age 14 to 30 per 1,000 at age 17 (Figure 5.6). The number of petitioned cases for white youths decreased by 2.4 percent from 1987 to 1988 (810,000 to 790,000) while it increased more than 7 percent for nonwhite youth (340,000 to 366,000) (Table 5.5). White youths were responsible for about 68 percent of all property, drug law, person, and public order cases, and non-whites were accountable for 32 percent (Figure 5.7). Comparing rates per 1,000 youth, the nonwhite delinquency case rate was, on average, twice the white rate, and the nonwhite rate of person offense cases was more than three times the white rate (Figure 5.8).

In 1988, 82,000 status offense cases were formally handled by the courts, a decrease of 2 percent between 1987 and 1988. Fifty-six percent of all formally processed status offenders were below the age of 16. These youth were involved in 65 percent of all runaway cases, 84 percent of truancy cases, 69 percent of ungovernable cases, but only 19 percent of all status liquor law violations (Figure 5.9). This pattern reverses with age. Status liquor law violations made up 57 percent of the offenses of youths 16 years or older and only 11 percent of those who were younger, while truancy represented 40 percent of the younger youth's offenses, dropping to 9 percent of those 16 or older (Figure 5.10). Liquor law violations, unlike other offenses which decrease with age, more than quadrupled between the ages of 15 and 17 (Figure 5.5).

Characteristics

While relatively few females are involved in violent crimes, females are involved in a much greater proportion of status offenses (41 percent). They represent nearly two-thirds of the runaway offenses and nearly half of the ungovernability cases. Liquor law violations are the only area in which the males dominate (76 percent) (Figure 5.11). Between 1987 and 1988, white status cases

the number of female cases decreased 1.4 percent. The male delinquency rate was almost five times greater than the female rate (Table 5.5), and while the rate increased for both with age, it rose much more sharply for males. The male's rate from 14 to

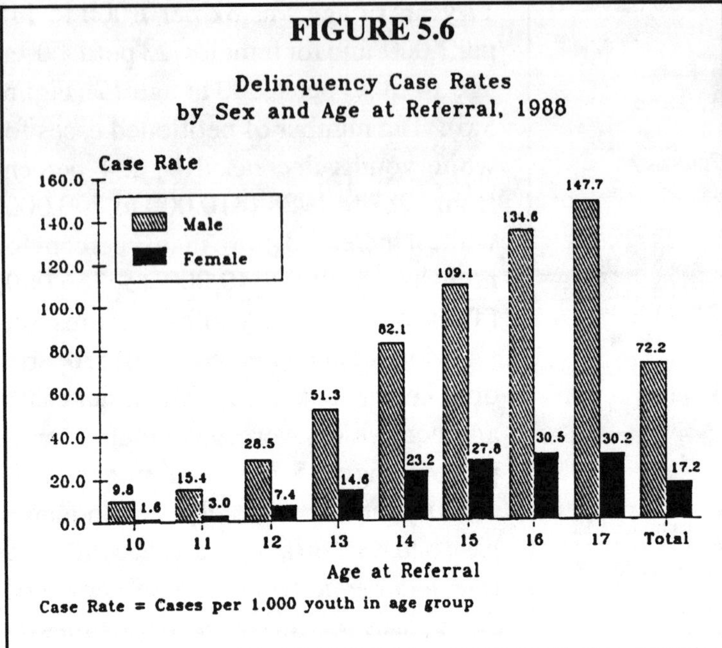

FIGURE 5.6

Delinquency Case Rates
by Sex and Age at Referral, 1988

Case Rate = Cases per 1,000 youth in age group

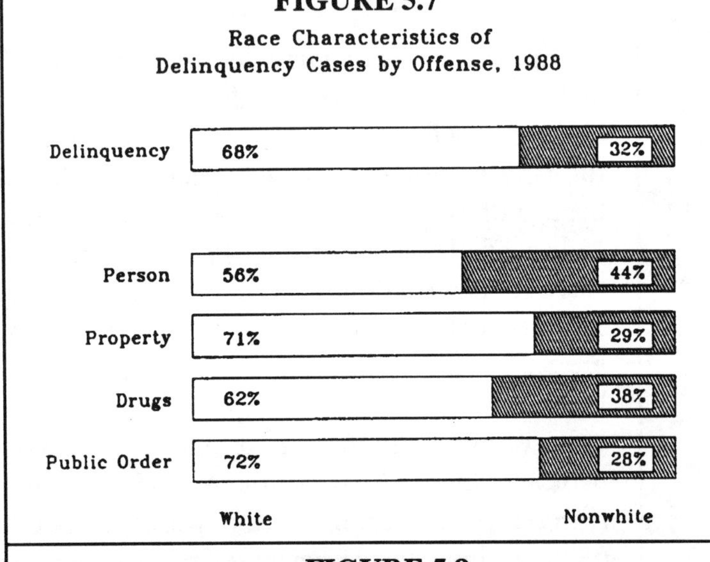

FIGURE 5.7

Race Characteristics of
Delinquency Cases by Offense, 1988

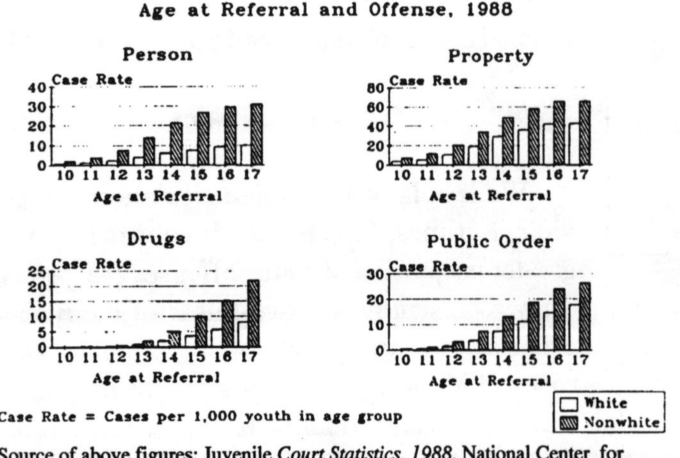

FIGURE 5.8

Delinquency Case Rates by Race,
Age at Referral and Offense, 1988

Case Rate = Cases per 1,000 youth in age group

Source of above figures: Juvenile *Court Statistics, 1988*, National Center for Juvenile Justice (WDC, December 1990)

declined by 3 percent, while nonwhite cases increased by 2 percent. The most striking difference between whites and non-whites is that 94 percent of the liquor law violations are committed by whites, while the other offenses are divided, on average, 80 percent white, 20 percent nonwhite (Figure 5.12). The rate, however, of delinquent youths per 1,000 is approximately twice as high for nonwhites at every age (Figure 5.13). In status offense cases, the reverse is true. The nonwhite rate is somewhat higher among younger juveniles, nearly the same at 15 and less than half at 17 years old. This is due to the high white rate of liquor law violations, more than 5 per 1,000 whites versus 1 per 1,000 nonwhites (Figure 5.14).

SOURCES OF REFERRAL AND SECURE DETENTION

Law enforcement agencies referred (sent on) to court 84 percent of delinquency cases, but only 41 percent of status offense cases, while parents, schools, victims, probation officers, and others referred the remaining cases (Figures 5.15 and 5.16). Among delinquency cases, police were most likely to refer drug and property offenses and least likely to refer public order cases. Among status cases, the police reported 91 percent of liquor law violations and one quarter of the runaway offenses. They were least likely to report ungovernable youth.

In 1988, 21 percent of delinquency offense cases and 10 percent of status offenders were held in confinement at some point between referral to court and final disposition. Youths charged with a person offense were held 24 percent of the time, violations of public order, 26 percent, and drug offenses were held 33 percent of the time. By contrast, status offenses were less likely to receive confine-

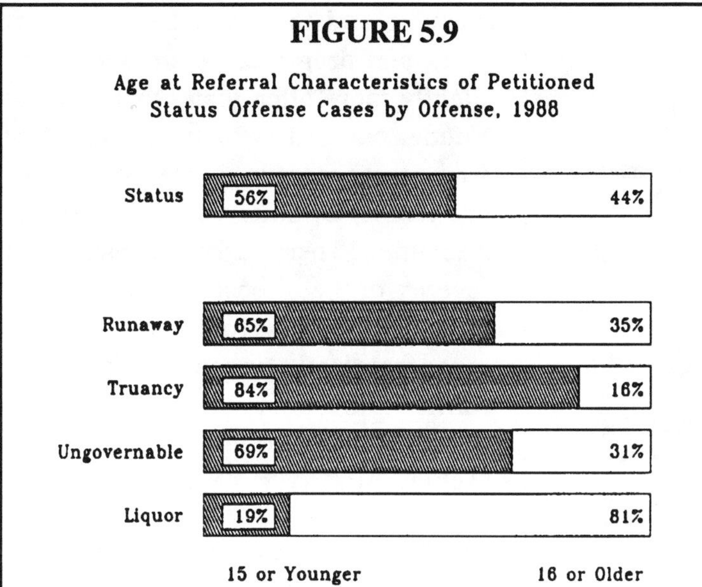

FIGURE 5.9

Age at Referral Characteristics of Petitioned
Status Offense Cases by Offense, 1988

FIGURE 5.10

Offense Characteristics of Petitioned Status
Offense Cases by Age at Referral, 1988

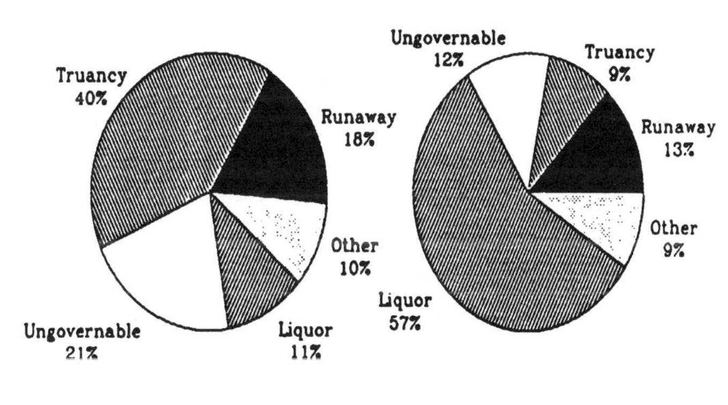

FIGURE 5.11

Sex Characteristics of Petitioned
Status Offense Cases by Offense, 1988

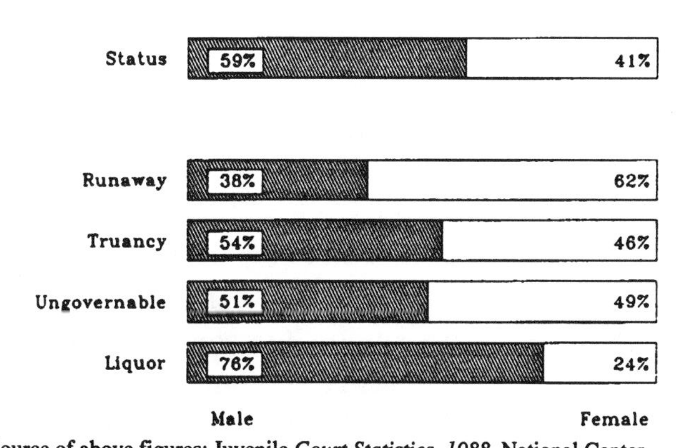

Source of above figures: Juvenile *Court Statistics, 1988,* National Center
for Juvenile Justice (WDC, December 1990)

ment; runaways were held in 25 percent of the cases, while truants and liquor law violators were held only about 4 percent of the time (Figures 5.17 and 5.18).

Drug and Alcohol Offenses

In 1989, drug and alcohol offenses accounted for 12 percent of juveniles detained, up from 8 percent in 1987 (Table 5.7). The BJS suggests that growth in the prison population before 1984 may have been linked to increases in incarceration for serious offenses. Much of the growth since 1984, however, has resulted from the increase in drug violations and the even greater increase in the probability of going to jail or prison for drug offenders.

Furthermore, the Bureau of Justice Statistics reports that victims believe their offenders were under the influence of drugs or alcohol in 38 percent of the offenses, if the offender were male, 17 percent if the offender were female. Interestingly, victims report that offenders younger than 20 years of age appeared to be under the influence in 29 percent of the situations, but in only 18 percent of the offenses commited by persons 21 or older. It is important to note that in an additional one-third to one-half of the situations, the victims could not determine whether the victim was or was not under the influence of a substance, but the victim could not eliminate the possibility (Table 5.8).

Adjudication

In 1988, 559,000 delinquency cases were formally petitioned. A small percentage (2 percent) were waived to criminal court, 58 percent were adjudicated, and the rest were dismissed by the judge, usually with some sanction such as a fine or community service (nonadjudicated) (Table 5.9). Person offenses were most

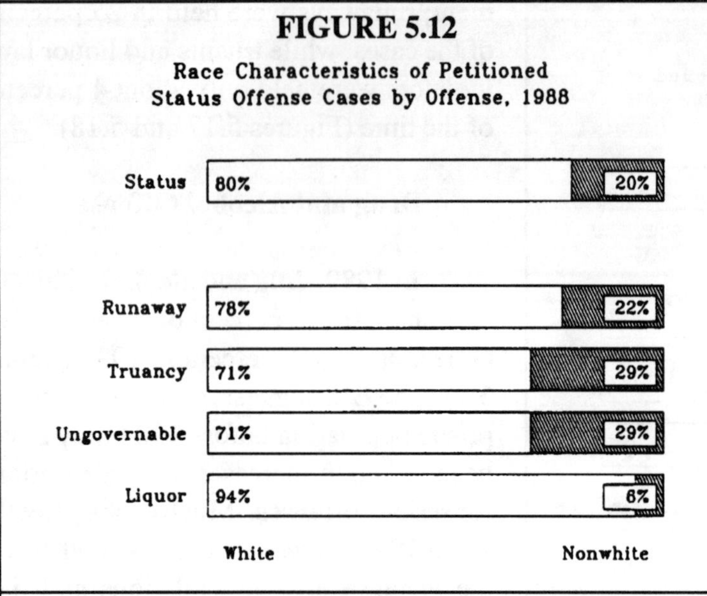

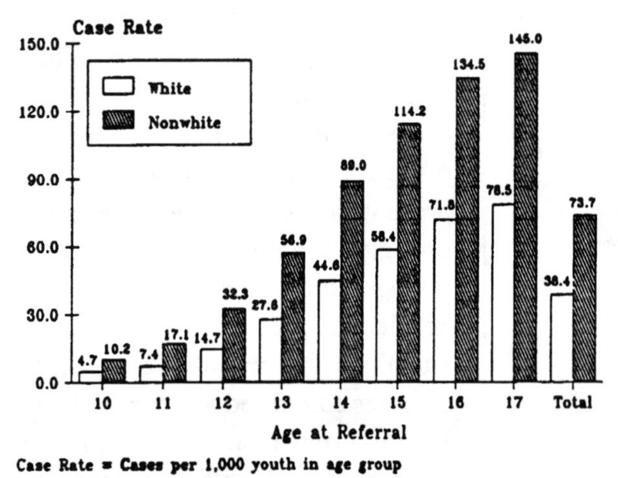

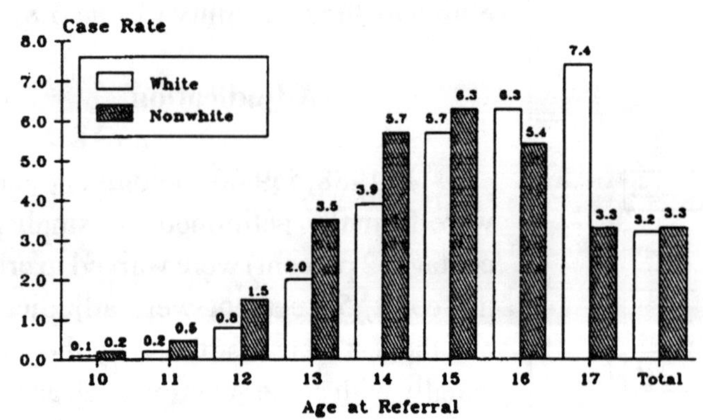

Source of above figures: Juvenile *Court Statistics, 1988*, National Center for Juvenile Justice (WDC, December 1990)

often waived to criminal court (4 percent), and drug cases were adjudicated slightly more often than other offenses. Youths charged with public order offenses were more often placed in a juvenile facility or otherwise removed from the home (30 percent), not because of the severity of the offense, but because this category includes youth who have escaped from institutions and probation and parole violators. Probation was the most common disposition in all categories (Table 5.10).

Sixty-one percent of the 82,000 formally petitioned status offense cases in 1988 were adjudicated. Sixty percent of that 61 percent were given probation, the most common disposition. The rest were divided between placement out of the home (18 percent), released (7 percent), or sanctioned with fines or community service ("Other") in 15 percent of the cases (Table 5.11). Table 5.12 shows the dispositions of each category of status offense. Liquor law violations were the only offenses having a large percentage (42) of "other" dispositions. "Other," in this case, refers to fines or referrals to a treatment center. The highest rate of youths placed outside the home, approximately one-third, were those adjudicated ungovernable.

CHANGING PHILOSOPHIES

Over the last fifteen years, the handling of status crimes has changed. The Juvenile Justice and Delinquency Prevention Act of 1974 (PL 93-415) offered substantial federal funds to states on the condition that they try to reduce the detention of status offenders. The primary responsibility for status offenders had been transferred from the juvenile courts to child welfare agencies. As a result, the character of the juvenile courts' activities

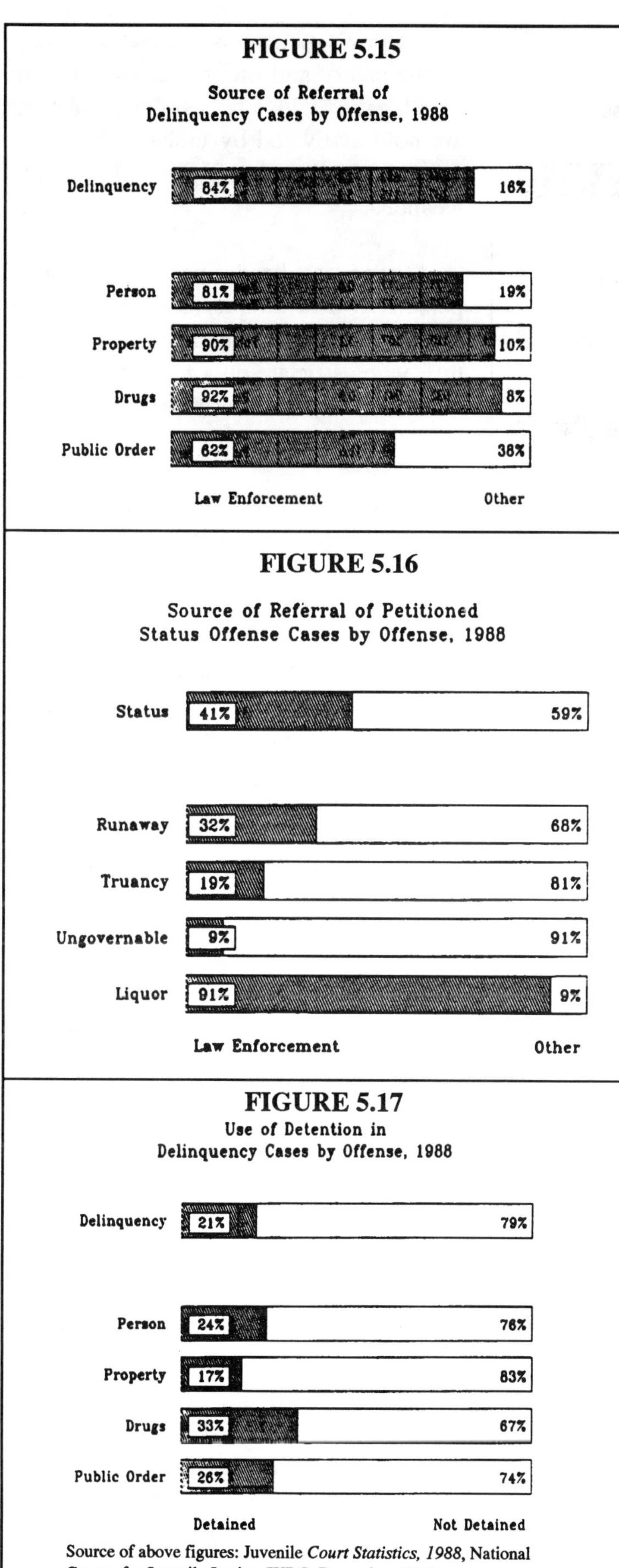

FIGURE 5.15

Source of Referral of
Delinquency Cases by Offense, 1988

FIGURE 5.16

Source of Referral of Petitioned
Status Offense Cases by Offense, 1988

FIGURE 5.17

Use of Detention in
Delinquency Cases by Offense, 1988

Source of above figures: Juvenile *Court Statistics, 1988*, National Center for Juvenile Justice (WDC, December 1990)

changed with delinquency offense cases making up the majority of the cases. Prior to this many juvenile detention centers contained a substantial number of young people whose only "crime" was that their parents could no longer control them. By not routinely institutionalizing the adolescents, the courts were showing that the youth were seen as deserving the same rights as adults. The logical extension of this has been that children are now being legally treated as if they were adults.

Traditionally, the philosophical difference between juvenile delinquency proceedings and adult criminal proceedings had been that the juvenile offender was viewed as misguided and correctable rather than as a criminal. Juveniles were "delinquent," not guilty; they received treatment, not punishment; juvenile proceedings took place in a closed court to protect the offender and his or her family; there were wide discretionary powers for probation officers, the court and correction agencies, depending on a youth's past history. Long-term incarceration was rare; and cases were disposed of quickly with a broad range of disposition alternatives.

The current trend in juvenile justice is to treat juveniles more like adults. On the one hand, if they are treated like adults, chronic offenders may receive adult sentences, removing them from society, and getting away from the notion of rehabilitation and replacing it with punishment for a crime committed. On the other hand, in an adult court, juveniles will be entitled to open court-room proceedings and jury trials and avoid a closed system over which they have no control.

YOUTH GANGS

Although gangs have been a part of American life since the early 18th cen-

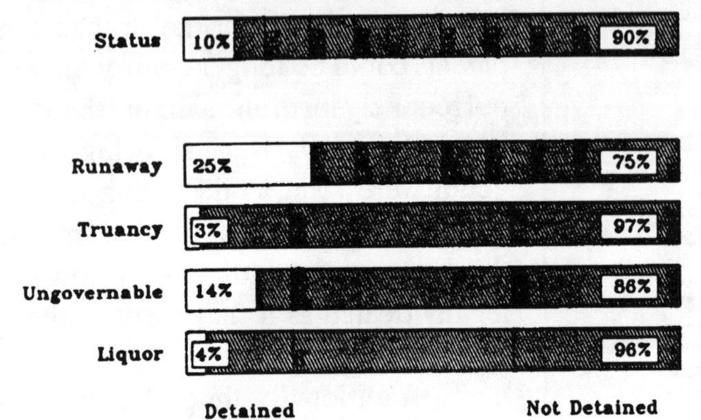

FIGURE 5.18

Use of Detention in Petitioned Status Offense Cases by Offense, 1988

Source: Juvenile *Court Statistics, 1988,* National Center for Juvenile Justice (WDC, December 1990)

TABLE 5.7

Types of offenses and other reasons for which male and female juveniles were held in public juvenile facilities: 1987 and 1989.

	1987			1989		
	Total	Male	Female	Total	Male	Female
Total juveniles	53,503	46,272	7,231	56,123	49,443	6,680
Delinquent offenses[a]	50,269	44,757	5,512	53,037	47,843	5,194
Offenses against persons	13,300	12,297	1,003	14,327	13,210	1,117
Violent—Murder, forcible rape, robbery, and aggravated assault	7,943	7,438	505	8,566	7,976	590
Other—Manslaughter, simple assault, sexual assault	5,357	4,859	498	5,761	5,234	527
Property offenses	23,431	21,272	2,159	22,780	20,849	1,931
Serious—Burglary, arson larceny/theft, and motor vehicle theft	15,746	14,595	1,151	15,181	14,112	1,069
Other—Vandalism, forgery, counterfeiting, fraud, stolen property, unauthorized use of a motor vehicle	7,685	6,677	1,008	7,599	6,737	862
Alcohol/drug offenses	4,161	3,733	428	6,586	6,067	519
Public order offenses	2,380	1,864	516	2,788	2,406	382
Probation violations	4,200	3,183	1,017	4,920	3,942	978
Other delinquent offenses[b]	2,797	2,408	389	1,636	1,369	267
Nondelinquent reasons	3,234	1,515	1,719	3,086	1,600	1,486
Status offenses[c]	2,523	1,198	1,325	2,245	1,128	1,117
Abuse/neglect[d]	429	190	239	426	205	221
Other[e]	29	20	9	113	78	35
Voluntarily admitted	253	107	146	302	189	113

[a] Offenses that would be criminal if committed by adults.

[b] Includes unknown and unspecified delinquent offenses.

[c] Offenses that would not be criminal for adults, such as running away, truancy, and incorrigibility.

[d] Also includes those held for emotional disturbance or mental retardation.

[e] Includes all other unspecified reasons for detention or commitment.

Source: *Children in Custody, 1989,* Office of Juvenile Justice and Delinquency Prevention, (WDC, 1991)

tury, today's gangs pose a greater threat to public safety and order than ever before. Youth gangs originated as social clubs, but are now motivated by violence, intimidation, and the illegal trafficking of drugs and weapons.

A gang can be defined as a group of persons with a unique name, identifiable marks or symbols, who claim a territory or turf, who associate on a regular basis, and who often engage in criminal or antisocial behavior.

The increasing violence among youth today is leading more and more juveniles into criminal court. "Today we are arresting more gang members than ever before; we are getting more convictions than ever before; and we are getting longer sentences than ever before, but ironically, we have more gangs than ever before," Frank Radke, the Commanding Officer of the Gang Crimes Section of the Chicago Police Department declared in a conference on gang crime. When we think of juvenile crime today, we often think of street gangs.

Drugs and Gangs

Some gang activity occurs because of turf wars, and some is drug related. Schools are often extensions of the street for juvenile gang and drug activity. Law enforcement experts report growing evidence that drugs are contributors to increases in gang violence. The extremely high profits and the abundance of cocaine have contributed to the spread of gangs all across the nation.

Characteristics of violent offenders under the influence of drugs or alcohol, as reported by victims

Offender characteristics[a]		Percent of violent crime incidents where victim perceived the offender to be:						
		Not under the influence	Under the influence					Not known if under the influence
	Total		Total	Alcohol only	Drugs only	Both	Not sure which substance	
Sex								
Male	100%	19%	38%	23%	6%	6%	2%	43%
Female	100	34	27	17	6	3	1[b]	38
Both sexes	100	17	47	23	13	11	—[b]	37
Race								
White	100%	23%	42%	28%	5%	7%	2%	35%
Black	100	18	27	12	9	4	2	55
Other	100	18	39	20	8[b]	6[b]	4[b]	43
Age								
20 or younger	100%	29%	23%	14%	5%	3%	1%[b]	48%
21 or older	100	18	45	28	8	8	2	37
Mixed ages	100	11	44	27	4[b]	12	2[b]	44
Relationship to victim								
Nonstranger	100%	31%	40%	24%	6%	8%	1%	28%
Stranger	100	13	35	22	7	5	2	52

Note: Percents may not total 100% because of rounding. For incidents with more than one offender, data show incidents in which at least one offender was under the influence. Crimes committed by mixed racial groups are not presented.

— Less than 0.5%.

[a] Describes single and multiple offenders.

[b] Estimate is based on 10 or fewer sample cases; see source.

Source: *Drugs and Crime Facts, 1990*, Bureau of Justice Statistics, (WDC, 1991)

TABLE 5.9

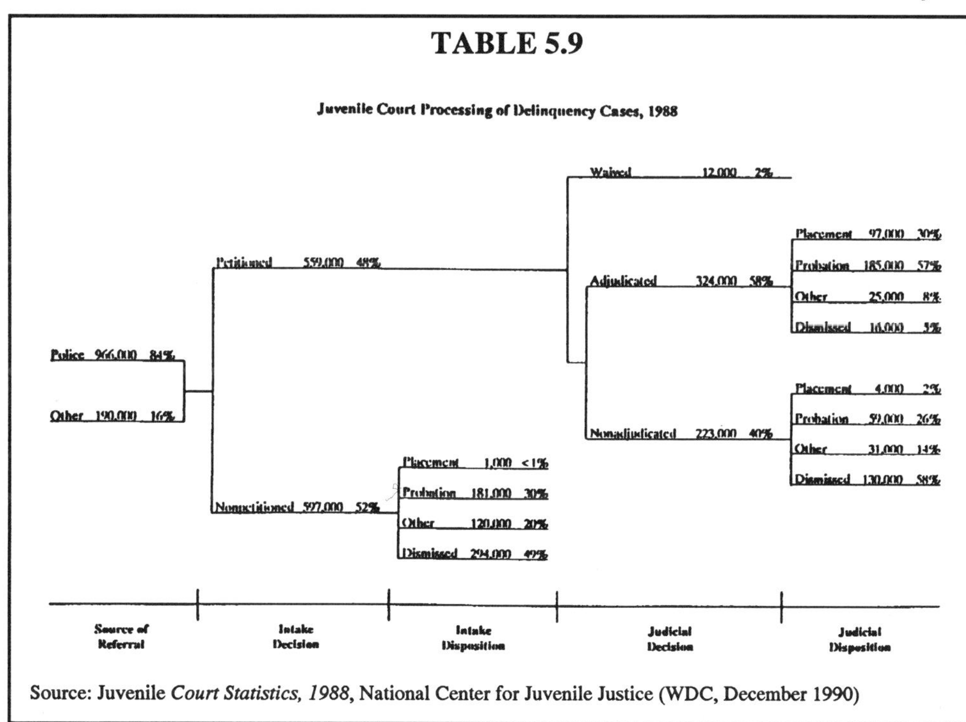

Juvenile Court Processing of Delinquency Cases, 1988

Source: Juvenile *Court Statistics, 1988*, National Center for Juvenile Justice (WDC, December 1990)

Young Juveniles

One of the most disturbing aspects of the gang problem is the number of young children involved. Older gang members recruit 8, 9, and 10 year-olds to sell drugs and be lookouts because the penalties are very minimal for juveniles that young. Ironically, the change in the status offense laws discouraging detention for juveniles has given older gang members a persuasive argument to recruit young children. It is hard for many underprivileged 9 and 10 year-olds to turn away from the lure of earning $200 a week for being a lookout for a crack house, especially if there are no negative consequences. The gangs also serve as families for children whose own families may be dysfunctional. "We don't have to intimidate youngsters to recruit them. They want to be with us. We know what they need," a gang member told officials. Gangs provide emotional support, shelter, and clothing — in essence, what the child's family may not be providing. Nonetheless, some children are intimidated into joining gangs either out of fear or for protection from other gangs.

CHILDREN IN CUSTODY

What are the courts doing with the growing population of juvenile offenders? In about one third of the formally and informally petitioned cases of delinquency and status offenses, the court ordered a youth placed outside the home. There are many different types of facilities for youth including juvenile detention centers, shelters, reception and diagnostic centers, training schools, camps,

The Jamaican Posse is an example of an organized drug gang (not necessarily made up of juveniles). These gangs are not only well established in the drug trade, they are extremely violent. The Drug Enforcement Administration estimates that posses are responsible for 40 percent of the crack cocaine business in the United States.

TABLE 5.10

Juvenile Court Processing of Delinquency Cases Within Offense Categories, 1988

Person Offenses

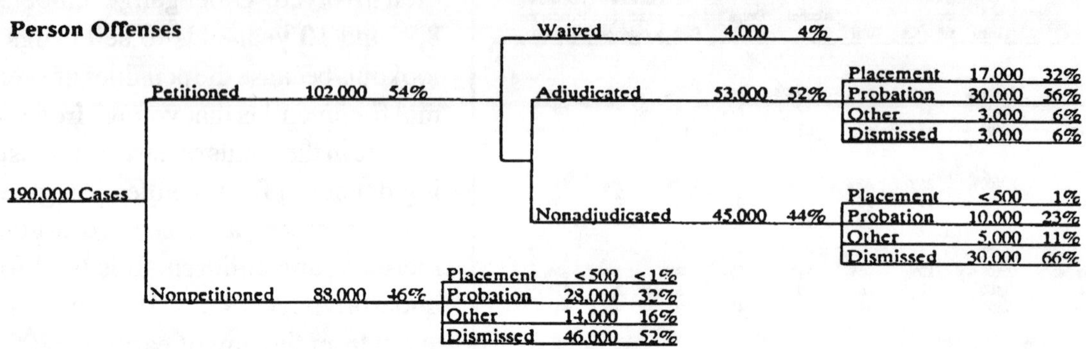

Property Offenses

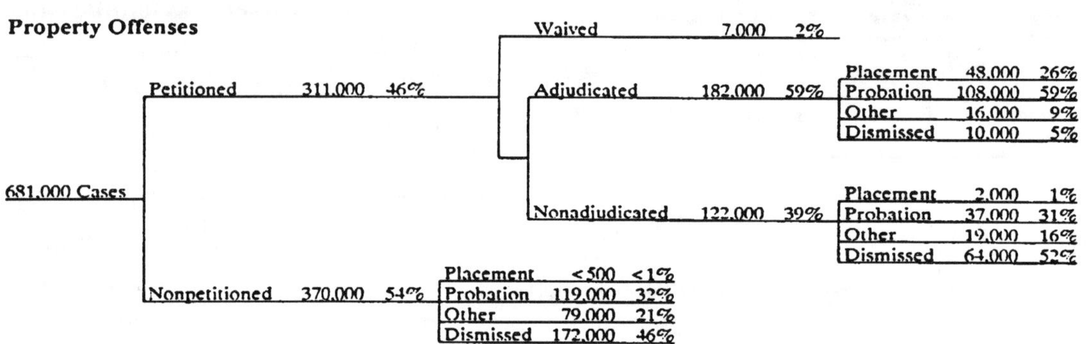

Drug Offenses

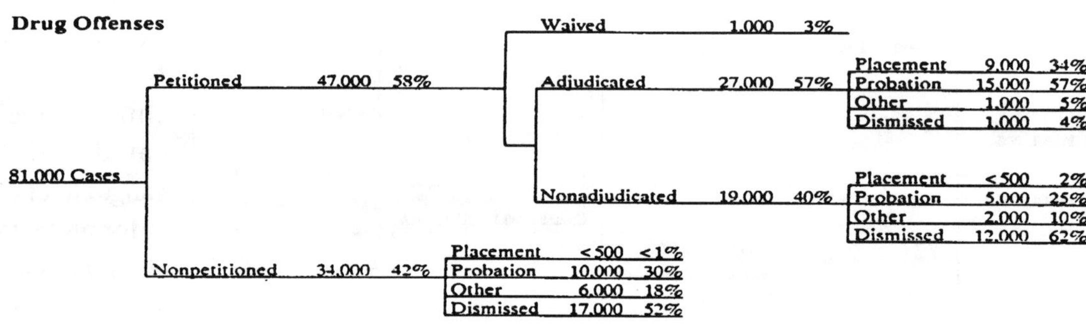

Public Order Offenses

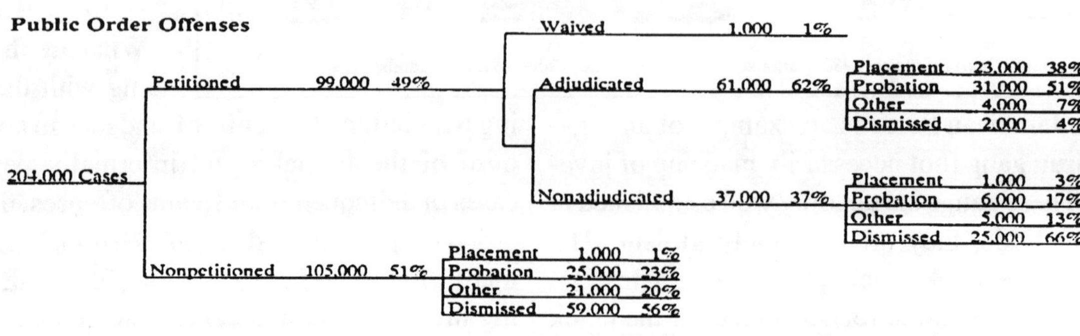

Source: Juvenile *Court Statistics, 1988*, National Center for Juvenile Justice (WDC, December 1990)

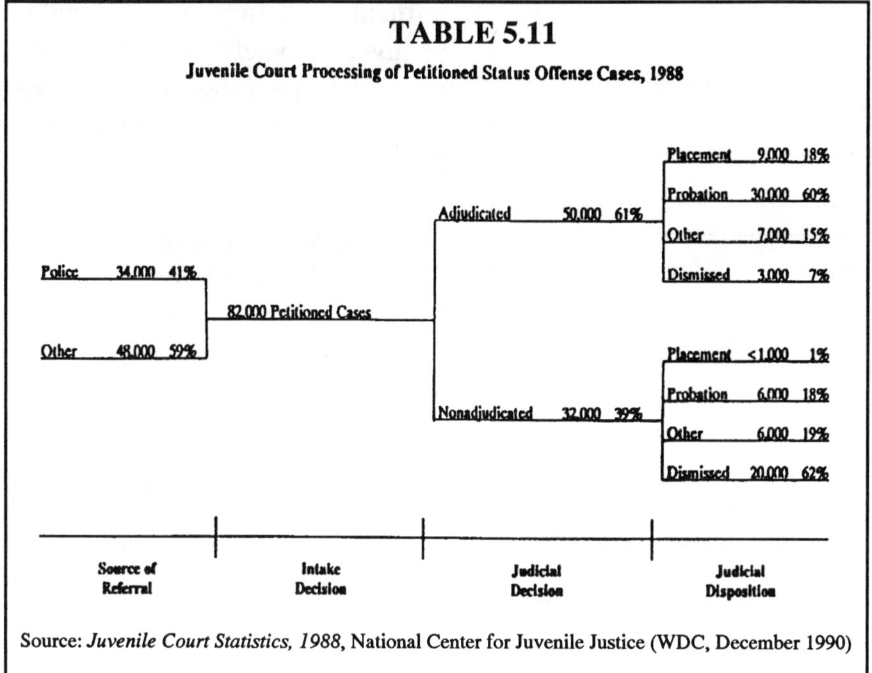

TABLE 5.11

Juvenile Court Processing of Petitioned Status Offense Cases, 1988

Source: *Juvenile Court Statistics, 1988*, National Center for Juvenile Justice (WDC, December 1990)

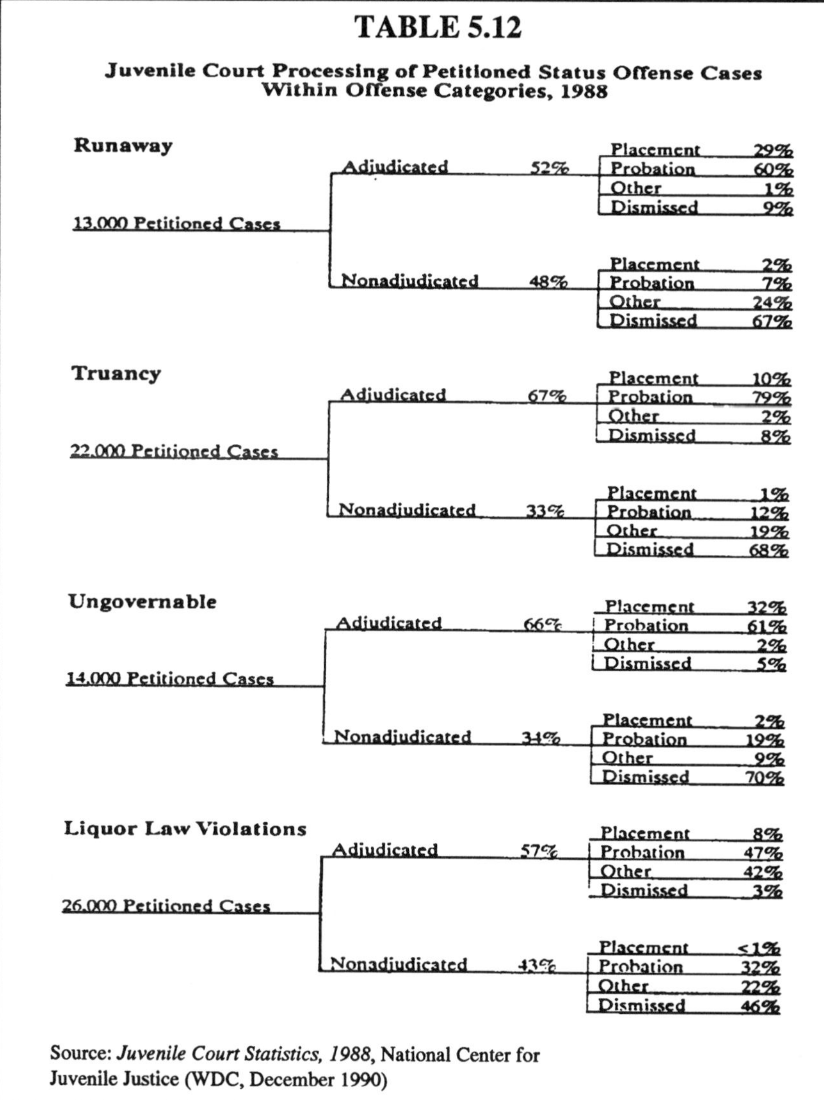

TABLE 5.12

Juvenile Court Processing of Petitioned Status Offense Cases Within Offense Categories, 1988

Source: *Juvenile Court Statistics, 1988*, National Center for Juvenile Justice (WDC, December 1990)

ranches, and group homes. Not all of the placed youths are accused delinquent and status offenders. Some are placed for treatment or as a result of abuse, dependency, or neglect. Some are held temporarily while other arrangements are being made.

More than half (55 percent) of the public institutions were long-term and the rest (45 percent) were short-term. Long-term facilities held two-thirds of the juveniles in custody, primarily those who had been committed for a criminal offense or had been placed for treatment. Short-term facilities housed mainly young people awaiting judgment, commitment, or placement. There are two different types of facilities within the private/public sector. There are institutional environments which impose restrictions on residents' movement and limit access to the community, and there are open environments which allow greater movement and more access to the community. These include shelters, ranches, forestry camps or farms, halfway homes and group homes. About 59 percent of youth were in an institutional environment, while the remaining 41 percent were held in open environment facilities.

A 1989 census (1991, "Children in Custody," WDC: Office of Juvenile Justice and Delinquency Prevention) found that 56,123 young people were

TABLE 5.13

Selected demographic characteristics of juveniles held in public juvenile facilities on census days: 1987 and 1989.

	1987	1989	Percent change
Total juveniles	53,503	56,123	+5%
Sex			
Male	46,272	49,443	+7%
Female	7,231	6,680	−8%
Minority status			
Nonminority[a]	23,375	22,201	−5%
Minority	30,128	33,922	+13%
Black[b]	20,898	23,836	+14%
Hispanic[c]	7,887	8,671	+10%
Other	1,343	1,415	+5%
Age on date of census			
9 years and under	73	45	−38%
10–13 years	2,811	3,276	+17%
14–17 years	43,898	44,894	+2%
18 years and over	6,721	7,908	+18%

[a] Includes whites not of Hispanic origin.

[b] Includes blacks not of Hispanic origin.

[c] Includes both whites and blacks of Hispanic origin.

Source: *Children in Custody, 1989*, Office of Juvenile Justice and Delinquency Prevention, (WDC, 1991)

TABLE 5.14

Characteristics of youth in long-term, State-operated juvenile institutions, yearend 1987

	Percent of youth			
Characteristics	Total	11–14 years old	15–17 years old	18 years and older
Sex				
Male	93.1%	92.4%	93.2%	93.3%
Female	6.9	7.6	6.8	6.7
Race				
White	53.1%	46.4%	53.8%	54.6%
Black	41.1	46.7	40.3	40.5
Other[*]	5.7	6.9	5.9	4.8
Ethnicity				
Hispanic	18.9%	10.1%	15.5%	30.7%
Non-Hispanic	81.1	89.9	84.5	69.3
Education				
8th grade or less	12.7%	46.0%	9.5%	4.5%
7th or 8th grade	41.0	51.5	48.8	18.2
Some high school	43.6	2.5	41.1	67.7
High school graduate	2.9	0	.8	9.6
Median education	8 yrs	7 yrs	8 yrs	10 yrs
Number of youth	25,024	3,096	15,130	6,798

Note: Percents may not add to 100% due to rounding.

[*] Includes American Indians, Alaska Natives, Asians, and Pacific Islanders.

Source: *Survey of Youth in Custody, 1987*, Bureau of Justice Statistics, (WDC, 1988)

confined to publicly-run state and local juvenile detention, correctional, and shelter facilities — about 221 juveniles in custody per 100,000 juveniles.

Characteristics of Youth in Custody

There were more than seven times as many male offenders (88 percent) in custody in public institutions at the time of the 1989 census than females (12 percent). Females were more often placed in private facilities; in 1986, they accounted for 31 percent of the juveniles in private facilities. In public facilities, whites were 40 percent of the population, blacks, 42 percent, Hispanics, 15 percent, and other races, 2 percent. The number of white juveniles decreased slightly (5 percent) between 1987 and 1989, while the number of black and Hispanic juveniles increased 14 and 10 percent respectively. Juveniles under 9 years old represented 0.1 percent of those in custody, 6 percent were 10 to 13 year-olds, 80 percent were 14 to 17 years old, and 14 percent were 18 years or older (Table 5.13).

Nineteen out of 20 (95 percent) juveniles were held for delinquent offenses. Four percent were in custody for status offenses, and approximately 1 percent were detained or committed because they were abused, neglected, or were other nonoffenders or voluntary admissions. Although the number of juveniles in custody increased by 5 percent between 1987 and 1989, the number held for serious, violent offenses including murder, non-negligent manslaughter, robbery and aggravated assault increased 8 percent. The number of juveniles held for drug or alcohol offenses increased 58 percent (Table 5.7).

TABLE 5.15

Current offense of youth in long-term, State-operated juvenile institutions, by sex, race, and age, yearend 1987

Age and current offense	Percent of youth						
		Sex		Race		Ethnicity	
	Total	Male	Female	White	Black	Hispanic	Non-Hispanic
Less than 18 years old:							
Total	100.0%	100.0%	100.0%	100.0%	100.0%	100.0%	100.0%
Violent offenses	39.3	39.8	32.0	32.9	47.8	40.8	39.1
Murder[a]	1.8	1.7	3.0	2.0	1.4	1.7	1.8
Negligent manslaughter	.6	.4	2.9	.6	.7	1.1	.5
Kidnaping	.3	.4	0	.2	.4	.4	.3
Rape	2.4	2.6	0	1.8	3.3	1.0	2.6
Other sexual assault	3.5	3.7	1.0	4.3	2.8	2.3	3.7
Robbery	13.1	13.3	10.6	10.8	15.9	15.8	12.6
Assault	16.3	16.5	14.7	11.9	21.4	16.8	16.3
Other violent	1.2	1.3	0	1.2	1.2	1.4	1.2
Property offenses	45.6	46.0	40.8	51.1	38.6	35.9	47.3
Burglary	23.8	24.2	18.6	27.2	19.4	20.1	24.4
Larceny/theft	7.3	7.4	5.3	8.8	6.3	3.1	8.0
Motor vehicle theft	7.8	7.8	8.2	8.2	7.1	7.3	7.9
Arson	1.8	1.9	.4	2.1	1.5	.9	1.9
Fraud	1.1	.6	7.4	1.7	.5	1.2	1.1
Stolen property	1.4	1.4	.9	1.1	1.7	.7	1.5
Other property	2.5	2.6	0	2.7	2.1	2.6	2.4
Drug offenses	5.6	5.4	7.7	4.2	7.4	14.3	4.1
Possession	2.9	2.6	6.9	2.7	3.5	6.3	2.3
Trafficking	2.5	2.6	.8	1.3	3.8	8.0	1.6
Other drug	.2	.2	0	.3	.1	0	.2
Public-order offenses	7.2	7.0	10.1	8.8	5.4	5.0	7.5
Weapons	1.9	1.9	1.2	1.6	2.2	1.0	2.0
Other public-order	5.3	5.1	8.9	7.2	3.2	4.0	5.5
Juvenile status offenses[b]	2.2	1.6	9.3	2.7	1.6	4.2	1.8
Other offenses	.2	.2	0	.3	0	0	.2
18 years and older:							
Total	100.0%	100.0%	100.0%	100.0%	100.0%	100.0%	100.0%
Violent offenses	52.3	52.2	53.0	48.2	56.0	60.3	48.7
Murder[a]	7.1	7.2	...	8.1	5.6	9.3	6.1
Negligent manslaughter	2.2	2.3	...	2.5	1.8	2.2	2.2
Kidnaping	1.4	1.0	...	2.0	.4	2.3	1.0
Rape	5.1	5.4	...	4.4	5.8	5.4	4.9
Other sexual assault	1.6	1.8	...	2.5	.4	.8	2.0
Robbery	18.0	16.9	...	14.0	22.6	18.4	17.8
Assault	16.6	17.2	...	14.5	18.9	21.3	14.5
Other violent	.3	.4	...	.2	.5	.4	.3
Property offenses	29.0	30.1	14.5	34.2	22.6	21.8	32.2
Burglary	17.1	17.5	...	21.4	11.5	13.3	18.8
Larceny/theft	3.5	3.8	...	4.5	2.6	2.2	4.2
Motor vehicle theft	3.3	3.5	...	3.3	3.7	2.5	3.7
Arson	1.0	1.0	...	.9	.8	.8	1.1
Fraud	1.4	1.3	...	1.6	.9	1.9	1.2
Stolen property	2.3	2.5	...	2.2	2.7	1.2	2.8
Other property	.4	.4	...	.3	.2	0	.5
Drug offenses	11.3	10.5	23.2	8.8	14.9	11.1	11.4
Possession	5.6	5.4	...	5.2	6.1	6.1	5.5
Trafficking	5.4	4.8	...	3.7	8.1	5.8	5.6
Other drug	.3	.3	...	0	.7	0	.4
Public-order offenses	6.8	6.6	9.3	8.4	5.5	6.4	7.0
Weapons	2.5	2.2	...	2.2	3.0	2.7	2.3
Other public-order	4.3	4.4	...	6.1	2.4	3.7	4.7
Juvenile status offenses[b]	.3	.3	0	0	.8	0	.5
Other offenses	.3	.3	0	.4	.2	.4	.2

Note: Percents may not add to 100% due to rounding.
...Too few cases to provide reliable estimate.

[a] Includes nonnegligent manslaughter.
[b] Includes noncriminal juvenile offenses, such as truancy, running away, and incorrigible behavior.

Source: *Survey of Youth in Custody, 1987*, Bureau of Justice Statistics, (WDC, 1988)

The "Survey of Youth in Custody" (1988, WDC) taken by the Bureau of Justice Statistics, of a sample of 2,621 juveniles confined in long-term, public institutions, gives a more detailed picture of seriously-troubled youth. The survey included California's Youth Authority facilities, resulting in more than a quarter of the sample who were between 18 and 21 years old. Also, because of California's population, there were a higher number of Hispanics included than a nationwide survey likely would have. The survey found that 93 percent of residents were male, 53 percent, white, 41 percent, black, 6 percent, other minorities. Of the total number of juveniles, 19 percent were Hispanic (Table 5.14). Thirty-nine percent were held for violent offenses, 46 percent for property offensse, 5.5 percent for drug offenses, and 7 percent for public order offenses. Just over 2 percent were being held on status offense charges. Blacks of both age groups were more likely to have committed a violent or drug offense than other groups, and Hispanic juveniles were more likely to be confined for drug offenses, especially drug trafficking (Table 5.15). Almost 43 percent of the juve-

TABLE 5.16

Family structure and peer group involvement of youth in long-term, State-operated juvenile institutions, yearend 1987

	Percent of youth		
	Total	Less than 18 years old	18 years and older
Person(s) lived with while growing up	100.0%	100.0%	100.0%
Both parents	29.8	27.8	35.2
Mother only	48.4	50.2	43.7
Father only	5.6	5.9	4.9
Grandparents	10.0	10.3	9.1
Other relative	2.8	2.4	3.9
Friends	.2	.2	.3
Foster home	1.6	1.6	1.5
Agency or institution	.1	.2	.1
Other	1.4	1.3	1.4
Family member ever incarcerated*			
No	48.2%	47.2%	51.0%
Yes	51.8	52.8	49.0
Mother	8.8	9.4	7.3
Father	24.4	25.9	20.4
Brother or sister	25.1	23.7	28.8
Other relative	13.1	14.4	9.5
Had group of friends who were involved with crime			
No	68.7%	69.3%	67.1%
Yes	31.3	30.7	32.9
With others at time of current offense			
No	38.0%	37.2%	40.4%
Yes	62.0	62.8	59.6

*Percents add to more than 100% because more than one family member may have been incarcerated.

Source: *Survey of Youth in Custody, 1987*, Bureau of Justice Statistics, (WDC, 1988)

niles had been arrested more than five times and 20 percent had more than 10 arrests behind them. More than 80 percent of those surveyed reported that they had used an illegal drug, and almost 40 percent who used drugs had begun before the age of 12. Nearly half (47.6 percent) reported being under the influence of drugs or alcohol at the time of their current offense.

About 70 percent of the juveniles did not live with both parents while growing up, more than half reported that a family member had served time, and a quarter said that their fathers had been incarcerated. The youth in custody had a lower level of education than the general population. About 77 percent had an eighth grade education, but less than a tenth had finished high school. (In the general population, 79 percent of youth have a high school diploma.) (See Table 5.16.)

CHRONIC OFFENDERS ARE RESPONSIBLE FOR MOST JUVENILE CRIME

A 1988 study, "Court Careers of Juvenile Offenders," conducted by Howard Snyder for the Office of Juvenile Justice and Delinquency Prevention (results published in "Study Sheds New Light on Court Careers of Juvenile Offenders," 1988, WDC) showed that a youth's second appearance in court under the age of 16 is a good predictor of future delinquency. The youths most likely to have more than one referral were originally charged with burglary, truancy, motor vehicle theft, or robbery. Those youths who committed a serious crime were not the only ones to become repeat offenders — only 5 percent of all the adjudicated juveniles were referred because of violent offenses, and less than 1 percent had more than one violent offense referral. The younger the offender, however, the more likely it was that the youth would later be referred to the court for a violent offense.

CHAPTER VI

PRISONS AND JAILS

*Anyone who contemplates breaking the law must know
that he or she will be caught, will be prosecuted and will
spend time in a jail or a prison.*
Former United States Attorney General Dick Thornburgh

*"No legal action can deter if it is not perceived as punitive by
those who are subject to it, and whether or not sanctions deter
depends in part on the extent to which they are perceived as severe."*
Jack Gibbs, *Crime, Punishment and Deterrence*, 1975, N.Y.: Elsevier

The terms "prison" and "jail" are frequently used interchangeably. Jails, however, are generally local (usually city or county) institutions used to confine individuals awaiting trial or other legal disposition or adults serving short sentences. Prisons, on the other hand, are used for convicted criminals sentenced to lengthy terms. Figure 6.1 shows the number of adult offenders in correctional institutions in 1990 and the increase since 1985. The United States imprisons a larger share of its population than any other nation. According to a 1992 study by the Sentencing Project ("Americans Behind Bars"), a private research and advocacy group, the U.S. incarceration rate is 455 per 100,000 persons, compared to the second-placed South African rate of 311 per 100,000 persons. In contrast, Sweden incarcerates 44, and Japan imprisons 42 out of 100,000 persons (Figure 6.2). The Soviet Union is not included in the 1992 study because it no longer exists as a single nation, but the Sentencing Project's 1991 report showed that the Soviet Union imprisoned 268 persons per 100,000 inhabitants as of 1991.

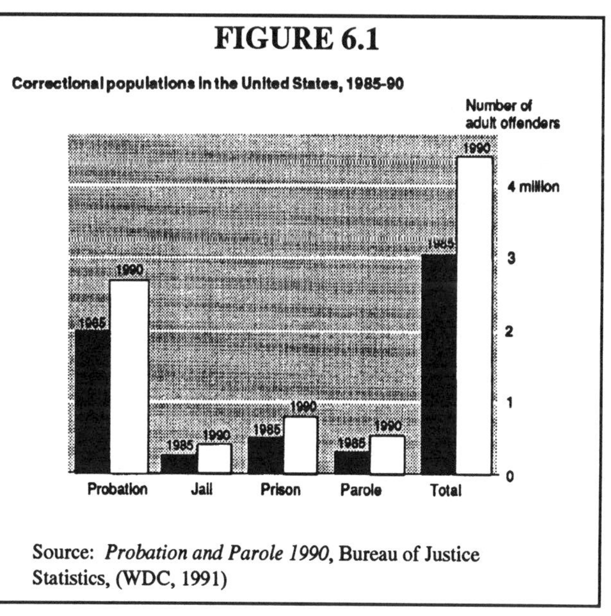

Source: *Probation and Parole 1990*, Bureau of Justice Statistics, (WDC, 1991)

JAIL INMATES

On June 30, 1990, the United States held an estimated 405,320 persons in jail, 2.5 percent more than a year earlier ("Jail Inmates 1990," WDC, 1991, Bureau of Justice Statistics). This means that one in every 457 adult residents of the United

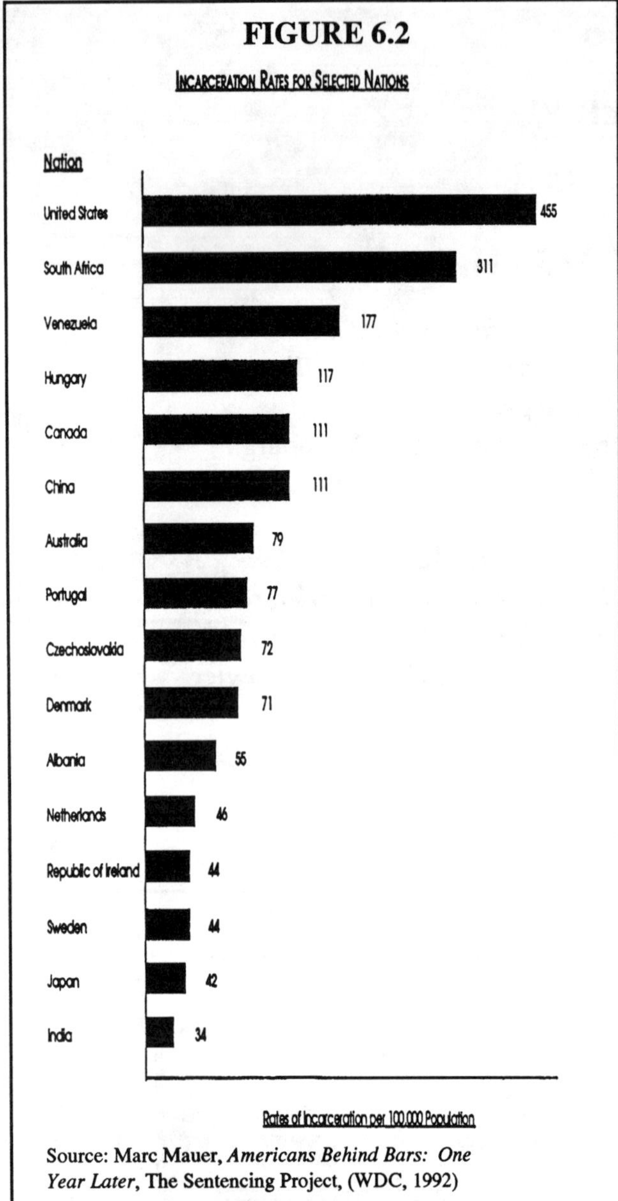

Source: Marc Mauer, *Americans Behind Bars: One Year Later*, The Sentencing Project, (WDC, 1992)

TABLE 6.1

Jail population: One-day count and average daily population, by legal status and sex, 1989-90

| | Number of jail inmates | | |
| | Annual Survey of Jails | | Percent change, |
	1989	1990	1989-90
One-day count			
All inmates	395,553	405,320	2.5%
Adults	393,303	403,019	2.5
Male	356,050	365,821	2.7
Female	37,253	37,198	--
Juveniles*	2,250	2,301	2.3
Average daily population			
All inmates	386,845	408,075	5.5%
Adults	384,954	405,935	5.5
Male	349,180	368,091	5.4
Female	35,774	37,844	5.8
Juveniles*	1,891	2,140	13.2

Note: Data for 1-day counts are for June 30, 1989, and June 29, 1990.
—Less than 0.5%.
*Juveniles are persons defined by State statute as being under a certain age, usually 18, and subject initially to juvenile court authority even if tried as adults in criminal court. Because less than 1% of the jail population were juveniles, caution must be used in interpreting any changes over time.

Source: *Jail Inmates, 1990*, Bureau of Justice Statistics, (WDC, 1991)

States was in jail on that day. The jail population is very fluid with an estimated 20 million admissions and releases in 1990. Jails house the following persons:

· individuals pending arraignment and awaiting trial, conviction and sentencing;
· probation, parole, and bail bond violators;
· temporarily detained juveniles awaiting transfer to juvenile facilities;
· mentally ill pending transfer to health facilities;
· military people under protective custody, those in contempt of court, and witnesses for the court;
· convicted inmates before being released into the community;
· transfer inmates to state and federal authorities.

Jails are a neglected part of the corrections system. They frequently fail to meet minimum standards for space, care, and staffing and are forced to mix a wide range of inmates from hardened criminals awaiting trial, to drunks, to those who have not yet been convicted (and may never be), to those with serious mental problems or addictions. Because the stay in jail is usually brief, medical care, recreation, and opportunities for work or activity are frequently minimal.

Population

The Bureau of Justice (BJS) statistics for 1990 show that over the preceding year, the average daily jail population of males increased 5.4 percent and the average daily female population rose 5.8 percent (Table 6.1). On June 30th of 1990, 49 percent of the adults in jail were convicted inmates

TABLE 6.2

Conviction status of adult jail inmates, by sex, 1989-90

	Number of jail inmates in Annual Survey of Jails	
	1989	1990
Total number of adults	393,303	403,019
Convicted	189,012	195,661
Male	171,181	177,619
Female	17,831	18,042
Unconvicted	204,291	207,358
Male	184,869	188,202
Female	19,422	19,156

Note: Data are for June 30, 1989, and June 29, 1990. Annual Survey of Jails data may underestimate the number of convicted inmates and overestimate the number of unconvicted inmates. Some facility records do not distinguish inmates awaiting sentence (or other convicted persons) from unconvicted inmates. The 1989 Survey of Inmates of Local Jails figures indicate that 43% of the inmates were unconvicted and 57% were convicted.

Source: *Jail Inmates, 1990*, Bureau of Justice Statistics, (WDC, 1991)

TABLE 6.3

Demographic characteristics of jail inmates, 1990

Characteristic	Percent of jail inmates
Total	100%
Sex	
Male	91
Female	9
Race	
White	51
Male	46
Female	5
Black	47
Male	43
Female	4
Other*	2
Male	1
Female	—
Ethnicity	
Hispanic	14
Male	13
Female	1
Non-Hispanic	86
Male	78
Female	8

Note: Data are for June 29, 1990. Race was reported for 90% of the inmates in 1990. Detail may not add to total because of rounding.
—Less than 0.5%.
*Native Americans, Aleuts, Asians, and Pacific Islanders.

Source: *Jail Inmates, 1990*, Bureau of Justice Statistics, (WDC, 1991)

TABLE 6.4

Twenty-five largest jurisdictions in 1990: Average daily population and 1-day count, June 30, 1989, and June 29, 1990

Jurisdiction	Number of jails in jurisdiction		Average daily population during		Population on	
	1989	1990	1989	1990	June 30, 1989	June 29, 1990
Los Angeles County, CA	8	8	22,426	21,984	22,100	21,810
New York City, NY	14	14	16,500	17,538	16,597	16,916
Cook County, IL	--	--	7,000	6,825	7,081	7,169
Dallas County, TX	4	4	6,800	6,960	6,043	5,306
Harris County, TX	2	3	8,206	5,694	8,199	5,633
San Diego County, CA	11	12	4,477	5,089	4,987	4,803
Shelby County, TN	2	2	4,452	4,932	4,838	4,894
Philadelphia County, PA	7	7	4,277	4,813	4,566	4,821
Dade County, FL	8	8	4,773	4,551	4,726	4,758
Orange County, CA	3	3	4,281	4,370	4,527	4,402
Santa Clara County, CA	10	7	4,316	4,177	4,162	4,217
Maricopa County, AZ	7	6	3,905	3,887	3,896	4,260
Alameda County, CA	4	4	3,110	3,610	3,214	3,505
New Orleans Parish, LA	--	--	3,700	3,604	3,663	3,550
Sacramento County, CA	3	3	3,321	3,095	2,966	3,233
Broward County, FL	3	3	2,979	3,059	2,844	2,788
Tarrant County, TX	2	3	2,420	2,958	2,698	3,339
Orange County, FL	3	2	2,831	2,890	3,305	3,031
San Bernardino County, CA	2	2	2,404	2,852	2,395	2,909
Baltimore City, MD	5	4	2,734	2,678	2,783	2,708
Fulton County, GA	4	4	2,278	2,517	2,316	3,151
Kern County, CA	3	3	2,302	2,383	2,291	2,595
Bexar County, TX	1	1	1,943	2,352	2,284	2,339
Fresno County, CA	3	3	1,829	2,309	2,101	2,246
Riverside County, CA	4	4	1,849	2,110	1,479	2,111

--These jurisdictions provided a single report covering all of their jail facilities.

Source: *Jail Inmates, 1990*, Bureau of Justice Statistics, (WDC, 1991)

which includes those awaiting sentencing or serving a sentence and those returned to jail because they had violated the conditions of their probation or parole. The remaining inmates (51 percent) were unconvicted, awaiting trial or arraignment, or on trial (Table 6.2). One out of every 241 men and one in every 2,581 women in the United States was in jail on that date. White inmates made up 51 percent of the population, blacks 47 percent, and the remaining two percent were of other races. Hispanics (a portion of both white and black populations) were 14 percent of the inmates (Table 6.3).

JAIL OVERCROWDING

Overcrowding in correctional facilities is a major problem. Bed space increased 7 percent from 1978 to 1983 and then jumped 30 percent in the following five years. The 1990 BJS survey reveals that the number of jail inmates increased 2.5 percent since 1989 (after a 15 percent increase from 1988 to 1989), while total rated capacity of the nation's jails rose 6 percent. Jails were operating at 104 percent of capacity in 1990, down from 108 percent in 1989. Twenty-eight percent of jurisdictions had at least one jail under court order to limit its population. One solution to overcrowding has been the early release of many prisoners.

LARGE JAIL POPULATIONS

On June 30, 1990, over 80 percent of the nation's jail population was housed in the 832 jails

TABLE 6.5

Jurisdictions under court order to reduce population or to improve conditions of confinement, 1989 and 1990

| | Number of jurisdictions with large jail populations | | | | | |
| | Total | | Ordered to limit population | | Not ordered to limit population | |
	1989	1990	1989	1990	1989	1990
Total	508	508	134	142	374	366
Jurisdictions under court order citing specific conditions of confinement	156	152	125	128	31	24
Subject of court order:						
Crowded living units	127	128	115	119	12	9
Recreational facilities	71	67	55	56	16	11
Medical facilities or services	60	50	45	41	15	9
Visitation practices or policies	51	42	40	37	11	5
Disciplinary procedures or policies	49	32	39	25	10	7
Food service	36	36	29	30	7	6
Administrative segregation procedures or policies	40	26	33	23	7	3
Staffing patterns	57	51	47	43	10	8
Grievance procedures or policies	44	34	35	28	9	6
Education or training programs	27	16	20	14	7	2
Fire hazards	27	14	24	11	3	3
Counseling programs	24	20	17	17	7	3
Inmate classification	47	37	38	32	9	5
Library services	51	50	36	41	15	9
Other	14	14	10	11	4	3
Totality of conditions	38	37	33	34	5	3

Some jurisdictions had a jail or jails under court order for more than one reason.

Source: *Jail Inmates, 1990*, Bureau of Justice Statistics, (WDC, 1991)

TABLE 6.6

Impact of inmates held for other authorities, 1989-90

| | Number of jurisdictions/inmates | |
	1989	1990
Jurisdictions with large jail populations	508	508
Jurisdictions holding inmates for other authorities:*	446	444
Federal	250	246
State	341	346
Local	229	225
Jurisdictions holding inmates because of crowding	259	262
All inmates in jurisdictions with large jail populations	322,314	327,917
Inmates being held for other authorities:	42,053	37,965
Federal	7,301	8,182
State	31,814	26,277
Local	2,938	3,506
Inmates being held because of crowding elsewhere:	29,358	24,238

Note: Data are for June 30, 1989, and June 29, 1990, and cover all jurisdictions with an average daily inmate population of 100 or more at the time of the 1988 Census of Local Jails.
*Detail adds to more than total because some jurisdictions hold inmates for more than one authority.

Source: *Jail Inmates, 1990*, Bureau of Justice Statistics, (WDC, 1991)

of 508 jurisdictions. Of the 25 largest jurisdictions (Table 6.4), 10 were located in California, four in Texas, and three in Florida. One-fourth of the jurisdictions with large jail populations had at least one jail under court order to reduce the number of inmates or to improve conditions of confinement (Table 6.5). More than half of these jurisdictions (52 percent) were holding inmates because of crowding elsewhere, principally the state prisons (Table 6.6).

POPULATION DENSITY

The population density of a jail is measured three ways: space per inmate, number of persons sharing a housing unit, and the amount of time spent in the housing unit. The 1988 census of local jails found that the average jails used 50.9 square feet per inmate, housing 2.5 inmates per unit. This represents a 6 percent decrease of space, although there was virtually no change in inmates per unit since the previous census in 1983 (Table 6.7). The American Correctional Association recommends that each inmate have 60 square feet of floorspace. The density however, varies widely from small jails (fewer than 50 inmates) to large jails (250 or more inmates). Small jails averaged 60.6 feet per inmate, while the largest jails of 1,000 or more inmates averaged only 46 square feet of space (Table 6.8). Large jails also had more multiple occupancy housing than small jails. Jails with 1,000 or more inmates housed an average of 3.4 persons per unit; small jails averaged two persons.

In 1988, 28 percent of jails housed five or more inmates per unit. Sixty-one percent of all inmates lived in these high density jails. Nearly 41 percent of inmates in cells with two persons were in space rated for one inmate. More than half the inmates in cells with three persons were confined in a cell meant for fewer persons (Table 6.9). The average number of hours per day that inmates are kept confined to their cells has not changed since 1983; it remains at 13.5 hours, 35 percent higher than is recommended by the ACA (Table 6.10).

TABLE 6.7

Percent of local jail inmates, average square feet, number of inmates per housing unit, and hours in housing unit per day, by region, size of unit, housing type, and size of facility, 1983 and 1988

	Percent of inmates		Average square feet per inmate		Average number of inmates per unit		Average number of hours inmates confined in unit	
	1983	1988	1983	1988	1983	1988	1983	1988
All jails	100.0%	100.0%	54.3 sq. ft.	50.9 sq. ft.	2.4	2.5	13.5 hours	13.5 hours
Region								
Northeast	16.4%	16.8%	55.6 sq. ft.	54.2 sq. ft.	1.6	1.8	11.8 hours	11.8 hours
Midwest	17.6	14.9	57.9	58.4	2.0	2.0	12.5	13.0
South	40.0	41.8	53.4	48.3	2.6	2.7	14.4	14.3
West	26.0	26.5	52.3	48.8	3.7	3.3	13.9	13.8
Persons per unit								
1 person	27.1%	25.4%	66.8 sq. ft.	68.2 sq. ft.	1.0	1.0	12.4 hours	12.6 hours
2 persons	14.3	17.7	48.4	39.2	2.0	2.0	12.2	12.2
3-5	15.0	11.8	45.9	40.7	3.6	3.6	13.6	13.6
6-49	33.3	31.1	52.0	48.9	12.7	13.4	15.4	15.1
50 or more	10.3	14.0	49.1	47.5	71.6	78.5	12.0	13.3
Housing unit use								
General	89.2%	88.5%	52.8 sq. ft.	49.8 sq. ft.	2.5	2.6	13.4 hours	13.4 hours
Special	4.0	4.0	57.8	55.0	1.4	1.6	18.3	17.7
Other	6.9	7.5	71.9	61.9	2.6	2.6	12.8	12.5
Size of facility								
Fewer than 50	16.4%	11.6%	64.4 sq. ft.	60.6 sq. ft.	1.8	1.9	13.2 hours	14.3 hours
50-249	31.2	25.7	54.8	53.5	2.4	2.4	13.1	13.6
250-499	17.4	17.2	57.2	52.3	2.5	2.5	14.1	13.6
500-999	17.2	18.5	50.2	47.8	2.5	2.3	13.8	13.3
1,000 or more	17.9	27.0	45.1	45.7	3.2	3.4	14.0	13.3

Note: Averages for square footage, number per unit, and hours confined are all computed by using the number of inmates reported to be in each unit and comparing this to its physical dimensions, average across units, or duration of confinement as appropriate. See *Methodology* for an example. Special housing units are reserved for disciplinary, protective custody, or administrative segregation, while other housing is any other nongeneral housing such as an infirmary or diagnostic unit.

Source: *Population Density in Local Jails, 1988*, Bureau of Justice Statistics, (WDC, 1990)

STATE AND FEDERAL PRISONS

Prisoners can be sent to either federal or state prisons. A person who is convicted of breaking a federal law or of being involved in an interstate crime could be sent to one of the 47 federal penitentiaries, correctional institutions, or prison camps located throughout the nation. Individuals may also serve time in a federal prison if their crime is committed against a federal institution (bank, post office, or federally-insured credit union) or a federal officer (FBI, Drug Enforcement Administration, or U.S. Treasury agent). About one-third of the federal prisoners are considered dangerous to others. For this reason, the federal prison system has established a security designation system that ranks prisons from one to six. The higher the number, the more security is provided at the insti-

TABLE 6.8

Size of facility	Average square feet per jail inmate	
	1983	1988
Fewer than 50	64.4	60.6
50-249	54.8	53.5
250-499	57.2	52.3
500-999	50.2	47.8
1,000 or more	45.1	45.7

TABLE 6.9

Occupancy by five or fewer inmates in housing units, by rated capacity of the units, 1988

Number of inmates in unit	Number	Rated capacity of housing unit						
		One	Two	Three	Four	Five	More than five	Unrated
One	86,913	89.3%	8.4%	.3%	.8%	0	.3%	.9%
Two	60,422	40.5	53.4	1.2	3.5	.1	.8	.5
Three	17,781	21.5	33.2	15.1	23.0	1.0	5.1	1.1
Four	14,256	1.4	8.6	1.7	74.0	2.3	10.7	1.3
Five	8,355	0	2.5	1.6	50.1	12.3	31.7	1.8

Source of both tables: *Population Density in Local Jails, 1988*, Bureau of Justice Statistics, (WDC, 1990)

TABLE 6.10

Size of facility	In 1988, the average number of:	
	Inmates per unit	Hours per day in unit
Fewer than 50	1.9	14.3
50-249	2.4	13.6
250-499	2.5	13.6
500-999	2.3	13.3
1,000 or more	3.4	13.3

Source: *Prisoners in 1989*, Bureau of Justice Statistics, (WDC, 1990)

TABLE 6.11

Change in the State and Federal prison populations, 1980-91

Year	Number of inmates	Annual percent change	Total percent change since 1980
1980	329,821		
1981	369,930	12.2%	12.2%
1982	413,806	11.9	25.5
1983	436,855	5.6	32.5
1984	462,002	5.8	40.1
1985	502,752	8.8	52.4
1986	545,378	8.5	65.4
1987	585,292	7.3	77.5
1988	631,990	8.0	91.6
1989	712,967	12.8	116.2
1990	773,124	8.4	134.4
1991	823,414	6.5	149.7

Note: All counts are for December 31 of each year and may reflect revisions of previously reported numbers.

Source: *Prisoners in 1991*, Bureau of Justice Statistics, (WDC, 1992)

tution. A prison camp, therefore, would be rated one, while the maximum security penitentiary at Marion, Illinois is rated six. Those convicted of murder, burglary, or larceny/theft might wind up in a state prison unless the crime was committed outside a state jurisdiction, such as in Washington, D.C., on the high seas, on government reservations or territories, or involved crossing state lines (kidnapping or transporting automobiles, for example).

Prison Population

The Bureau of Justice Statistics (BJS) regularly surveys the nation's correctional facilities. The most recent survey counted prisoners in 1991 (1992, "Prisoners in 1991," WDC: Department of Justice Statistics). By year-end the number of state and federal prisoners had reached a record 823,414. This was an increase of nearly 150 percent since 1980 (Table 6.11). The 1991 growth rate of 6.5 percent (down from 8.4 in 1990) translated into a nation-wide need for nearly 967 new prison bedspaces per week. This was a reduction from the 1,157 per week needed in 1990 and was the lowest annual growth rate since 1984. The Criminal Justice Institute had also gathered statistics on correctional institutions in 1988. They found that as of January 1, 1989, there were 1,199 prisons in operation. Of those, 11 percent were maximum security, 11 percent were high/close, 28 percent were medium, 25 percent were minimum, and 25 percent were community facilities. Community-based facilities are those where half or more of the residents leave regularly (unaccompanied) for work, study, school, or other activity.

Types of Prisons

Prisoners with sentences of more than one year (also known as sentenced prisoners) accounted for 96 percent of the 1991 prison population. The remaining prisoners had shorter sentences or were awaiting trial in states with combined prison-jail systems. At year-end, 12,225 prisoners were held in local jails because of prison overcrowding, a drop from 17,574 in 1990. Despite a decline in both the population at the highest risk of committing crimes and a drop in crime according to the *National Crime Survey*, the rate of prisoners per 100,000 population continues to rise steadily. Since 1980, the rate has more than doubled from 139 to 310 at the end of 1991. Overall, the number of sentenced prisoners nationwide has increased by 123 percent since 1980. During 1991, the percentage growth of total prisoners and sentenced prisoners increased the most in the Northeast (7.5 percent and 17 percent, respectively). The South has the highest net gain in sentenced prisoners per 100,000 residents (309) (Table 6.12).

TABLE 6.12

Prisoners under the jurisdiction of State or Federal correctional authorities, by region and jurisdiction, yearend 1990 and 1991

Region and jurisdiction	Total			Sentenced to more than 1 year			Incarceration rate, 1991*
	Advance 1991	Final 1990	Percent change, 1990-91	Advance 1991	Final 1990	Percent change, 1990-91	
U.S. total	823,414	773,124	6.5%	789,261	739,142	6.8%	310
Federal	71,608	65,526	9.3	56,696	50,403	12.5	22
State	751,806	707,598	6.2	732,565	688,739	6.4	287
Northeast	131,813	123,392	6.8%	127,934	119,063	7.5%	248
Connecticut	10,977	10,500	4.5	8,585	7,771	10.5	262
Maine	1,621	1,523	6.4	1,600	1,480	8.1	127
Massachusetts	9,058	8,273	9.5	8,998	7,899	13.9	150
New Hampshire	1,533	1,342	14.2	1,533	1,342	14.2	132
New Jersey	23,483	21,128	11.1	23,483	21,128	11.1	300
New York	57,862	54,895	5.4	57,862	54,895	5.4	319
Pennsylvania	23,388	22,290	4.9	23,386	22,281	5.0	192
Rhode Island	2,772	2,392	15.9	1,749	1,586	10.3	172
Vermont	1,119	1,049	6.7	738	681	8.4	125
Midwest	155,469	145,793	6.6%	155,140	145,480	6.6%	254
Illinois	29,115	27,516	5.8	29,115	27,516	5.8	246
Indiana	13,008	12,736	2.1	12,876	12,615	2.1	226
Iowa	4,145	3,967	4.5	4,145	3,967	4.5	144
Kansas	5,903	5,777	2.2	5,903	5,777	2.2	230
Michigan	36,423	34,267	6.3	36,423	34,267	6.3	387
Minnesota	3,472	3,176	9.3	3,472	3,176	9.3	78
Missouri	15,411	14,943	3.1	15,411	14,943	3.1	294
Nebraska	2,506	2,403	4.3	2,389	2,286	4.5	146
North Dakota	492	483	1.9	441	435	1.4	68
Ohio	35,750	31,822	12.3	35,750	31,822	12.3	323
South Dakota	1,374	1,341	2.5	1,374	1,341	2.5	190
Wisconsin	7,870	7,362	6.9	7,841	7,335	6.9	158
South	301,265	284,029	6.1%	291,807	275,217	6.0%	332
Alabama	16,760	15,665	7.0	16,400	15,365	6.7	392
Arkansas	7,709	6,766	13.9	7,667	6,718	14.1	314
Delaware	3,721	3,471	7.2	2,406	2,241	7.4	342
District of Col.	10,251	9,947	3.1	6,893	6,798	1.4	1,168
Florida	46,533	44,387	4.8	46,531	44,380	4.8	346
Georgia	23,644	22,345	5.8	22,859	21,605	5.8	342
Kentucky	9,799	9,023	8.6	9,799	9,023	8.6	261
Louisiana	20,464	18,599	10.0	20,307	18,599	9.2	486
Maryland	19,291	17,848	8.1	17,824	16,734	6.5	366
Mississippi	9,070	8,375	8.3	8,848	8,084	9.5	335
North Carolina	18,899	18,411	2.7	18,288	17,764	2.9	270
Oklahoma	13,376	12,285	8.9	13,376	12,285	8.9	414
South Carolina	18,312	17,319	5.7	17,173	16,208	6.0	473
Tennessee	11,502	10,388	10.7	11,502	10,388	10.7	227
Texas	51,677	50,042	3.3	51,677	50,042	3.3	297
Virginia	18,755	17,593	6.6	18,755	17,418	7.7	297
West Virginia	1,502	1,565	-4.0	1,502	1,565	-4.0	82
West	163,259	154,384	5.7%	157,684	148,979	5.8%	290
Alaska	2,720	2,622	3.7	1,841	1,851	-.5	344
Arizona	15,415	14,261	8.1	14,843	13,781	7.7	398
California	101,808	97,309	4.6	98,515	94,122	4.7	320
Colorado	8,347	7,671	8.8	8,347	7,671	8.8	247
Hawaii	2,688	2,533	6.1	1,979	1,708	15.9	172
Idaho	2,211	1,961	12.7	2,211	1,961	12.7	212
Montana	1,478	1,425	3.7	1,478	1,425	3.7	182
Nevada	5,879	5,322	10.5	5,879	5,322	10.5	477
New Mexico	3,119	3,187	-2.1	3,016	3,067	-1.7	191
Oregon	6,760	6,492	4.1	6,760	6,492	4.1	229
Utah	2,624	2,496	5.1	2,605	2,474	5.3	149
Washington	9,156	7,995	14.5	9,156	7,995	14.5	183
Wyoming	1,054	1,110	-5.0	1,054	1,110	-5.0	225

Note: The advance count of prisoners is conducted immediately after the calendar year ends. Prisoner counts for 1990 may differ from those reported in previous publications. Counts for 1991 are subject to revision as updated figures become available. Explanatory notes for each jurisdiction are reported in the appendix.
*The number of prisoners with sentences of more than 1 year per 100,000 resident population.

Source: *Prisoners in 1991*, Bureau of Justice Statistics, (WDC, 1992)

TABLE 6.13

Prisoners under the jurisdiction of State or Federal correctional authorities, by sex of inmates, yearend 1990 and 1991

	Men	Women
Total		
Advance 1991	775,723	47,691
Final 1990	729,135	43,989
Percent change, 1990-91	6.4%	8.4%
Sentenced to more than 1 year		
Advance 1991	745,193	44,099
Final 1990	698,707	40,436
Percent change, 1990-91	6.7%	8.6%
Incarceration rate, 1991*	599	34

*The number of prisoners with sentences of more than 1 year per 100,000 residents on December 31, 1991.

Source: *Prisoners in 1991*, Bureau of Justice Statistics, (WDC, 1992)

CHARACTERISTICS OF PRISONERS

Gender

The female prison population increased at a faster rate during 1991 (8.4 percent) than the number of male inmates (6.4 percent). The number of sentenced male prisoners (599 per 100,000 males in the resident population), however, was 18 times higher than for sentenced females (34 per 100,000). Nationwide, women accounted for 5.8 percent of prisoners in 1991 (Table 6.13).

Race

An ethnic breakdown of the prison population by the Criminal Justice Institute in its *Corrections Yearbook* shows that in the state and federal system in 1991, 36 percent of prisoners were black, 51 percent white, 8 percent Hispanic, a little more than 1 percent Oriental, and almost 3 percent Native American. However, the percentages by state vary tremendously, reflecting characteristics of their populations. The District of Columbia's prison population is over 97 percent black, Hawaii's is 54 percent Oriental (this includes Pacific Islanders), New Mexico's is 55 percent Hispanic, and Vermont is 100 percent white (Table 6.14).

The Sentencing Project, "Young Black Men and the Criminal Justice System: A Growing National Problem" (Marc Mauer, 1990, WDC), reveals that on a single day in 1989, nearly one in four black men ages 20 to 29 was on probation, in jail, in prison, or on parole. In contrast, 6 percent of white men and a little over 10 percent of Hispanic men in the same age group were under some form of correctional jurisdiction. More black women were also under supervision than white or Hispanic women — one in 37 black women versus one in 100 white women and one in 56 Hispanic women. Blacks make up an increasing share of drug arrests, an offense which has grown by 31 percent from 1986 to 1988, making them the fastest growing category of offenders.

Prison Overcrowding

Preliminary reports by the Bureau of Justice Statistics indicate that the states' prison population grew 6.4 percent in 1991, pushing virtually every state past their intended capacity despite court orders in 37 states to reduce overcrowding. Four billion dollars was authorized in new prison construction in 1989 in addition to $4.4 billion in 1988, but this has not kept up with the growing prison population.

Prison Capacity

Several different systems are used to measure prison capacity. Rated capacity is the number of beds or inmates assigned by a rating official to institutions within the jurisdiction; operational capacity is the number of inmates that can be accommodated based on a facility's staff, programs and services; design capacity is the number of inmates that planners or architects intended for the facility. BJS's 1991 statistics ("Prisoners in 1991") included lowest and highest capacity figures for the institution. Prisons require some reserve capacity to operate efficiently. Cells need repair, space has to be available for isolation, protective custody or emergencies. At the end of 1991, seven states reported that they were operating below 95 percent of their highest capacity. The Federal prison system and 45 jurisdictions operated at 100 percent or more of their lowest capacity, and 38 of these had populations that met or exceeded their highest reported capacity (Table 6.15). Overall, state prisons were operating at 116 percent of their highest capacities and 131 percent of their lowest capacities. Prisons in the South were operating closest to reported capacity on each measure (Table 6.16).

TABLE 6.15

Reported Federal and State prison capacities, yearend 1991

Region and jurisdiction	Rated capacity	Operational capacity	Design capacity	Population[a] as a percent of Highest capacity	Lowest capacity
Federal[b]	43,753	...	...	146	146
Northeast					
Connecticut	9,935	10,928	...	100	110
Maine	1,193	1,193	1,193	136	136
Massachusetts	...	...	5,650	160	160
New Hampshire	1,318	1,542	1,162	99	132
New Jersey	...	...	14,898	155	155
New York	58,687	55,699	48,363	99	120
Pennsylvania	...	...	15,915	147	147
Rhode Island	3,042	3,042	2,789	91	99
Vermont	647	862	647	130	173
Midwest					
Illinois	23,961	23,961	20,217	122	144
Indiana	11,934	14,211	...	92	109
Iowa	3,003	3,003	3,003	138	138
Kansas	...	6,622	...	89	89
Michigan	26,209	...	...	139	139
Minnesota	3,414	3,414	3,414	102	102
Missouri	15,056	15,411	...	100	102
Nebraska	...	...	1,706	147	147
North Dakota	...	576	576	85	85
Ohio	...	...	20,783	172	172
South Dakota	1,189	1,130	1,189	116	122
Wisconsin	6,497	6,497	6,497	121	121
South					
Alabama	14,604	14,604	14,604	115	115
Arkansas	...	7,335	...	105	105
Delaware	2,915	3,138	2,015	119	185
District of Columbia	9,788	9,508	8,101	105	127
Florida	53,652	47,572	36,470	87	128
Georgia	...	22,895	...	103	103
Kentucky	8,455	8,270	...	116	119
Louisiana	15,493	15,493	15,493	132	132
Maryland	...	18,880	13,984	102	138
Mississippi	8,524	8,098	8,524	106	112
North Carolina	16,126	19,646	...	96	117
Oklahoma	8,964	11,243	...	119	149
South Carolina	16,138	16,138	12,335	114	149
Tennessee	9,409	9,349	9,642	98	100
Texas	47,770	50,698	62,212	83	108
Virginia	13,970	13,970	13,970	134	134
West Virginia	1,585	1,644	1,736	87	95
West					
Alaska	2,523	2,602	...	105	108
Arizona	...	14,994	...	103	103
California	...	...	55,692	183	183
Colorado	...	7,416	6,239	112	133
Hawaii	...	2,569	1,656	105	162
Idaho	...	2,086	1,831	106	121
Montana	1,117	1,441	1,117	103	132
Nevada	6,166	6,166	5,014	95	117
New Mexico	3,236	3,236	3,236	96	96
Oregon	...	6,690	...	101	101
Utah	3,131	2,890	...	84	91
Washington	5,452	6,710	6,710	137	168
Wyoming	88	777	619	136	198

... Data not available.

[a] Excludes inmates who had been sentenced to State prison but were held in local jails because of crowding and who were included in the total prisoner count.

[b] Excludes prisoners housed in contract or other non-Federal facilities.

Source: *Prisoners in 1991*, Bureau of Justice Statistics, (WDC, 1992)

Prison Commitments

Changes in attitude towards criminal behavior have influenced criminal justice policies. Increasing complaints that judges were inconsistent in their sentencing and racially biased have led at least 25 states and the federal judicial system to adopt some form of determinate sentencing. California's formula weighs the seriousness of the crime with the offender's past history to give a prescribed sentence of either prison or probation and length of sentence. This eliminates much of the judge's leeway, and a recently released study by the Rand Corporation (appearing in the February 1990 issue of the journal *Science*) claims that racial bias in sentencing has all but been eliminated.

One of the results of determinate sentencing is that more criminals are being incarcerated, overloading the system. Other causes of the overload include more drug arrests (Figure 6.3), a decline in parolees, and the stiffening of criminal laws which have created new classes of felonies. New crimes, such as being a repeat offender, are being identified. When a state prison system is under court order, prisoners have to be shuffled to make room. Some prisoners are held longer in local jails, others are given early release for good behavior, and some states have housed prisoners almost anywhere, including in barges and tents. In 1990, in 37 states some prisons or entire penal systems were under court order to remedy overcrowding or conditions such as inadequate medical care or other problems that result from too large a prison population.

PRISON EXPENSE

In 1991, Americans spent $20.1 billion on building and operating prisons, according to the Edna McConnell Clark Foundation. The Justice Department reports that figuring in probation and parole expenses raises the figure to $26.2 billion. Spending on prisons is the second fastest-growing item in state budgets after Medicaid, increasing 13 percent per year since 1986. With many states facing budget crises, spending for prisons diverts money from programs for education, health, and job training that many criminologists believe might prevent crime.

The effectiveness of the vast expenditures on prisons is sharply debated. John DeIulio, professor of politics at Princeton University, claims that the typical criminal, when freed, commits 12 crimes a year, at an estimated annual cost of $27,600. Comparing this to a 1987 Justice Department finding that the annual cost of incarcerating a criminal was $25,000, Mr. DeIulio concluded that the monetary price of imprisonment to society is less than the damage done by a criminal if free.

TABLE 6.16

State prison population and capacity, by region, 1991

Region	Prison population	Highest capacity	Lowest capacity	Population as a percent of Highest capacity	Lowest capacity
U.S. total	749,318	647,160	572,487	116%	131%
Northeast	131,452	112,717	100,552	116	131
Midwest	155,469	123,582	117,147	126	133
South	299,219	297,351	247,364	101	121
West	163,178	113,510	107,424	144	152

Note: Population counts exclude prisoners sentenced to State prison but held in local jails.

Source: *Prisoners in 1991*, Bureau of Justice Statistics, (WDC, 1992)

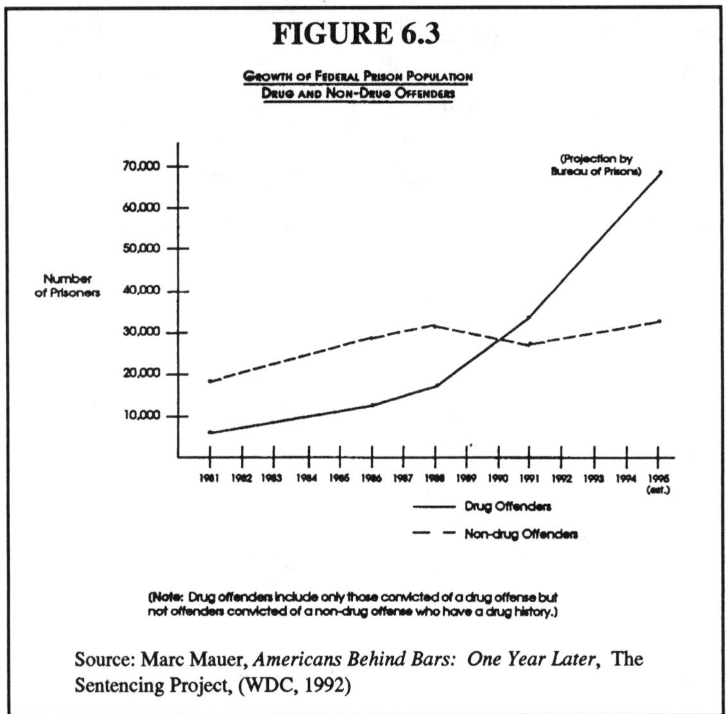

FIGURE 6.3

Source: Marc Mauer, *Americans Behind Bars: One Year Later*, The Sentencing Project, (WDC, 1992)

Reducing Prison Cost

In recent years, some prisons have established factories and workshops. Inmates are paid small wages for employment, and they also participate in vocational education programs. In some prisons, such as the New York State prison system, work is mandatory, and inmates may be penalized if they refuse to work. This tough approach has raised concern among prisoners' rights groups. Correction officials claim, however, that mandatory work accomplishes three objectives, (1) forces inmates to assume some of the $25,000 cost of imprisonment, (2) prepares them to hold jobs after their release, and (3) counters a growing feeling among the citizens that prisons have become too easy for inmates.

TABLE 6.17

Adults on probation, 1990

Region and jurisdiction	Probation population, 1/1/90	1990 Entries	1990 Exits	Probation population, 12/31/90	Percent change in probation population during 1990	Number on probation on 12/31/90 per 100,000 adult residents
U.S. total	2,521,525	1,637,557	1,489,448	2,670,234	5.9%	1,443
Federal	59,106	20,388	21,272	58,222	-1.5%	31
State	2,462,419	1,617,169	1,468,176	2,612,012	6.1	1,411
Northeast	449,418	219,442	202,854	466,006	3.7%	1,198
Connecticut	42,842	28,738	24,940	46,640	8.9	1,838
Maine	6,851	4,698	4,000	7,549	10.2	821
Massachusetts	88,529	44,486	60,556	72,459	-18.2	1,554
New Hampshire	2,991	1,775	1,620	3,146	5.2	379
New Jersey	64,398	33,540	25,597	72,341	12.3	1,220
New York	136,686	47,656	39,076	145,266	6.3	1,058
Pennsylvania	89,491	46,111	38,275	97,327	8.8	1,071
Rhode Island	12,231	9,294	6,159	15,366	25.6	1,975
Vermont	5,399	3,144	2,631	5,912	9.5	1,408
Midwest	538,394	392,972	364,127	567,839	5.5%	1,289
Illinois	93,944	58,870	57,115	95,699	1.9	1,128
Indiana	61,177	65,388	58,482	68,683	12.3	1,680
Iowa	13,722	346	173	13,895	1.3	675
Kansas	21,675	12,683	12,175	22,183	2.3	1,222
Michigan	122,459	100,151	89,171	133,439	9.0	1,952
Minnesota	58,648	31,394	30,719	59,323	1.2	1,849
Missouri	44,158	25,000	26,836	42,322	-4.2	1,113
Nebraska	12,627	17,767	15,740	14,654	16.1	1,275
North Dakota	1,644	523	436	1,731	5.3	374
Ohio	78,299	59,049	53,968	83,380	6.5	1,036
South Dakota	2,757	3,995	3,592	3,160	14.6	635
Wisconsin	27,284	17,806	15,720	29,370	7.6	815
South	984,909	695,398	638,295	1,042,012	5.8%	1,643
Alabama	25,519	14,251	12,084	27,686	8.5	928
Arkansas	15,552	3,531	3,100	15,983	2.8	924
Delaware	9,701	6,393	3,871	12,223	26.0	2,430
District of Columbia	10,132	8,070	8,460	9,742	-3.8	1,988
Florida	192,731	266,244	248,194	210,781	9.4	2,093
Georgia	125,147	76,042	66,349	134,840	7.7	2,838
Kentucky	8,062	3,030	3,610	7,482	-7.2	274
Louisiana	32,295	13,310	15,414	30,191	-6.5	1,009
Maryland	84,456	44,435	45,993	82,898	-1.8	2,291
Mississippi	7,333	3,138	2,250	8,221	12.1	450
North Carolina	72,325	41,981	36,477	77,829	7.6	1,550
Oklahoma	24,240	12,565	12,394	24,411	.7	1,057
South Carolina	31,623	14,405	13,741	32,287	2.1	1,258
Tennessee	30,906	21,925	20,112	32,719	5.9	894
Texas	291,156	151,767	134,566	308,357	5.9	2,538
Virginia	19,085	11,951	9,733	21,303	11.6	455
West Virginia	4,646	2,360	1,947	5,059	8.9	375
West	489,698	309,357	262,900	536,155	9.5%	1,385
Alaska	3,335	1,993	1,729	3,599	7.9	952
Arizona	27,340	11,978	8,921	30,397	11.2	1,133
California	284,437	173,883	152,620	305,700	7.5	1,388
Colorado	28,037	22,310	19,236	31,111	11.0	1,279
Hawaii	10,960	6,442	5,735	11,667	6.5	1,409
Idaho	4,025	2,024	1,672	4,377	8.7	627
Montana	3,459	1,873	1,280	4,052	17.1	702
Nevada	7,065	3,518	2,883	7,700	9.0	851
New Mexico	5,660	9,650	9,016	6,294	11.2	589
Oregon	31,878	15,742	9,989	37,631	18.0	1,777
Utah	5,524	3,596	3,290	5,830	5.5	532
Washington	74,918	54,791	44,892	84,817	13.2	2,353
Wyoming	3,060	1,557	1,637	2,980	-2.6	937

Source: *Prisoners in 1991*, Bureau of Justice Statistics, (WDC, 1992)

drug and alcohol abuse, low self-esteem, and are hostile to others, especially those in authority. If society has failed them, how is prison going to succeed? Prisoners bring their own society into prison with them. It revolves around drugs, smuggling, extortion, predatory sexual behavior, and violence. Prisons are characterized by overcrowding, lack of privacy, noise, racial tension, boredom, violent sex, infectious disease, and hopelessness. Under these conditions it would be surprising, indeed, if prisoners were rehabilitated. Norval Morris, professor of law and criminology at the University of Chicago, believes that increased imprisonment has made no difference in the crime rate. He pointed out that while the United States doubled the number of inmates from 1980 to 1990, the crime rate at the end of the decade was about the same as it was at the beginning.

ALTERNATE SENTENCING

With no sign that the flow of prisoners will let up and 37 states under court order to control prison overcrowding, interest is growing in alternative sanctions for lesser or first-offenders, reserving prison sentences for the worst offenders.

Probation

Traditionally, probation (a period of time under court supervision rather than a prison sentence) was a counseling and supervisory relationship between offender and officer. Today it is becom-

What is the Solution?

Is prison the answer to crime? It is the primary method the government uses to show that it takes crime seriously and will not let it go unpunished. It keeps dangerously violent criminals off the street, but does it rehabilitate or punish? Prisoners are society's failures, mostly men, who have had failed relationships with their families, schools, and jobs. They suffer disproportionately from physical abuse,

ing more of a law enforcement relationship. In New York in 1989, almost 38 percent of the criminals who had been given probation were sent to prison for violating rules. Five years before, it was 26 percent of the probationers. In Los Angeles, a single probation officer is expected to handle as many as 1,000 criminals. Rand Corporation studies show that while the prison population increased 45 percent over the last decade, those on probation increased 75 percent. The probationers are mostly male, unemployed, 20 to 30 years old, and many are illiterate. The most common offense, by far, is possession or selling of drugs.

Probation Characteristics

The BJS reports ("Probation and Parole 1990," 1991, WDC: Bureau of Justice Statistics) that there were 2,670,234 adults on probation on January 31, 1990 (Table 6.17). A 1986 Rand Corporation study of persons on probation found that 46 percent were felons, 40 percent had committed a misdemeanor, and 12 percent had been charged with driving under the influence. Males made up 84 percent of the probationers, and of the jurisdictions which provided the information, 70 percent were white, 29 percent black, and 1 percent, native American. Hispanics made up 13 percent of those probationers from agencies which reported the information. Eighty-one percent successfully completed their sentences, while 12 percent were returned to prison either for the same sentences or new ones. If success, however, is measured by the proportion of probationers who are rearrested or rearraigned during a follow-up period, the rates are much lower. They range from 10 to 15 percent failure for minimum supervision cases (often offenses like drunk driving) to 50 to 60 percent failure for maximum or intensive supervision cases. Joan Petersilia and Susan Turner, in "Prison versus Probation in California: Implications for Crime and Offender Recidivism" (1986, California: the Rand Corporation), concluded that,

In our opinion, felons granted probation present a serious threat to public safety. During the 40-month follow-up period of our study, 65 percent of the probationers in our subsample were rearrested, 51 percent reconvicted, 18 percent were reconvicted of serious violent crimes (homicide, rape, weapons offenses, assault, and robbery), and 34 percent were reincarcerated. Moreover, 75 percent of the official charges filed against our subsample involved burglary/theft, robbery and other violent crimes — the crimes most threatening to public safety.

Why are felons given probation? Historically, there are three reasons for giving probation; prison is used for repeat offenders, prisons are overcrowded, and judges fear that the threat to society is even greater from released prisoners than probationers. In the Rand Corporation study, the authors found that this third argument may well be true. The recidivism (a relapse into crime) rate of felons in California was 72 percent for prisoners versus 63 percent of probationers.

TABLE 6.18

How long do inmates stay in Boot Camp programs, and what is the average daily cost per inmate?

Among 23 jurisdictions, the average length of the Boot Camp program is 4 months. The average daily cost per inmate is $42.52 in the 16 reporting agencies.

	Program Length (mos.)	Daily Cost Per Inmate		Program Length (mos.)	Daily Cost Per Inmate
AL[1]	4.5	14.96	NH	4.0	44.00
AZ	4.0	45.83	NY	6.0	80.52
AR	3.8		NC[6]	3.0	38.34
CO	3.0		OH	3.0	
FL[2]	3.4	39.73	OK	4.0	34.71
GA	3.0	39.82	SC	3.0	34.25
ID[3]	5.0	23.00	TN	3.0	63.04
IL	4.0		TX	3.0	43.57
KS[4]	6.0	32.27	VA	3.0	
LA[5]	6.0		WY	3.0	47.89
MI	3.3	72.00	FED	6.0	
MS	4.0	26.39	Average	4.0	$42.52

[1]Ranges 3 to 6 mos. [2]Ranges 3 to 4 mos. [3]Ranges 4 to 6 mos. [4]Cost is projected. [5]Maximum is 6 mos. [6]Cost estimated.

Source: *The Corrections Yearbook, 1991*, Criminal Justice Institute, (South Salem, NY, 1991)

TABLE 6.19

State	Maximum Annual SI Capacity*	1987 Prison Population	SI Capacity As A % Of Prison Population
Georgia	800	16,291	4.9%
Oklahoma	570	9,596	5.9%
Mississippi	760	6,561	11.6%
New York	1,000	38,449	2.6%
Louisiana	360	14,300	2.5%
South Carolina	496	11,022	4.5%
Florida	348	32,228	1.1%

*Maximum annual capacity equals SI bedspace × 365 ÷ average length of stay.

TABLE 6.20
Shock Incarceration Treatment Components

Jurisdiction	Program Length	Drug/ Alcohol Counseling	Reality Therapy	Relaxation Therapy	Individual Counseling	Recreation Therapy	Theraputic Community
Georgia	90 days						
Oklahoma	120 days	X	X	X	X	X	
Mississippi	90 days		X	X	X		
Orleans Parish	120 days	X			X		
Louisiana	90-180 days	X	X		X		
South Carolina	90 days	X				X	
New York	180 days	X	X		X	X	X
Florida	90-120 days	X	X	X			

Source of both tables: *Shock Incarceration: An Overview of Existing Programs*, National Institute of Justice, (WDC, 1989)

INTENSIVE SUPERVISION PROGRAM

A possible solution to the dilemma is Intensive Supervision Programs (ISP's), an alternative to prison or probation. An example of an ISP is described by the Oregon Department of Corrections, "...the offender will be visited by a probation officer two or three times per week, who will phone on the other days. The offender will be subject to unannounced searches of his home for drugs and have his urine tested regularly for alcohol and drugs. He must strictly abide by other conditions set by the court — not carrying a weapon, not socializing with certain persons — and he will have to perform community service and be employed or participate in training or education. In addition, he will be strongly encouraged to attend counseling and/or other treatment, particularly if he is a drug offender" (Joan Petersilia, 1990, "When Probation Becomes More Dreaded Than Prison," WDC: *Federal Probation*). ISP, according to Joan Petersilia, is in the conflicting position of having to appear punitive enough to be acceptable to the "get-tough" public and, on the other hand, appearing too punitive to prisoners. When given the choice of serving time or ISP, one-third of non-violent offenders in New Jersey chose prison.

Petersilia points out that prison is not always the deterrent it is meant to be. Sanctions are most effective if social standing is injured and the offender feels he may be excluded from his group. Having a prison record is not as stigmatizing as it once was. In some social milieus it is common for peers and family to have done time. Such a high proportion of black men end up incarcerated, that, for some, prison is a part of life, not a terrible dishonor. In gangs, imprisonment can even confer status. Petersilia adds that, "the grim fact — and national shame — is that for most people who go to prison, the conditions inside are not all that different from the conditions outside." For some

87

it is even an improvement, providing food, shelter, medical care, and a community. Ironically, social programs and job training are often more available inside prisons than outside. "Prisons are becoming the place where we provide services to our poor people," claims Robert Gangi, executive director of the Correctional Association of New York, a nonpartisan prison watchdog agency. Moreover, the offender often finds a large social network on "the inside." The warden of a penitentiary described it: "When a new guy comes up here it's almost a homecoming — undoubtedly there are people from his neighborhood and people who know him." ISP, however, does change your social standing. To be isolated and restricted within your own community can be harder to handle than prison. The intrusions, lack of privacy, and curfews are more stressful to the offender within his normal community than within a prison where such limitations are considered normal.

TABLE 6.21

Adults on parole, 1990

Region and jurisdiction	Parole population, 1/1/90	1990 Entries	1990 Exits	Parole population, 12/31/90	Percent change in parole population during 1990	Number on parole on 12/31/90 per 100,000 adult residents
U.S. total	456,803	358,820	284,216	531,407	16.3%	287
Federal	21,422	9,790	9,519	21,693	1.3%	12
State	435,381	349,030	274,697	509,714	17.1%	275
Northeast	110,749	71,214	53,017	128,946	16.4%	332
Connecticut	322	49	80	291	-9.6	11
Massachusetts	4,688	5,774	5,742	4,720	.7	101
New Hampshire	477	408	363	522	9.4	63
New Jersey	20,062	13,019	9,783	23,298	16.1	393
New York	36,885	23,273	17,321	42,837	16.1	312
Pennsylvania	47,702	28,225	19,270	56,657	18.8	623
Rhode Island	393	276	348	321	-18.3	41
Vermont	220	190	110	300	36.4	71
Midwest	55,773	50,053	40,133	65,693	17.8%	149
Illinois	14,550	16,349	13,228	17,671	21.5	208
Indiana	3,456	2,965	2,643	3,778	9.3	92
Iowa	1,900	1,572	1,361	2,111	11.1	103
Kansas	5,089	3,107	2,445	5,751	13.0	317
Michigan	9,890	8,994	6,983	11,901	20.3	174
Minnesota	1,699	2,249	2,075	1,873	10.2	58
Missouri	7,545	4,746	3,095	9,196	21.9	242
Nebraska	490	840	698	632	29.0	55
North Dakota	138	136	158	116	-15.9	25
Ohio	6,464	5,788	4,307	7,945	22.9	99
South Dakota	510	571	461	620	21.6	124
Wisconsin	4,042	2,736	2,679	4,099	1.4	114
South	183,715	117,556	85,498	215,773	17.4%	340
Alabama	5,724	2,225	1,979	5,970	4.3	200
Arkansas	3,657	2,402	2,088	3,971	8.6	230
Delaware	1,013	676	406	1,283	26.7	255
District of Columbia	4,915	3,268	2,837	5,346	8.8	1,091
Florida	2,318	645	899	2,064	-11.0	20
Georgia	17,437	16,611	11,402	22,646	29.9	477
Kentucky	3,133	2,210	2,160	3,183	1.6	117
Louisiana	9,177	6,220	6,520	8,877	-3.3	297
Maryland	9,862	7,715	6,385	11,192	13.5	309
Mississippi	3,349	1,657	1,528	3,478	3.9	190
North Carolina	7,559	9,148	6,824	9,883	30.7	197
Oklahoma	1,993	1,990	747	3,236	62.4	140
South Carolina	3,386	1,129	972	3,543	4.6	138
Tennessee	10,511	5,914	5,098	11,327	7.8	309
Texas	91,294	46,476	28,044	109,726	20.2	903
Virginia	7,444	8,790	7,186	9,048	21.5	193
West Virginia	943	480	423	1,000	6.0	74
West	85,144	110,207	96,049	99,302	16.6%	256
Alaska	533	542	507	568	6.6	150
Arizona	2,048	4,087	3,424	2,711	32.4	101
California	57,515	91,379	81,332	67,562	17.5	307
Colorado	1,974	2,149	1,727	2,396	21.4	98
Hawaii	1,287	527	389	1,425	10.7	172
Idaho	238	275	270	243	2.1	35
Montana	752	406	347	811	7.8	141
Nevada	2,417	1,620	1,187	2,850	17.9	315
New Mexico	1,151	1,277	1,204	1,224	6.3	115
Oregon	5,794	5,805	3,576	8,023	38.5	379
Utah	1,277	1,244	960	1,561	22.2	143
Washington	9,832	741	958	9,615	-2.2	267
Wyoming	326	155	168	313	-4.0	98

Note: Five States estimated numbers in one or more categories. Maine eliminated parole in 1976.

Source: *Probation and Parole 1990*, Bureau of Justice Statistics, (WDC, 1991)

HOUSE ARREST AND ELECTRONIC MONITORING

Some non-violent offenders are sentenced to house arrest in which they are legally ordered to remain confined in their own homes. They are allowed to leave only for medical purposes or to go to work. Some are required to perform a certain number of hours of community service, and if they are employed, to repay the cost of probation and/or restitution. Electronic monitoring is a recent and fast-growing addition to the house arrest concept. Two years ago, about 20 states used it. Today, experts estimate that 10,000 men and women in more than 40 states are being monitored. A small radio transmitter is attached to the offender in a non-removable bracelet or anklet. Some systems send a signal to a small monitoring box which is programmed to phone a Department of Corrections computer if the signal is broken; other systems randomly call probationers, and the computer makes a voice verification of the prisoner; or a special device is inserted into the electronic monitor, sending a confirmation to the computer. Electronic monitoring costs much less than the $40,000 required to build a new prison cell. In Florida, monitoring costs are $6.41 a day versus $38.14 to house, feed, and guard a prisoner. Florida requires monitored convicts to be employed to help keep their families off welfare, and to pay taxes, restitution to victims, court costs, and $40.00 a month for the monitoring.

House arrest frees space in prisons and jails and costs far less to administer. The offender stays with his/her family and is able to earn money to help defray the costs as well as to support his or her family. In Florida, 66 percent of all those under house arrest (monitored or not) successfully completed their terms of probation. That still means that 34 percent got into some kind of trouble. As of June 30th, 1989, of the 47,812 men and women under house arrest since October 1983, 22 have been arrested for murder. The addition of electronic monitoring adds an extra measure of security, although officials believe that at least one or two of those murders were committed by monitored prisoners. Other objections to the practice include, on one side, the potential of infringing a prisoner's diminishing rights, and on the other, that the punishment is not severe enough.

SHOCK INCARCERATION

Shock incarceration is one of the most controversial new trends in corrections, consisting of a military-type boot camp for three to six months as an alternative to prison. It was first tried in Georgia in December 1983, and by the end of 1991, 38 programs were operating in 23 states. The average length of stay is four months, and the estimated average daily cost per inmate is $42.52 (Table 6.18)(Criminal Justice Institute, 1991, NY: *The Corrections Yearbook*). The programs are popular with politicians and the public, and they get positive media attention. The program is both punitive in its rigid discipline and rehabilitative in the self-esteem it claims to confer upon successful completion of the program. The hoped-for results of shock incarceration are to motivate prisoners, teach respect for oneself and others, and break the destructive cycles of behavior. Table 6.19 shows the

TABLE 6.22

State prison releases, by method, 1977-90

| | | | | Percent of prison releases | | | | | | |
| | | | | Conditional releases | | | | Unconditional releases | | |
Year	Total releases from prison	All	Discretionary parole	Supervised mandatory release	Probation	Other[a]	Expiration of sentence	Commutation	Other
1977	115,213	100%	71.9%	5.9%	3.6%	1.0%	16.1%	1.1%	.4%
1978	119,796	100	70.4	5.8	3.3	2.3	17.0	.7	.5
1979	128,954	100	60.2	16.9	3.3	2.4	16.3	.4	.6
1980	136,968	100	57.4	19.5	3.6	3.2	14.9	.5	.8
1981	142,489	100	54.6	21.4	3.7	3.1	13.9	2.4	`1.0
1982	157,144	100	51.9	24.4	4.8	3.6	14.4	.3	.6
1983	191,237	100%	48.1%	26.9%	5.2%	2.5%	16.1%	.5%	.6%
1984	191,499	100	46.0	28.7	4.9	2.7	16.3	.5	.9
1985	203,895	100	43.2	30.8	4.5	3.0	16.9	.4	1.2
1986	230,672	100	43.2	31.1	4.5	4.6	14.8	.3	1.4
1987	270,506	100	40.6	31.2	4.4	5.7	16.2	1.0	.9
1988	301,378	100	40.3	30.6	4.1	6.0	16.8	1.0	1.2
1989	364,434	100%	39.1%	30.5%	4.4%	8.9%	16.0%	.2%	.9%
1990	304,682	100%	40.5	29.6	5.8	10.6	10.1	.1	.9

Note: The data are from the National Prisoner Statistics reporting program. The total releases from State prison are those for which the method of release was reported. Deaths, unspecified releases, transfers, and escapes were not included. Altogether, 419,783 persons were released or removed from State prisons in 1990.

[a]Other conditional releases include prisoners discharged under special procedures that included early release because of crowding, supervised work furloughs, release to home detention, release to community residence, release to special programs with required supervision, supervised reprieves, and emergency releases. Approximately 93% of the 41,837 "other conditional releases" in 1990 occurred in 5 States: Arizona, Connecticut, Florida, Georgia, and Oregon.

Source: *Probation and Parole 1990*, Bureau of Justice Statistics, (WDC, 1991)

proportion of prison inmates incarcerated by the first states to use shock incaceration.

The components of the treatment vary from state to state depending on the eligibility requirements for the participants and the approach taken by the state. All the programs include physical training and regular drill-type exercise, housekeeping and maintenance of the facility, and most require hard labor. Oklahoma and Louisiana are the exception, using this time for vocational, educational, or treatment programs. Georgia and Mississippi do not offer any educational programs, but other states do, some with notable success. Drug and alcohol counseling, reality therapy, relaxation therapy, individual counseling, and recreation therapy are other components that are incorporated into shock incarceration programs. Table 6.20 shows the various counseling components that the states include in their programs. All the programs have elaborate regulations that describe in minute detail all aspects of communication, dress, movement, eating, hygiene, etc. Obedience to rules reinforces the submission to authority and develops competency in handling a challenge that is both tedious and demanding.

Does SI work? No careful study has yet been completed that weighs the differences in the programs, the seriousness of the crimes of the participants, and what their chances for recidivism would be if they had been sent to prison instead. In a three-year follow-up, the Georgia Department of Corrections found that 38.5 percent of their SI graduates returned to prison, similar to offenders who had been sent to prison instead, but the study did not use carefully constructed comparison groups.

PAROLE

At yearend 1990, 456,803 offenders were on parole (a conditional, supervised release from prison) in the United States. The parole population grew 16.3 percent during 1990. The greatest growth was in the Midwest, which increased parole population by an average of 17.8 percent. Texas was the state with the highest ratio of parolees to residents, 903 per 100,000 adults. The District of Columbia had, by far, the highest ratio, however, at 1091 per 100,000 adults (Table 6.21). More than 85 percent of inmates released from prison go into supervised programs in the community. There are three kinds of releases. *Supervised mandatory release* is most common in jurisdictions with determinate sentencing, conditionally releasing inmates at the end of their sentence (with time off for good behavior) into a parole portion of their sentence. *Discretionary parole release* is a decision made by a parole board based on statutory or administrative determination of eligibility. An *unconditional prison release* is given when the offender's obligation to serve a sentence has been fully satisfied. In 1990, 40 percent of released prisoners were released into discretionary parole, 30 percent received a supervised mandatory release; 5.3 percent were given probation, and 14 percent were unconditionally released at the end of their sentence. The proportion of supervised mandatory releases from prison increased fivefold from 6 percent of all releases in 1977 to nearly 30 percent in 1990. In contrast, prisoners released by a parole board decision declined from 72 percent to 41 percent in 1990 (Table 6.22).

CHAPTER VII

WHITE-COLLAR CRIME

A DEFINITION

The *Dictionary of Criminal Justice Data Terminology* defines white-collar crime as, "nonviolent crime for financial gain committed by means of deception by persons . . . having professional status or specialized technical skills." This definition emphasizes the status of the defendant rather than the nature of the offense. An offense-centered definition used by the Bureau of Justice Statistics defines white-collar crime as, "nonviolent crime for financial gain committed by deception."

Following is a list of the specific crimes that the Bureau of Justice includes in white-collar crime:

• Counterfeiting — the manufacture or attempted manufacture of a copy of a negotiable instrument (coins, currency, securities, stamps, and official seals) with value set by law or possession of such a copy without authorization and with intent to defraud.

• Embezzlement — the misappropriation or illegal disposal of property entrusted to an individual with intent to defraud the legal owner or intended beneficiary. Embezzlement differs from fraud in that it involves a breach of trust that existed between the victim and the offender.

• Forgery — the alteration of something written by another or writing something that claims to be either the act of another or to have been done at a time or place other than was in fact the case.

• Fraud — the intentional misrepresentation of fact to unlawfully deprive a person of his or her property or legal rights without damage or threatened or actual injury to persons.

• White-collar regulatory offenses — the violation of federal regulations and laws other than those listed above including import and export (not including drug offenses), antitrust, transportation, food and drug, labor and agricultural offenses.

CORPORATE CRIME

Tracking white-collar crime, and especially corporate crime, is generally much more complicated than tracking other crimes. There often is no one single offender nor one victim to report the crime. White-collar crime is often based on establishing trust between the victim and the offender before any crime is committed. Building trust expands the time frame of the crime, permitting repeated victimizations of an unsuspecting victim. Corporate crime costs can run into billions of dollars, but because these losses are frequently spread out over so many uninformed victims it does not raise the same outrage or leave the same scars that an armed robbery of a few hundred dollars can leave. Corporations are so complex and powerful that the rules of justice that apply to individuals are often applied differently to business. One factor is that there often is no single person to take the blame. A board of directors is not imprisoned for a corporate wrongdoing; instead the corporation is fined. The government rarely studies corporate crime. In addition to the complexity of the issues, government funding for such studies is not available.

The first large-scale investigation of corporate crime, "Illegal Corporate Behavior," published by the now defunct Law Enforcement Assistance Administration in 1979, remains the only government study. It revealed that corporate executives believed unethical and illegal practices were common and that lawbreaking can be part of standard operating procedure within some corporations. The greater goals of the corporation take precedence over the ethical beliefs of the executives. A variety of defenses offered by lawbreaking corporations included:

1. Government measures constitute interference with the free enterprise system.

2. The government is to blame because the added costs of regulation and bureaucratic procedures cut heavily into profits.

3. The government is to blame because most of their regulations are incomprehensible and too complicated.

4. The government is to blame because the things they regulate are unimportant.

5. There is little deliberate intent; most violations are errors of omission rather than commission. Many are mistakes.

6. Other concerns in the same line of business are doing it too, and so there is no reason why we shouldn't also benefit.

7. Although it is true, as in price-fixing cases, that some violations may involve millions of dollars, the damage is so diffused among a large number of consumers that, individually, there is little loss.

8. If there is no increase in corporate profits, a violation is not wrong.

9. Violations are caused by economic necessity.

10. The corporation has changed its practices and, therefore, is no longer in violation.

Different types of ethical violations linked to corporate crime include: misrepresentation in advertising, deceptive packaging, the lack of social responsibility in television commercials, the sale of harmful and unsafe products, the sale of virtually worthless products, restricting development and built-in obsolescence, polluting the environment, kickbacks and payoffs, unethical influences on government, unethical competitive practices, personal gain for management, unethical treatment of workers, and the victimization of local communities by corporations.

Penalties

"Illegal Corporate Behavior" investigated 582 of the largest publicly-owned corporations for two years (1975-76) for corporate violations and enforcement actions. Despite using four different sources, the authors felt these figures represented a one-third undercount of government actions.

Forty percent of the corporations had no judicial or administrative actions taken against them, showing that it is possible to honestly run a large-scale business. Sixty percent had at least one violation, while 40 percent of those had repeated violations including one corporation that had 62 government actions taken during the two-year period (more than two and half per month). Motor vehicle, drug, and oil refining corporations accounted for almost half of all violations and 40 percent of those were rated as serious or moderate (Table 7.1).

Corporate actions that harm the economy were more likely to receive greater penalties than those affecting consumer product quality which were less severely sanctioned (punished). Monetary penalties in 80 percent of the cases were $5,000 or less. In only 1 percent were the penalties over $1 million. Corporate executives are rarely held accountable for the actions of the corporation. The study found that in only 1.5 percent of all enforcement actions was a corporate officer convicted for failure to carry out his legal responsibilities. Of the 56 federally convicted executives in the study, 62.5 percent received probation, 21 percent received suspended sentences, and 29 percent went to jail. For the statistics on sanctions imposed by industry type, see Table 7.2.

Corporate crimes, despite their potential to do extensive damage, are not regarded with the same fear as "street crime." Personal attacks are far more frightening, even to persons who have never been physically assaulted, than the seemingly remote possibility of dying a slow death due to air pollution or buying defective tires or using a dangerous drug. Except in certain spectacular cases that receive extensive media coverage, such as the savings and loan fraud (see below) the consequences of corporate misbehavior are generally ignored.

Crime or Questionable Business Practices ?

Bristol-Myers Squibb Co., a major pharmaceutical company, was recently fined $3.5 million and required to build a $30 million waste-water treatment plant for violating the Clean Water Act by discharging chemicals into a Syracuse lake. This is the biggest penalty leveled on a company for pollution since the *Exxon Valdez* oil spill.

In 1987, when Northrup Corp. contracted to build B-2 Stealth bombers, the radar evading airplanes were expected to cost $430 million each. In 1992, they are expected to cost $2.2 billion each and the main purpose of the planes, to penetrate Soviet airspace and knock out Moscow's mobile missiles, is no longer critical. If the planes are canceled, however, termination clauses in Northrup's contract would cost taxpayers as much as $1.6 billion to cover the defense contractor's investment in the program. Questionable accounting practices have hidden the true cost of the planes

TABLE 7.1

INDUSTRY TYPE BY PRIMARY VIOLATION TYPE

INDUSTRY TYPE		PRIMARY VIOLATION TYPE [1]													
		Total		Administrative		Environmental		Financial		Labor		Manufacturing		Trade	
		Violations	Percent	Violations	Percent	Violations	Percent	Violations	Percent	Violations	Percent	Violations	Percent	Violations	Percent
MINING AND OIL PRODUCTION	T	17	1.2	1	0.8	10	2.0	0	0.0	1	0.6	2	0.4	3	4.8
	S/M	8	1.2	1	2.9	1	1.9	0	0.0	1	0.6	2	0.6	3	4.9
FOOD	T	96	6.7	4	3.3	11	2.2	5	12.3	12	6.7	54	10.5	7	11.0
	S/M	49	7.4	2	5.9	3	5.7	5	13.2	12	7.5	20	6.3	7	11.5
APPAREL	T	4	0.3	0	0.0	0	0.0	1	2.4	2	1.1	0	0.0	1	1.6
	S/M	3	0.5	0	0.0	0	0.0	0	0.0	2	1.2	0	0.0	1	1.6
PAPER, FIBER, WOOD	T	81	5.7	3	2.4	50	10.1	0	0.0	15	8.3	1	0.2	10	15.9
	S/M	28	4.2	2	5.9	3	5.7	0	0.0	22	7.5	1	0.3	10	16.4
CHEMICAL	T	115	8.1	13	10.6	55	11.1	1	2.4	15	8.3	21	4.1	7	11.0
	S/M	49	7.4	3	8.8	12	22.6	1	2.6	10	6.2	16	5.0	7	11.5
OIL REFINING	T	289	20.1	6	4.9	229	46.2	25	61.1	9	5.1	8	1.6	10	15.9
	S/M	70	10.4	5	14.7	19	35.8	23	60.5	9	5.6	4	1.3	8	13.1
METAL MANUFACTURING	T	88	6.2	8	6.5	71	14.3	0	0.0	4	2.3	3	0.6	2	3.2
	S/M	13	2.0	3	8.8	3	5.7	0	0.0	2	1.2	3	0.9	2	3.3
METAL PRODUCTS	T	28	2.0	8	6.5	3	1.0	0	0.0	9	5.1	4	8.8	3	3.3
	S/M	13	2.0	0	0.0	0	0.0	0	0.0	7	4.4	4	1.3	2	3.3

[1] Thirteen "other" violations were excluded from the non-total columns of this table. This includes 2 serious or moderate "other" violations.

Source: *Illegal Corporate Behavior*, National Institute of Law Enforcement and Criminal Justice, (WDC, 1979)

from Congress, making the first planes look less expensive and subsequent ones nearly doubling in price. The Air Force agreed to the contracts and demands made by Northrup because the military desperately wanted the B-2s and the creative bookeeping made the project easier to sell to the American public. No other aircraft program has included as much money in protection against cancellation, a contract provision which was successfully kept secret from the Congress for three years.

THE SAVINGS AND LOAN DISASTER

The best way to rob a bank is to own it.
(a joke from the height of the crisis)

The largest financial fraud of the past decade was the savings and loans debacle. It was at least a decade in the making, involving the government, several members of Congress, and shady, risk-taking directors of federally-insured savings institutions. Constantly rising estimates predicted that it would cost each and every person in this country at least $1,200 to repair the damage.

In the 1980s, deregulation prompted changes in the laws, allowing savings banks to offer higher rates of interest and higher levels of insurance to individual depositors in order to attract more savers and help reduce inflation. The banks were also permitted a wider scope of investments, encouraging riskier loans to finance the higher interest they then were offering. Construction in the booming Southwest was one of the prime sources of investments, financed by loans from high-living owners of savings banks who were, in some cases, plundering their own banks. Some bankers conspired with real estate developers to "roll over" land and artificially inflate the value of the property. The easy money and lack of government supervision attracted criminals who saw an easy way to make a lot of money that was guaranteed by the government insurance on savings accounts.

FIGURE 7.2

INDUSTRY TYPE BY SANCTION TYPE

INDUSTRY TYPE		PRIMARY SANCTION TYPE[*]											
		Total		Monetary Penalty		Unilateral Order		Consent Order		Warning		Injunction	
		Sanctions	Percent	Sanctions	Percent	Sanctions	Percent	Sanctions	Percent	Sanctions	Percent	Sanctions	Percent
MINING AND OIL PRODUCTION	T	16	1.1	7	2.1	3	1.2	4	2.2	1	0.2	1	5.6
	S/M	7	1.0	1	1.0	2	1.5	3	2.3	0	0.0	1	5.6
FOOD	T	106	7.4	12	3.6	24	9.5	17	9.5	50	8.1	1	5.6
	S/M	60	8.6	10	9.7	18	13.5	14	10.6	15	5.0	1	5.6
APPAREL	T	4	0.3	1	0.3	0	0.0	2	1.1	0	0.0	0	0.0
	S/M	4	0.6	1	1.0	0	0.0	2	1.5	0	0.0	0	0.0
PAPER, FIBER, WOOD	T	95	6.6	27	8.0	23	9.1	15	8.4	28	4.1	0	0.0
	S/M	35	5.0	22	21.4	7	5.3	4	3.1	1	0.3	0	0.0
CHEMICAL	T	110	7.7	25	7.4	13	5.2	25	14.0	44	7.1	0	0.0
	S/M	35	7.9	13	12.6	4	3.0	21	16.0	15	5.0	0	0.0
OIL REFINING	T	248	17.3	192	57.0	25	9.9	14	7.8	11	1.8	4	22.2
	S/M	56	8.0	23	22.3	16	12.0	9	6.9	3	1.0	4	22.2
METAL MANU-FACTURING	T	98	6.9	27	8.0	18	7.1	19	10.6	32	5.2	1	5.6
	S/M	25	3.6	8	7.8	5	3.8	8	6.1	3	1.0	1	5.6
METAL PRODUCTS	T	35	2.5	4	1.2	16	6.4	7	3.9	6	1.0	1	5.6
	S/M	18	2.6	3	2.9	4	3.0	6	4.6	4	1.3	1	5.6

Source: *Illegal Corporate Behavior*, National Institute of Law Enforcement and Criminal Justice, (WDC, 1979)

When oil prices plummeted in the Southwest, the scheme began to fall apart. Real estate and oil businesses funded by these risky loans were going bankrupt, pulling the banks down with them. As problems began to surface, some bank owners turned to their Congressional connections to help them out. Having paved the way with substantial contributions to politicians' campaigns, they tried to buy their way out of trouble. Five senators were accused of helping Charles Keating Jr. by intervening with regulators investigating his Lincoln Savings and Loan. Keating had given the senators $1.3 million in contributions. Jim Wright (D - TX), then Speaker of the House, was forced out of office, technically over improprieties over the income from a book, which deflected attention from his activities protecting fraudulent bank owners.

Already, by the end of 1987, 435 savings and loans had less cash on hand than is considered the minimum amount for safety (banks must have cash available for depositors to make withdrawals at will), and 500 more banks were insolvent, regulators called them the "living dead." This represented nearly one-third of the savings and loan industry, and at last count, the crisis was expected to cost the country a staggering minimum of $500 to $700 billion.

BANK FRAUD

The FBI reported that banks, credit unions, and savings and loans lost $1.3 billion to fraud and embezzlement in 1989. This was based on 13,486 cases investigated and is undoubtedly not the total figure. Banks were the hardest hit — they reported losses of $779.5 million in 11,102 completed cases (cases which led to an arrest); savings and loans reported $491.2 million in 1,896 cases; and credit unions suffered the least with $13.3 million in losses in 488 cases.

The figures for 1988 were nearly twice as high as 1989 with 2.2 billion in fraud and embezzlement losses. Commercial banks lost $1.6 billion, savings and loans lost $587.9 million, and credit unions lost $20.2 million. These high losses were dramatically greater than the losses a decade earlier. Bank losses were 21 times higher than in 1978, savings and loans increased 103 times, and credit union losses were seven times greater. According to Anthony Adamski, chief of financial crimes at the FBI, in 1978, crimes were primarily committed by bank tellers and loan officers and were on a relatively small scale. Today, 80 percent of all employee-related crime, with an average of $1 million per theft, is committed by financial officers at the bank.

COMPUTER CRIME

Computer-assisted crime is now a major part of white-collar crime and, like corporate crime, is often unrecorded. The National Institute of Justice has defined different computer abuses as:

Computer Abuse — a broad range of intentional acts that may or may not be specifically prohibited by criminal statutes. Any intentional act involving knowledge of computer use or technology … if one or more perpetrators made or could have made gain and/or one or more victims suffered or could have suffered loss.

Computer Fraud — any crime in which a person uses the computer either directly, or as a vehicle, for deliberate misrepresentation or deception, usually to cover up the embezzlement or theft of money, goods, services, or information.

Computer Crime — any violation of a computer crime statute.

Computers and their technology (printers, modems, computer bulletin boards) are used for credit card fraud, counterfeiting, bank embezzlement, theft of secret documents, vandalism, and any kind of illegal activity that can be facilitated by the use of the computer. Experts have placed the annual value of computer crime at anywhere from $550 million to $5 billion a year, although even that may be an underestimate because victims try to hide the crime. Few companies want to admit that their computer security has been breached and that their confidential files or accounts are vulnerable. Computer crime has unlimited possibilities for damage. A study by the National Research Council ("Computers at Risk: Safe Computing in the Information Age") concluded that "Tomorrow's terrorist may be able to do more damage with a keyboard than with a bomb."

There is no centralized data bank for computer crime statistics. The FBI says that the crime is too new for the agency to have developed meaningful statistics. The Secret Service reported that arrests in violation of the federal Computer Fraud and Abuse Act of 1986 (PL 99-474) increased from 19 in 1988 to 120 in 1990.

Senator Leahy (D - VT) has proposed changes in Title XXVII of the Violent Crime Control and Law Enforcement Act of 1991. The revised Computer Fraud and Abuse Act has passed the House and has been re-introduced to the Senate in 1992. The current statute on federal computer crime requires that the offender gain "unauthorized access to federal interest computers." Today's computer abusers can cause extensive damage through remote computers without ever technically "gaining access" to the federal interest computer. The new bill is intended to place the focus on the violator's harmful intent and resulting harm rather than on "access." The bill proposes to make it a felony to cause harm to a computer or the information stored within it by transmitting a program or code. Furthermore, the bill would expand the jursidiction of the Act to include computers involved in interstate commerce and not just "federal interest computers."

Types of Computer Crime

Computer crime is faceless and bloodless, and the financial gain can be huge. A common computer crime involves tampering with accounting and banking records especially through electronic funds transfers: wire transfers, cash management systems which allow the customer to have electronic access to an account, automatic teller machines, and internal banking procedures including on-line teller terminals and computerized check processing.

The police have found that the ATM (automatic teller machine) thefts do not involve the typical white-collar offender. People arrested for ATM fraud have extensive prior records, including violent crimes, which leads police to conclude that ATM fraud may, in part, be replacing robberies and burglaries.

Computer crimes involving large sums of money, however, are more likely to be committed by someone within the company, someone with a grudge, or someone known as a "Robin Hood," a person who will steal only from the rich (although they rarely distribute it to the poor). One convicted embezzler's morals dictated that he never take more than $20,000 from any one account so as not to exceed the bank's insurance liability.

The Game

Computer crime often starts as a challenge or an opportunity for the criminal that appears too easy to pass up. Mike Hansen, now a computer crime and security consultant, explained his reasoning for committing the perfect financial crime, "Each day that I went into that wire transfer room it was like I was viewing a pile of money sitting on a table. I could reach in and grab a whole handful. I thought that surely there would be visible safeguards to prevent me. I looked around and discovered there weren't any." Hansen's ultimate theft of over $8 million worth of diamonds achieved through an illegal wire transfer started as a game. He wanted to show the financial community how easy it was to commit the perfect financial crime. The challenge of outwitting the computer gives some computer crime the appearance of being an elegant game like chess, a game of intelligence where no one gets hurt.

Robert T. Morris Jr.'s case was a highly publicized example of what allegedly began as a game. Morris, a Cornell graduate student, introduced a "worm" into the Internet Network of computers.

The worm multiplied, clogging the memories of 6,200 computers nationwide until they could no longer function. Morris was the first person convicted under the Computer Fraud and Abuse Act. He was sentenced to three years probation, a $10,000 fine, 40 hours of community service, and $91 a month to cover his probation supervision.

Espionage Through Computers

A more serious computer crime that also began as a game is detailed in Clifford Stoll's *The Cuckoo's Egg* (1989, New York: Doubleday). Stoll, an astrophysicist turned systems manager, noticed a 75-cent accounting error as part of his job tracking the bookkeeping for a thousand accounts who used computer time at the laboratory where he worked. Errors of a few pennies in a computer's bookkeeping often signals a deeply buried problem somewhere in the computer program. Starting as an afternoon's entertainment, Stoll ended up tracking down a spy network in West Germany that was breaking into computers all over the world and selling military secrets to the KGB (the former USSR's secret police). It began with half a dozen hackers (computer geniuses who compulsively devote their time to matching wits with computers) who had formed a group called the Chaos Computer Club. One member, code-named Hagbard, teamed with an independent hacker, Markus Hess, to steal secrets from United States computer systems. Hagbard used Hess, who was in it for the challenge, to sell secrets to the KGB to support a cocaine habit. Stoll patiently tracked their activity for 10 months, setting computer traps and supplying them with false information until the FBI and the German government could charge them with espionage.

Crackers

Hackers who have abused the system are now being called "crackers" to distinguish them from those who use the system legally. A new vocabulary has appeared to describe different types of computer abuse. **Logic bombs** are programs set to go off at a certain time to empty computer memories or sabotage programs. **Worms**, like viruses, attack programs but they do not attach themselves; they float independently through cyberspace (cyberspace is a term taken from science fiction and refers to the general computer environment). Computer hackers use tricks such as **masquerading,** assuming the identity of someone with legal access to a system, usually by guessing the password. **Trojan horses** are hard-to-detect programs that alter computer instructions enabling fraud and sabotage. **Salami attacks** take small amounts from many accounts so that the loss will be overlooked, while **scanning** uses high speed sequencing (sorting) to figure out telephone numbers, credit card numbers, and passwords. **Social engineering** is a cynical term used to describe conning someone with access to a system to divulge the password.

PBX Fraud

A PBX is a small computer that operates as an automatic switchboard for any location that has multiple telephone lines, which includes most companies of over a half a dozen or so employees. Hackers can easily penetrate the systems and make thousands of dollars of phone calls which will not be detected by the company until the telephone bill arrives in, perhaps, a box rather than an envelope because it is so large. Telecommunications fraud costs an estimated $1.2 billion to $2 billion a year. The three major long distance companies (AT&T, MCI, and Sprint) are reluctant to reveal how vulnerable their services are, and the victimized companies usually do not want customers to know that their computer systems have been infiltrated. The telephone companies and their customers battle over who will be responsible for the enormous bills, while the culprits almost always get away with the crime.

The perpetrators sell access to long distance lines, often to new immigrants who do not realize that they are breaking the law, running up thousands of dollars in overseas calls. Pacific Mutual Life Insurance Company was charged $200,000 in toll fraud over three days by hackers who gained

TABLE 7.3

Total Arrest Trends, Sex, 1982–1991

[7,073 agencies; 1991 estimated population 161,135,000; 1982 estimated population 147,670,000]

Offense charged	Males						Females					
	Total			Under 18			Total			Under 18		
	1982	1991	Percent change	1982	1991	Percent change	1982	1991	Percent change	1982	1991	Percent change
TOTAL	6,581,698	7,583,006	+15.2	1,135,879	1,171,409	+3.1	1,291,401	1,754,397	+35.9	298,313	343,586	+15.1
Murder and nonnegligent manslaughter .	12,624	15,308	+21.3	1,178	2,352	+99.7	1,868	1,758	−5.9	101	113	+11.9
Forcible rape	22,216	26,318	+18.5	3,247	4,035	+24.3	209	300	+43.5	52	59	+13.5
Robbery	104,636	118,485	+13.2	27,908	30,559	+9.5	8,265	11,088	+34.2	1,984	2,951	+48.7
Aggravated assault	177,849	286,496	+61.1	23,223	39,942	+72.0	26,019	45,197	+73.7	4,153	7,071	+70.3
Burglary	322,005	265,410	−17.6	127,501	88,359	−30.7	23,947	26,570	+11.0	9,321	8,293	−11.0
Larceny-theft	629,462	717,967	+14.1	214,960	225,220	+4.8	269,622	339,180	+25.8	78,444	90,922	+15.9
Motor vehicle theft	82,343	131,346	+59.5	28,684	56,266	+96.2	8,075	14,523	+79.9	3,511	7,123	+102.9
Arson	12,028	11,261	−6.4	4,676	5,501	+17.6	1,769	1,699	−4.0	628	540	−14.0
Violent crime[1]	317,325	446,607	+40.7	55,556	76,888	+38.4	36,361	58,343	+60.5	6,290	10,194	+62.1
Property crime[2]	1,045,838	1,125,984	+7.7	375,821	375,346	−.1	303,413	381,972	+25.9	91,904	106,878	+16.3
Crime Index total[3]	1,363,163	1,572,591	+15.4	431,377	452,234	+4.8	339,774	440,315	+29.6	98,194	117,072	+19.2
Other assaults	298,435	573,138	+92.0	43,219	80,812	+87.0	50,379	113,037	+124.4	11,726	24,889	+112.3
Forgery and counterfeiting	44,233	44,213	[4]	4,344	3,686	−15.1	21,354	23,717	+11.1	1,951	1,842	−5.6
Fraud	121,657	149,977	+23.3	13,897	7,149	−48.6	78,533	108,815	+38.6	3,664	2,616	−28.6
Embezzlement	4,338	5,651	+30.3	365	447	+22.5	1,957	3,492	+78.4	136	238	+75.0
Stolen property; buying, receiving, possessing	83,088	102,699	+23.6	21,628	28,268	+30.7	10,881	13,789	+26.7	2,211	3,154	+42.7
Vandalism	145,775	194,424	+33.4	65,166	84,863	+30.2	15,216	23,921	+57.2	5,956	7,675	+28.9
Weapons; carrying, possessing, etc.	120,144	147,686	+22.9	17,609	31,339	+78.0	10,000	11,359	+13.6	1,228	2,146	+74.8
Prostitution and commercialized vice ...	24,065	25,628	+6.5	658	455	−30.9	64,971	50,242	−22.7	1,583	516	−67.4
Sex offenses (except forcible rape and prostitution)	50,045	67,215	+34.3	8,362	11,725	+40.2	3,777	5,232	+38.5	563	850	+51.0
Drug abuse violations	386,128	581,184	+50.5	51,647	48,153	−6.8	61,432	116,248	+89.2	9,951	5,872	−41.0
Gambling	23,969	10,265	−57.2	780	759	−2.7	2,892	1,582	−45.3	36	24	−33.3
Offenses against family and children	28,457	46,315	+62.8	782	1,668	+113.3	3,817	11,302	+196.1	451	855	+89.6
Driving under the influence	1,002,453	925,267	−7.7	18,009	9,364	−48.0	122,615	139,795	+14.0	2,380	1,497	−37.1
Liquor laws	260,854	290,936	+11.5	72,057	60,499	−16.0	47,303	68,030	+43.8	22,132	23,018	+4.0
Drunkenness	797,552	542,380	−32.0	25,181	12,573	−50.1	71,898	62,882	−12.5	4,125	2,274	−44.9
Disorderly conduct	366,052	391,517	+7.0	56,904	67,963	+19.4	68,573	99,710	+45.4	12,711	17,776	+39.8
Vagrancy	24,052	26,360	+9.6	2,720	1,753	−35.6	3,235	3,170	−2.0	555	266	−52.1
All other offenses (except traffic)	1,344,537	1,788,508	+33.0	208,473	170,647	−18.1	245,405	373,181	+52.1	51,371	46,348	−9.8
Suspicion (not included in totals)	6,313	7,117	+12.7	1,762	2,132	+21.0	1,095	1,469	+34.2	429	619	+44.3
Curfew and loitering law violations	54,526	45,931	−15.8	54,526	45,931	−15.8	15,025	16,725	+11.3	15,025	16,725	+11.3
Runaways	38,175	51,121	+33.9	38,175	51,121	+33.9	52,364	67,853	+29.6	52,364	67,853	+29.6

[1] Violent crimes are offenses of murder, forcible rape, robbery, and aggravated assault.
[2] Property crimes are offenses of burglary, larceny-theft, motor vehicle theft, and arson.
[3] Includes arson.
[4] Less than one-tenth of 1 percent.

Source: *Crime in the U.S., 1991 - Uniform Crime Reports*, FBI, (WDC, 1992)

access through the building's remote telephone control of the lights and thermostat. Teenagers in New York gained access to a publisher's voice mail (computerized message service) system, causing over $2 million in damage in retaliation for a misunderstanding about a free poster offer.

The Secret Service does not have the resources to bring a case to court for less than $50,000 in losses. In New York City, source of an estimated 95 percent of all toll fraud, the district attorney refused cases under $100,000 in damages. MCI spent $12,000 pursuing a case against two defendants responsible for over $300,000 in telecommunications theft. The perpetrators were sentenced to 500 and 300 hundred hours of community service, respectively.

Computer Forgery

As technology advances, forgers are able to use sophisticated computers, scanners (a machine that

TABLE 7.4

SOURCE OF SHRINKAGE ESTIMATES (MEAN PERCENTS) BY STORE TYPE

Source	Department Store	Discount Store	Specialty Apparel	Specialty Hard Goods	Specialty Other	Home Centers	Drug Store	Grocery, Etc.	Other	Total
Employee Theft	35.2%	38.0%	39.8%	43.0%	39.7%	33.5%	38.5%	40.6%	36.1%	38.0%
Shoplifting	32.0%	24.9%	29.6%	24.9%	27.5%	25.3%	31.3%	22.7%	14.6%	26.2%
Book Keeping Errors	26.5%	28.1%	24.5%	26.4%	26.3%	23.6%	14.5%	12.6%	17.7%	22.4%
Vendor Error	3.6%	7.0%	1.9%	3.4%	2.9%	5.7%	5.9%	9.5%	3.4%	4.9%
Other	2.7%	2.0%	4.2%	2.3%	3.6%	11.9%	9.8%	14.6%	27.9%	8.5%
Total	100%	100%	100%	100%	100%	100%	100%	100%	100%	100%
N=	73	46	67	39	55	38	36	68	34	456

"reads" a document and transfers it to the computer), and laser printers to make copies of more and more documents, including counterfeit checks, identification badges, driver's licenses, even dollar bills (the bills do not have the right feel, but they can be inserted into a stack of currency and an overworked bank teller may not catch the forgery). For example, a refund check from a company can be scanned into a computer where the name of the payee and the amount can easily be altered. Even color copiers can be used. Commuters on a New York railroad line were arrested for forging commuter passes with a color copier, and copied travelers checks were discovered in Los Angeles.

CREDIT CARD FRAUD

Credit card fraud losses, especially those caused by counterfeit cards, increased significantly between 1989 and 1990 for Visa International. Losses went from $259 million to $354 million, a 37 percent increase. Mastercard also reported that losses had almost doubled over the same year. Visa attributed the sharp rise to the theft of cards from the mail in the United States and to counterfeit cards, especially in the Far East. To prevent the use of fraudulent cards, a counterfeit-protection strip has been developed called a CVV (code verification values). Visa has given the issuing banks until April 1, 1993, to implement CVV or they will lose their insurance coverage for losses on counterfeit cards.

WOMEN IN WHITE-COLLAR CRIME

The "victimless" aspect of computer crime, and white-collar crime in general, seems to make it more appealing to women. In 1991, 38 percent of embezzlers were women, up from one out of six in the 1950s, and 35 percent of those charged with forgery were female. Women were responsible for 42 percent of the cases of fraud. This increase can be attributed to the much larger female work force and therefore the much greater opportunity to commit crimes. FBI statistics from 1982 to 1991 show the rate of female embezzlers rose 78.4 percent, while fraud rose 38.6 percent. (See Table 7.3.) A study done on gender and white-collar crime revealed that, frequently, the female criminal is a clerical worker who is helping a husband or lover, often to support his drug habit.

Among the FBI's ten most wanted women in 1991 was Valerie Finn, wanted since 1984 for wire fraud and theft of nearly $2 million. Ms. Finn was a seemingly shy company comptroller, living at home with her mother. Finn and her boyfriend, a professional motorcycle racer, used her position and expertise to plan a new life for themselves. Ms. Finn wired the money into two banks in New York and then to a precious-metals firm in Miami where she authorized the purchase of gold coins (about 186 pounds worth), which were then collected by the boyfriend. No one questioned the transfer because the company where she worked often

TABLE 7.5

USE OF LOSS PREVENTION SYSTEMS

	Department Store	Discount Store	Specialty Apparel	Specialty Hard Goods	Specialty Other	Home Centers	Drug Store	Grocery, Etc.	Overall Percent
Ink/Dye Tags	19.1%	2.7%	16.4%	0.0%	5.3%	0.0%	5.5%	1.5%	8.3%
Electronic Security Tags	36.9%	45.9%	65.6%	38.4%	41.0%	34.2%	47.2%	21.1%	40.0%
Visible Live CCTV	65.7%	64.8%	29.8%	61.5%	60.7%	65.7%	61.1%	71.2%	60.0%
Visible Simulated CCTV	17.8%	32.4%	25.4%	20.5%	17.8%	31.5%	27.7%	25.7%	24.8%
Covert CCTV	68.4%	62.1%	28.3%	33.3%	42.8%	42.1%	52.7%	51.5%	43.8%
Obvservation Mirrors	60.2%	89.1%	40.3%	43.5%	51.7%	68.4%	83.3%	66.6%	53.6%
Cables, Locks and Chains	87.6%	72.9%	56.7%	58.9%	44.6%	75.3%	38.8%	54.5%	62.8%
Subliminal Messaging Systems	0.0%	2.7%	2.9%	5.1%	3.5%	0.0%	5.5%	0.0%	1.9%
Security Display Fixtures	52.0%	35.1%	19.4%	30.7%	33.9%	47.3%	30.5%	15.1%	33.3%
Merchandise Alarms	56.1%	48.6%	25.3%	20.5%	23.2%	44.7%	36.1%	19.7%	35.3%
Average Number of Systems	4.6	4.4	3.1	3.1	3.1	4.1	3.9	3.3	

Percentages take into account the 37 stores that are classified as "other" (8.0% of total) but that are not mentioned in the the table.

made transactions of this size. When Finn failed to come to work the loss was discovered. Finn and her boyfriend are still fugitives.

RETAIL STORE THEFT

A survey of retail theft prepared for The National Retail Federation (1992, "National Retail Security Survey," *Security Magazine*) found that, of the different store categories, department and specialty stores suffered the most inventory shrinkage (the industry term for the difference between the recorded value of the inventory bought and sold and the value of the actual inventory at the end of the year). Shrinkage was lowest in stores which sell commonplace items like food and hardware or stores which sell bulky, hard-to-conceal items.

Respondents to the survey estimated that 38 percent of their losses were due to dishonest employees, 26.2 percent to shop-lifting, and 22.4 percent to bookkeeping errors. Department stores and drug stores attributed nearly one-third of their shrinkage to shop-lifting, while specialty hard goods stores and grocery stores thought employee theft was responsible for over 40 percent of their loss. (See Table 7.4.)

TABLE 7.6

Characteristics of persons arrested for Federal crimes, 1984-85

Percent of persons arrested who were:

Offense	Sex		Race		Ethnicity		Age		Education	
	Male	Female	White	Non-white	His-panic	Non-His-panic	40 and under	Over 40	No college	Attended college
All offenses	84%	16%	72%	28%	21%	79%	75%	25%	74%	26%
White collar	74%	26%	66%	34%	10%	90%	66%	34%	67%	33%
Tax fraud	88	12	93	7	2	98	33	67	56	44
Lending and credit fraud	82	18	81	19	5	95	60	40	51	49
Wire fraud	83	17	69	31	5	95	59	41	58	42
Other fraud*	75	25	62	38	15	85	64	36	65	35
Embezzlement	59	41	68	32	10	90	74	26	60	40
Forgery	70	30	52	48	11	89	80	20	83	17
Counterfeiting	86	14	76	24	9	91	73	27	76	24
Regulatory offenses	92	8	90	10	11	89	50	50	65	35
Nonwhite collar	87%	13%	74%	26%	26%	74%	78%	22%	78%	22%

Note: Data describe 22,580 persons interviewed by the Pretrial Services Agency during calendar years 1984-85. See Note, table 1. *See note a, table 1.

Stores reported that they instituted many policies to try to control loss. The most common were to place controls on refunds and voids (85.3 percent and 74.8 percent respectively). Among other techniques, stores also monitored trash removal (57.9 percent), interstore transfers (72.4 percent), unobserved exit supervision (62.6 percent), and controlled access to cash (74.6 percent). They also used loss-prevention systems including electronic security tags; visible real or simulated television monitors; cables, locks and chains; and even subliminal message systems. Table 7.5 shows the percentages of stores using the various systems.

The survey revealed that stores that pay well, use incentives or profit sharing, have low employee turnover, and promote from within have lower rates of shrinkage than stores that do not offer these benefits.

CHARACTERISTICS OF WHITE-COLLAR CRIME

The Bureau of Justice Statistics last published a report on white-collar crime in 1987, using data from 1985 ("White Collar Crime," WDC). The statistics revealed a very different profile of the white-collar criminal as compared to the violent criminal. (See Chapter I for the profile of the violent criminal.) Despite white-collar crime being more common for women than most other crimes, men still committed these crimes three times as often as women (74 percent versus 26 percent); 72 percent were white. A quarter of them were over 40 years old and slightly more than a quarter (26 percent) had a college education (Table 7.6).

During 1985, 10,733 defendants were convicted of federal white-collar crimes, an increase of 18 percent since 1980. More than half (54 percent) of the convictions were for different types of fraud (Table 7.7). Criminal cases were filed by the U.S. Attorneys against 55 percent of those accused of white-collar crimes in 1985. Those suspected of tax fraud (79 percent) and regulatory offenses (65 percent) were most frequently prosecuted. U.S. Attorneys declined to prosecute in 40 percent of the white-collar cases, compared to 26 percent of nonwhite-collar cases (Table 7.8). Whether these cases were subsequently prosecuted at a state or local level is not known.

Convictions

Eighty-five percent of white-collar defendants were convicted in 1985 as compared to 78 percent of nonwhite-collar defendants. The highest conviction rate was for tax fraud at 91 percent, followed by embezzlement at 89 percent (Table 7.9). Although a greater percentage of white-collar defendants were convicted, they served lighter sentences than their nonwhite-collar counterparts. Forty percent of white-collar criminals were sentenced to an average of 29 months behind bars versus 54 percent of nonwhite-collar offenders sentenced to an average 50 months in prison. Only 7 percent of white collar offenders received sentences of more than five years, compared to 20 percent of nonwhite-collar offenders. (See Tables 7.10 and 7.11.)

TABLE 7.10

Percent of convicted Federal offenders sentenced to incarceration, by type of victim and prior record of offender, 1985

| | Percent of offenders sentenced to incarceration when victim was: | | | | | |
| | U.S. Government | | Lending and credit institution | | U.S Postal Service | |
Prior record of offender	Theft or larceny	Embezzlement or fraud*	Theft or larceny	Embezzlement or fraud	Theft or larceny	Embezzlement or forgery
No prior convictions	15%	18%	44%	27%	20%	16%
Convicted but not incarcerated	39	32	81	44	51	34
Previously incarcerated	58	55	92	71	78	80

Note: Includes all sentences to incarceration.   *Excludes tax fraud.

Source: *White Collar Crime*, Bureau of Justice Statistics, (WDC, 1987)

TABLE 7.11

Sentence lengths for convicted Federal offenders, 1985

| | | Percent sentenced to incarceration for: | | | |
Offense	Total	1 year or less	13 months to 5 years	Over 5 years	Number sentenced to incarceration
All offenses	100%	45%	39%	16%	14,226[a]
White collar	100%	49%	44%	7%	4,265
Tax fraud	100	62	33	5	571
Lending and credit fraud	100	48	49	4	216
Wire fraud	100	42	51	7	705
Other fraud	100	51	44	5	1,016
Embezzlement	100	62	33	6	487
Forgery	100	40	49	11	897
Counterfeiting	100	34	52	14	289
Regulatory offenses	100	71	27	1	84
Nonwhite collar	100%	44%	37%	20%	9,915

Note: Percents may not total to 100% because of rounding. Includes all sentences to incarceration.   [a]Includes 46 offenders whose offense type was unknown.

Source: *White Collar Crime*, Bureau of Justice Statistics, (WDC, 1987)

CHAPTER VIII

CRIME AND DRUGS

Drug addiction claims its victims like Dorothy and her friends in the Wizard of Oz. Most times individuals walk into it haphazardly and become enchanted with its effects. Unfortunately sweet dreams turn into nightmares. So, like the wicked witch from the West cast her spell — so has crack and cocaine. And like Dorothy, drug abusers are bewitched by the tantalizing and seducing powers of these chemical compounds. Juliana Williams testifying at the Hearings before the Permanent Subcommittee on Investigations — Drugs and Violence, June 26, 1989

The connection between the use of drugs and criminal activity has long been an issue in American society. Even before federal laws were passed in 1914 to control narcotics and other drugs, observers claimed a connection between drug use and criminal activity. Drug abuse is thought to encourage criminal behavior in several ways. It can reduce inhibitions, stimulate aggression, and interfere with the ability to earn an income. Drugs can destroy one's personal sense of morality. Once a person is involved in the illegal activity of using drugs, especially addictive drugs, there are few moral restrictions that will prevent that person from committing further criminal offenses. The need to get the money necessary to support a habit supersedes any other consideration.

For segments of society that are impoverished and underprivileged, drugs may be another negative aspect of the social condition of their lives. The same circumstances that might lead a person to begin committing crimes may also contribute to the development of drug habits. For example, the same conditions that limit opportunity and reduce an individual's commitment to society contribute to both drug abuse and criminal behavior. Some people enjoy taking risks and are willing, for whatever reason, to violate the law or seek experiences that they cannot get through legal means. The use of drugs, especially on a regular basis, may not begin until after they have already begun a life of crime. Drug abuse may, therefore, be only part of a more general lifestyle that also includes other types of criminal activity. Which came first however, the crime or the drug, is less important than the tremendous problem that drugs are causing in America today. Drugs can destroy everything Americans value — life, family, work, community.*

---

* This chapter focuses on the connection of drugs and street crime — how many were arrested for violating drug laws and what proportion of those arrested or sent to prison for various other crimes were using drugs. The chapter does not deal with the functioning of the huge criminal network designed to bring in and distribute drugs. For a complete discussion of where the drugs come from, how they get to the United States, and how they are distributed, see *Illegal Drugs and Alcohol: America's Anguish* (1992, Wylie, TX 75098: Information Plus, Inc).

TABLE 8.1

Total Estimated Arrests[1], United States, 1991

TOTAL[2]	14,211,900		
Murder and nonnegligent manslaughter	24,050	Embezzlement	14,000
Forcible rape	40,120	Stolen property; buying, receiving, possessing	170,000
Robbery	173,820	Vandalism	335,100
Aggravated assault	480,900	Weapons; carrying, possessing, etc.	232,300
Burglary	436,500	Prostitution and commercialized vice	98,900
Larceny–theft	1,588,300	Sex offenses (except forcible rape and prostitution)	108,000
Motor vehicle theft	207,700	Drug abuse violations	1,010,000
Arson	20,000	Gambling	16,600
		Offenses against family and children	99,400
		Driving under the influence	1,771,400
Violent crime[3]	718,890	Liquor laws	624,100
Property crime[4]	2,252,500	Drunkenness	881,100
		Disorderly conduct	757,700
Crime Index total[5]	2,971,400	Vagrancy	38,500
		All other offenses	3,240,000
Other assaults	1,041,200	Suspicion (not included in totals)	18,400
Forgery and counterfeiting	103,700	Curfew and loitering law violations	93,400
Fraud	427,800	Runaways	177,300

[1]Arrest totals based on all reporting agencies and estimates for unreported areas.
[2]Because of rounding, figures may not add to totals.
[3]Violent crimes are offenses of murder, forcible rape, robbery, and aggravated assault.
[4]Property crimes are offenses of burglary, larceny–theft, motor vehicle theft, and arson.
[5]Includes arson.

Source: *Crime in the United States*, Federal Bureau of Investigation, (WDC, 1992)

THE GOVERNMENT'S ROLE

The federal government is addressing the drug problem in two ways: reduction of supply through interdiction and enforcement and reduction of demand through education, prevention, and treatment. The 1993 federal budget proposal called for $28.5 billion to fight crime, of which $12.7 billion was for drug-related programs.

The administration request included over $1.6 billion for drug abuse prevention initiatives and prevention related research; $115 million for High-Risk Youth Prevention Programs; $61.9 million for the Drug Enforcement Administration (DEA); $2.3 billion for drug treatment; and an additional $133.6 million for Alcohol, Drug Abuse, and Mental Health Services in an effort to target hard-to-reach users — adolescents, those in the criminal justice system, pregnant women, and intravenous drug users. In addition, the budget asked for $480 million for military, law enforcement, and economic assistance to Bolivia, Columbia, and Peru and to target trafficking groups who import drugs to the United States, particularly New York City. Nearly $400 million was requested for the Organized Crime Drug Enforcement Task Forces.

While recent studies have found that drug use in adolescents has declined (see below), hard-core substance abuse has not. The Office of National Drug Control Policy (a federal agency) has singled out addicts, drug users over 35 years old, and minorities in inner cities as those primarily responsible for hard-core drug use. The federal drug strategy seeks to limit drug supply and demand by focusing on priorities which include deterring new and casual users, treating current users, dismantling trafficking organization, intercepting supply networks, and removing drug dealers from the streets. A new aspect to the drug strategy is to step-up the campaign against alcohol and tobacco use among minors.

Misdirected Research

The Government Accounting Office (GAO) has reported that federally funded research on drug treatment has been misdirected, with priority given to heroin use when cocaine is the most serious problem (1990, *Drug Abuse: Research on Treatment May Not Address Current Needs*). In 1989, 42 percent of the National Institute of Drug Abuse's (NIDA) research was devoted to heroin and other opiates; 35 percent for other addictions including marijuana, nicotine, and methamphetamines; and

TABLE 8.2

Arrests for Drug Abuse Violations, 1991

[Percent distribution]

	United States total	North-eastern States	Mid-western States	South-ern States	Western States
Total[1]	100.0	100.0	100.0	100.0	100.0
Sale/manufacture:	33.4	44.7	30.4	30.9	28.2
Heroin or cocaine and their derivatives	22.5	37.2	11.9	20.5	17.2
Marijuana	6.1	5.0	7.1	6.3	6.5
Synthetic or manufactured drugs	.8	1.2	.6	1.2	.2
Other dangerous nonnarcotic drugs	4.0	1.3	10.8	2.9	4.4
Possession:	66.6	55.3	69.6	69.1	71.8
Heroin or cocaine and their derivatives	32.8	33.2	22.4	30.4	38.1
Marijuana	22.4	18.5	34.2	28.3	16.0
Synthetic or manufactured drugs	1.4	1.2	1.2	2.6	.6
Other dangerous nonnarcotic drugs	10.1	2.3	11.8	7.7	17.0

[1] Because of rounding, percentages may not add to totals.

Source: *Crime in the United States*, Federal Bureau of Investigation, (WDC, 1992)

23 percent for cocaine research. NIDA defends its funding allocation by countering that the heavy opiate research is an effort to control the spread of AIDS through intravenous drug use. Furthermore, NIDA reports that funding of cocaine addiction research has increased sixfold between 1986 and 1989, but the that the results of this search will not be available for several years. The GAO contends that NIDA has not conducted enough follow-up research on the effectiveness of treatment and that NIDA's failure to consult with drug treatment practitioners has contributed to the misdirection of funds.

Finally, the GAO has determined that the method used to distribute block grants to the states is heavily weighted to states with high urban populations and that these states have received a greater share of drug treatment funding than their use warrants (1990, *Targeting Aid to States Using Urban Population as Indicator of Drug Use*). While drug use in urban areas is about three times higher than in rural ones, the cities may receive up to 15 times as much funding.

DRUG ARRESTS

The federal government has passed several anti-crime bills — the Comprehensive Crime Control Act of 1984 (PL 98-473), the Anti-Drug Abuse Act of 1986 (PL 99-570), and the Anti-Drug Abuse Act of 1988 (PL 100-690) — each one requiring harsher and more mandatory sentencing, preventive detention, and even the death penalty for certain drug-related crimes. More states have changed their sentencing from indeterminate to determinate sentencing, stressing deterrence and retribution. These laws are a factor in the rising rate of drug arrests. In 1989, the Justice Department reported that between 1980 and 1987, federal drug prosecutions increased by 153 percent, while the number of offenders sentenced to federal prisons grew by 177 percent.

The Uniform Crime Reports — Crime in the United States, 1991 compiled by the Federal Bureau of Investigations (1992, WDC) reported that 14,211,900 arrests took place in 1991. Of these, 1,010,000 arrests (7 percent) were for drug abuse violations. While the 1991 drug abuse violation arrest total was down 8 percent from the 1990 level, it was 7 percent higher than the 1987 rate, and 56 percent higher than in 1982. Another 1,771,400 arrests (12.5 percent) were for driving under the influence (usually of alcohol); 624,100 (4.4 percent) for violating liquor laws; and 881,100 (6 percent) for drunkenness. Altogether, these arrests involving drug or alcohol abuse accounted for almost one-third (30 percent) of all arrests. (See Table 8.1.)

Of the 1,010,000 arrests for drug abuse in 1991, two-thirds (66.6 percent) were for possession, while the rest were for the sale or manufacture of drugs. Most of the possession arrests (32.8 percent of all drug abuse violations) were for opium/cocaine (this includes heroin, morphine, and codeine), followed by marijuana (22.4 percent). Synthetic or manufactured drugs accounted for 1.4 percent, while other dangerous non-narcotic drugs (barbiturates, LSD, PCP) made up 10 percent of the arrests. One fifth (22.5 percent) of the drug violations were for the sale and manufacture of opium/cocaine; 6 percent for marijuana; 0.8 percent for synthetic narcotics; and 4 percent for dangerous non-narcotic drugs (Table 8.2).

TABLE 8.3

Total Arrests, Distribution by Age, 1991

[10,148 agencies; 1991 estimated population 189,961,000]

Offense charged	Total all ages	Age												
		13–14	15	16	17	18	19	20	21	22	23	24	25–29	30–34
TOTAL	10,743,755	421,380	322,492	390,342	422,446	488,565	503,467	503,622	466,20	416,047	395,884	385,429	1,838,683	1,540,824
Percent distribution[1]	100.0	3.9	3.0	3.6	3.9	4.5	4.7	4.7	4.	3.9	3.7	3.6	17.1	14.3
Murder and nonnegligent manslaughter	18,654	267	502	777	1,045	1,465	1,362	1,269	1,07.	967	762	666	2,810	2,143
Forcible rape	30,350	1,220	869	988	1,167	1,367	1,320	1,292	1,29.	1,140	1,136	1,157	5,501	4,550
Robbery	139,182	7,817	7,059	8,978	9,616	9,729	8,630	7,990	7,08.	6,093	5,619	5,318	23,404	15,763
Aggravated assault	368,483	11,102	9,437	12,678	14,509	15,677	15,899	15,772	15,83	14,411	14,157	13,798	67,370	55,994
Burglary	328,790	28,966	20,352	22,674	22,619	23,020	19,185	15,914	13,45	11,512	10,404	10,031	45,021	33,648
Larceny–theft	1,215,303	105,839	64,951	70,255	66,014	62,959	54,101	47,163	41,79	36,182	33,691	32,126	158,075	138,426
Motor vehicle theft	161,628	17,400	16,802	18,166	15,615	12,399	9,518	7,605	6,43	5,198	4,583	4,214	16,924	11,750
Arson	14,916	2,117	897	694	593	553	469	429	37.	355	282	299	1,532	1,309
Violent crime[2]	556,669	20,406	17,867	23,421	26,337	28,238	27,211	26,323	25,28.	22,611	21,674	20,939	99,085	78,450
Percent distribution[1]	100.0	3.7	3.2	4.2	4.7	5.1	4.9	4.7	4.	4.1	3.9	3.8	17.8	14.1
Property crime[3]	1,720,637	154,322	103,002	111,789	104,841	98,931	83,273	71,111	62,05	53,247	48,960	46,670	221,552	185,133
Percent distribution[1]	100.0	9.0	6.0	6.5	6.1	5.7	4.8	4.1	3.	3.1	2.8	2.7	12.9	10.8
Crime Index total[4]	2,277,306	174,728	120,869	135,210	131,178	127,169	110,484	97,434	87,33	75,858	70,634	67,609	320,637	263,583
Percent distribution[1]	100.0	7.7	5.3	5.9	5.8	5.6	4.9	4.3	3.	3.3	3.1	3.0	14.1	11.6
Other assaults	789,144	32,923	21,960	24,501	26,137	27,544	29,432	31,550	32,76	30,622	30,302	30,758	151,250	125,123
Forgery and counterfeiting	77,066	842	1,018	1,891	2,736	3,751	4,167	4,488	4,03	3,462	3,273	3,257	15,285	12,239
Fraud	292,597	2,275	2,642	2,168	3,263	6,930	10,091	12,663	13,22	13,144	13,277	13,354	61,618	52,123
Embezzlement	10,602	98	88	211	327	530	604	587	58	485	463	404	1,981	1,522
Stolen property; buying, receiving, possessing	130,579	8,043	6,939	8,680	9,494	10,462	8,780	7,360	6,24	5,202	4,710	4,219	17,839	12,934
Vandalism	252,469	29,410	17,742	19,100	17,318	13,945	11,951	10,565	9,49	7,921	7,098	6,561	29,376	21,473
Weapons; carrying, possessing, etc.	178,955	8,110	7,061	9,211	10,610	12,076	11,140	9,994	9,53	8,142	7,221	6,391	26,317	19,230
Prostitution and commercialized vice	81,536	113	123	278	526	1,479	2,274	3,047	3,87(	4,111	4,218	4,176	22,514	17,438
Sex offenses (except forcible rape and prostitution)	82,228	4,668	2,437	2,387	2,187	2,396	2,395	2,357	2,44:	2,313	2,294	2,437	12,687	12,297
Drug abuse violations	781,250	7,534	10,133	17,166	24,547	35,665	38,454	40,061	38,61:	35,837	34,509	33,974	166,221	136,893
Gambling	12,913	124	173	219	377	466	491	374	37(	316	293	322	1,489	1,588
Offenses against family and children	72,527	639	619	636	693	1,953	1,987	2,301	2,73:	2,653	2,584	2,852	15,063	14,509
Driving under the influence	1,288,876	215	563	3,299	9,173	23,617	33,415	42,522	56,891	53,782	53,027	53,064	270,717	239,119
Liquor laws	453,807	8,420	14,731	30,651	49,508	71,860	71,980	63,111	17,391	11,525	9,259	7,880	29,934	22,970
Drunkenness	657,119	1,725	2,413	4,095	7,870	16,809	19,549	21,716	25,98	23,642	22,862	22,419	118,804	117,177
Disorderly conduct	569,314	22,392	18,197	22,629	26,150	29,271	29,069	29,471	31,075	25,848	23,535	22,385	96,029	74,174
Vagrancy	31,262	475	446	622	593	1,106	970	853	849	744	747	750	4,673	5,921
All other offenses (except traffic)	2,480,902	52,290	42,026	58,049	73,072	100,902	115,632	122,560	122,18(	109,957	105,070	102,124	473,789	388,395
Suspicion	14,707	881	622	673	602	634	602	608	564	483	508	493	2,460	2,116
Curfew and loitering law violations	73,125	17,893	16,937	19,930	14,399	....	....	....	....	....	....	....	....	....
Runaways	135,471	47,582	34,753	28,736	11,686	....	....	....	....	....	....	....	....	....

Source: *Crime in the United States*, Federal Bureau of Investigation, (WDC, 1992)

Demographics

Those most frequently arrested for drug and alcohol offenses are between the ages of 25 and 34. In 1991, this group was 30 percent (303,114 arrests) of those arrested for drug abuse, while offenders who were under 25 years old were 10.3 percent (104,320 arrests) of those arrested. Alcohol violations (a combination of the numbers for driving under the influence, liquor law violations, and drunkenness) showed a similar age/arrest pattern with 10 percent (257,460 arrests) of those arrested under 25, and 33 percent (798,721 arrests) 25 to 34 years old (Table 8.3).

Since 1982 there has been a large increase in drug abuse arrests, especially for women. Women were arrested for drugs 89 percent more often in 1991 than a decade ago, while male arrests increased 50.5 percent. In 1991, white drug arrests made up almost 58 percent of the total, while black arrests were 41 percent. The remaining 0.8 percent was Native Americans or Asian/Pacific Islanders. White offenders committed most of the alcohol violations, representing 89 percent of driving under the influence, 87.3 percent of the liquor law violations, and 81.2 percent of drunkenness. Native Americans had more arrests for alcohol-related abuses than any other crime. They were

106

TABLE 8.4

Total Arrests, Distribution by Race, 1991

[10,075 agencies; 1991 estimated population 186,621,000]

Offense charged	Total arrests					Percent distribution[1]				
	Total	White	Black	American Indian or Alaskan Native	Asian or Pacific Islander	Total	White	Black	American Indian or Alaskan Native	Asian or Pacific Islander
TOTAL	10,516,399	7,251,862	3,049,299	115,345	99,893	100.0	69.0	29.0	1.1	.9
Murder and nonnegligent manslaughter	18,096	7,861	9,924	143	168	100.0	43.4	54.8	.8	.9
Forcible rape	29,767	16,306	12,960	259	242	100.0	54.8	43.5	.9	.8
Robbery	136,176	51,217	83,146	600	1,213	100.0	37.6	61.1	.4	.9
Aggravated assault	364,250	218,628	139,407	3,184	3,031	100.0	60.0	38.3	.9	.8
Burglary	323,670	222,817	94,688	2,844	3,321	100.0	68.8	29.3	.9	1.0
Larceny–theft	1,190,037	792,895	368,053	12,987	16,102	100.0	66.6	30.9	1.1	1.4
Motor vehicle theft	160,103	93,728	62,918	1,266	2,191	100.0	58.5	39.3	.8	1.4
Arson	14,738	11,309	3,164	132	133	100.0	76.7	21.5	.9	.9
Violent crime[2]	548,289	294,012	245,437	4,186	4,654	100.0	53.6	44.8	.8	.8
Property crime[3]	1,688,548	1,120,749	528,823	17,229	21,747	100.0	66.4	31.3	1.0	1.3
Crime Index total[4]	2,236,837	1,414,761	774,260	21,415	26,401	100.0	63.2	34.6	1.0	1.2
Other assaults	772,016	498,497	257,121	9,685	6,713	100.0	64.6	33.3	1.3	.9
Forgery and counterfeiting	74,869	48,535	25,264	418	652	100.0	64.8	33.7	.6	.9
Fraud	291,528	197,643	91,230	1,283	1,372	100.0	67.8	31.3	.4	.5
Embezzlement	10,565	7,202	3,195	74	94	100.0	68.2	30.2	.7	.9
Stolen property; buying, receiving, possessing	129,609	73,908	54,011	696	994	100.0	57.0	41.7	.5	.8
Vandalism	249,252	189,474	55,014	2,461	2,303	100.0	76.0	22.1	1.0	.9
Weapons; carrying, possessing, etc.	173,490	98,609	72,137	893	1,851	100.0	56.8	41.6	.5	1.1
Prostitution and commercialized vice	78,779	47,517	29,943	455	864	100.0	60.3	38.0	.6	1.1
Sex offenses (except forcible rape and prostitution)	80,838	63,185	15,985	828	840	100.0	78.2	19.8	1.0	1.0
Drug abuse violations	763,340	443,596	312,997	2,639	4,108	100.0	58.1	41.0	.3	.5
Gambling	12,464	5,581	5,843	16	1,024	100.0	44.8	46.9	.1	8.2
Offenses against family and children	70,945	47,304	20,942	763	1,936	100.0	66.7	29.5	1.1	2.7
Driving under the influence	1,270,713	1,129,876	115,724	14,846	10,267	100.0	88.9	9.1	1.2	.8
Liquor laws	448,880	391,991	43,576	10,610	2,703	100.0	87.3	9.7	2.4	.6
Drunkenness	625,127	507,571	102,307	13,544	1,705	100.0	81.2	16.4	2.2	.3
Disorderly conduct	558,504	365,765	182,414	7,185	3,140	100.0	65.5	32.7	1.3	.6
Vagrancy	30,755	15,735	14,341	605	74	100.0	51.2	46.6	2.0	.2
All other offenses (except traffic)	2,428,040	1,542,890	831,857	24,968	28,325	100.0	63.5	34.3	1.0	1.2
Suspicion	10,184	4,150	5,964	53	17	100.0	40.8	58.6	.5	.2
Curfew and loitering law violations	72,037	55,389	14,819	542	1,287	100.0	76.9	20.6	.8	1.8
Runaways	127,627	102,683	20,355	1,366	3,223	100.0	80.5	15.9	1.1	2.5

Source: *Crime in the United States*, Federal Bureau of Investigation, (WDC, 1992)

arrested for 2.4 percent of liquor law and 2.2 percent of drunkenness violations. (See Table 8.4.)

Increased Arrests Are Not Effective

A study by the General Accounting Office (1991, *The War on Drugs: Arrests Burdening Local Criminal Justice Systems*, WDC) found that increasing arrests without also expanding the capacity of the criminal justice system has been ineffective in deterring drug crime. The nation's criminal justice system has become overburdened with crowded court schedules, overworked attorneys and prosecutors, and overflowing jails, prisons, and drug treatment centers. The report stated,

For the criminal justice system to have an impact, it should convey to potential drug offenders that they will be held accountable for their illegal activities. Although generating additional prison capacity would appear to be the simplest solution, it is becoming a less feasible option as fiscal constraints are imposed at every level of government.

Efforts by cities to cope with the increased number of arrests have led to the increased use of plea bargaining, probation and parole, and early release programs, and these measures have weakened the criminal justice system. While less costly

TABLE 8.5

Pretrial status of defendants charged with drug offenses, 1988

Pretrial status	Percent of drug offense defendants
Total	100%
Released	72%
Financial total	36%
Surety	19
Full cash	10
Deposit	6
Other	1
Nonfinancial total	36%
Release on recognizance	30
Unsecured bail	7
Detained	28%

Note: Detail may not add to total because of rounding.

TABLE 8.6

Percent of felony defendants released before trial and median bail set, by type of offense, 1988

Most serious felony arrest charge	Percent released prior to case disposition	Median bail set
Murder	39%	$35,000
Rape	55	17,500
Robbery	52	7,500
Assault	69	5,000
Burglary	53	5,000
Theft	64	2,500
Drug offenses	72	3,500
Sales/trafficking	69	5,000
Other	75	2,500

Source of both tables: *Drugs and Crime Facts, 1990,* Bureau of Justice Statistics, (WDC, 1991)

than incarceration, these alternatives lack offender accountability.

Out on Bail

The Bureau of Justice Statistics (BJS), in "Felony defendants in large urban counties, 1988" (1990, WDC), found that, of those persons charged with a felony drug offense in 1988, 72 percent were released prior to case disposition, 26 percent were held with bail set, and 2 percent were held without bail. (See Table 8.5.) Eighty-two percent of drug defendants with no prior record were released, compared to 73 percent of those with at least one misdemeanor conviction, 58 percent of those with a prior non-violent felony conviction, and 62 percent of those with a prior violent felony conviction. Table 8.6 shows the percentage of defendants who were released by type of crime and amount of bail set.

DRUGS AND CRIME

Drug Use Forecasting (DUF)

The FBI statistics for drug and alcohol offenses do not show how many crimes, especially the more serious Index Crimes, happened because the offender was on drugs, was in a gang selling drugs, was trying to support an addiction, or was neglecting and abusing other family members because of drug addiction.

In 1987, the National Institute of Justice started the Drug Use Forecasting program. The aim of the program is to clarify the nature and extent of drug abuse by continuously tracking the drug use of arrestees in 24 major cities across the United States. The data is collected in central booking facilities in each city for approximately 14 consecutive evenings each quarter through voluntary and anonymous interviews and urine specimens from selected arrestees. Over 90 percent of the arrestees approached agreed to be interviewed, and over 80 percent of those interviewed agreed to give a urine specimen. DUF statistics are the minimum estimates in the male arrestee population because the sampling only includes a limited number of the men who were arrested on drug charges. All female arrestees were accepted for the sampling because of the small number of women arrested. Except for marijuana and PCP, which can remain in the system for several weeks, all the other drugs had been used by the arrestees in the preceding two or three days.

In 1990, 24 cities* collected data from male arrestees, while 21 also interviewed females. The percentage of males testing positive for any drug ranged from 30 percent in Omaha, NE to 78 percent in San Diego, CA. For women, the percentages ranged from 39 percent in Indianapolis, IN to 76 percent in Philadelphia, PA. In 18 of the DUF sites, 50 percent or more of male and female arrestees tested positive. In 14 of the 21 sites that tested both males and females, females tested positive as often, or more often, than did males. Drug use was prevalent in arrestees of all ages and races. (See Table 8.7.)

---

* Only 23 cities are listed in the tables. Miami was omitted.

TABLE 8.7

Any Drug Use by Male and Female Booked Arrestees*

City	Sex	% Positive Any Drug	% Positive by Age 15–20	21–25	26–30	31–35	36+	% Positive by Race Black	White	Hispanic	Other
Atlanta	Males	62	32	50	72	79	67	64	44	**	**
	Females	71	**	69	78	87	66	68	85	**	**
Birmingham	Males	64	43	68	70	74	62	65	58	**	**
	Females	67	41	52	80	79	58	67	66	**	**
Chicago	Males	73	55	80	82	80	74	73	63	78	**
Cleveland	Males	55	38	52	70	62	57	58	42	35	**
	Females	73	36	69	78	89	76	80	67	**	**
Dallas	Males	56	40	60	61	69	51	60	52	43	**
	Females	60	51	54	62	72	65	59	64	**	**
Denver	Males	48	47	50	51	47	42	54	45	46	24
	Females	55	39	61	62	56	47	67	48	44	**
Detroit	Males	51	35	41	57	67	64	51	55	**	**
	Females	74	51	80	78	73	76	74	74	**	**
Ft. Lauderdale	Males	60	44	58	67	68	56	69	52	30	**
	Females	66	56	68	71	67	61	71	63	**	**
Houston	Males	64	45	65	73	75	66	71	51	54	**
	Females	59	40	55	67	66	58	62	69	29	**
Indianapolis	Males	46	39	51	51	50	40	51	41	**	**
	Females	39	31	34	43	48	42	47	35	**	**
Kansas City	Males	45	36	38	54	60	41	50	32	**	**
	Females	64	46	69	84	66	39	67	58	**	**
Los Angeles	Males	65	50	59	66	76	70	76	69	53	**
	Females	71	36	68	81	79	76	76	78	56	**
Manhattan	Males	76	52	76	85	83	81	79	75	72	**
	Females	71	41	69	77	78	79	76	72	58	**
New Orleans	Males	61	48	67	71	67	56	62	48	**	**
	Females	60	35	56	68	70	60	61	54	**	**
Omaha	Males	30	24	34	29	32	32	35	28	8	**
Philadelphia	Males	76	65	74	86	84	69	78	66	77	**
	Females	76	51	76	81	87	76	78	72	66	**
Phoenix^A	Males	54	45	58	56	60	47	67	51	50	31
	Females	56	63	58	56	61	55	71	59	45	39
Portland^B	Males	62	61	63	67	68	55	63	65	52	36
	Females	61	45	60	70	63	59	62	60	**	**
St. Louis	Males	54	35	58	69	68	42	55	44	**	**
	Females	56	35	60	72	57	43	57	53	**	**
San Antonio	Males	51	45	53	57	58	46	61	53	47	**
	Females	41	25	38	49	48	43	51	45	37	**
San Diego	Males	78	62	76	86	86	79	82	78	78	**
	Females	75	59	74	74	82	80	84	72	67	**
San Jose	Males	55	54	52	58	66	50	62	55	56	33
	Females	57	36	50	65	67	54	67	54	61	**
Washington, D.C.	Males	56	28	56	68	70	61	57	51	**	**
	Females	73	56	67	76	87	73	75	61	**	**

Source: National Institute of Justice/Drug Use Forecasting Program

* Positive by urinalysis, January through December 1990
** Less than 20 cases
^A Site does not test males for methaqualone, barbiturates, and propoxyphene; does not test females for methaqualone and barbiturates
^B Site does not test for methadone, methaqualone, and propoxyphene

Multiple drug use was also found in subjects of all ages and races. San Diego reported the highest rates — 46 percent for males and 38 percent for females. The low ranged from 4 percent in Omaha for males and 9 percent in Atlanta, GA for females (Table 8.8).

Cocaine Use

The most frequently used drug was cocaine. Male arrestees testing positive for cocaine ranged from 10 percent in Omaha to 65 percent in New York City and Philadelphia. Of the 21 cities that tested females, 13 of them had higher rates for females than for males. Atlanta reported the highest female rate of 68 percent, followed closely by Cleveland, OH and Washington, DC (65 percent), Detroit, MI and Manhattan (NYC) (64 percent), and Philadelphia (63 percent). (See Table 8.9.) In some cities cocaine use had decreased. In Detroit, cocaine use among males decreased from 51 percent in 1988 to 50 percent in 1989, to 38 percent in

1990. Similar decreases over the three year period were seen in Portland, OR (40, 37, and 22 percent), Los Angeles, CA (60, 52, and 45 percent), and Manhattan (74, 72, and 65 percent). In New Orleans, LA, females testing positive for cocaine use rose from 40 percent in 1988 to 50 percent in 1990.

Marijuana

The percentage of males who tested positive for marijuana ranged from 4 percent in Atlanta to 42 percent in Portland. Similarly, females tested positive for marijuana only 1 percent of the time in Atlanta and 27 percent in Portland. More males than females tested positive for marijuana use in nearly every city (Table 8.10). Marijuana use was down in most DUF cities. In Detroit in 1988, 1989, and 1990, the rates went from 33 to 21 to 15 percent. For females the rates in New Orleans decreased from 25 percent to 18 percent to 12 percent in 1990. See Table 8.11 for opiate (heroin) use.

TABLE 8.9

Cocaine Use by Male and Female Booked Arrestees*

City		% Positive Cocaine	% Positive by Age: 15–20	21–25	26–30	31–35	36+	% Positive by Race: Black	White	Hispanic	Other
Atlanta	Males	59	27	50	71	74	62	61	35	**	**
	Females	68	**	67	74	83	66	67	70	**	**
Birmingham	Males	50	26	50	59	61	48	55	27	**	**
	Females	43	31	36	57	44	34	48	36	**	**
Chicago	Males	54	34	58	62	68	60	54	44	58	**
Cleveland	Males	45	26	40	61	54	47	52	18	15	**
	Females	65	32	64	69	84	58	73	53	**	**
Dallas	Males	43	22	43	51	58	42	50	31	29	**
	Females	46	24	43	52	55	55	51	40	**	**
Denver	Males	24	20	23	27	27	21	34	15	22	6
	Females	40	30	46	46	44	22	61	27	26	**
Detroit	Males	38	16	30	48	56	48	38	38	**	**
	Females	64	38	71	68	68	59	62	69	**	**
Ft. Lauderdale	Males	46	14	40	54	61	49	61	33	15	**
	Females	55	37	56	61	59	47	65	47	**	**
Houston	Males	53	32	54	65	62	55	63	33	39	**
	Females	49	34	46	62	50	46	55	51	24	**
Indianapolis	Males	18	10	17	20	26	17	28	6	**	**
	Females	13	11	10	14	16	18	22	8	**	**
Kansas City	Males	30	14	21	39	47	30	35	12	**	**
	Females	54	26	59	73	58	31	58	42	**	**
Los Angeles	Males	45	28	34	48	60	54	63	29	38	**
	Females	56	18	51	65	68	57	68	48	43	**
Manhattan	Males	66	32	62	78	78	73	70	63	60	**
	Females	64	28	62	69	76	73	71	63	50	**
New Orleans	Males	51	37	60	55	58	49	54	23	**	**
	Females	50	29	52	58	58	44	52	40	**	**
Omaha	Males	10	3	13	14	11	9	16	6	4	**
Philadelphia	Males	66	50	64	79	77	58	71	40	68	**
	Females	63	41	62	66	80	61	69	48	59	**
Phoenix	Males	29	15	28	35	35	27	55	17	34	7
	Females	34	38	36	32	39	28	65	26	30	14
Portland	Males	22	11	21	19	30	23	38	14	33	14
	Females	34	17	33	44	30	36	48	27	**	**
St. Louis	Males	42	26	46	56	54	32	48	10	**	**
	Females	44	32	47	57	45	31	49	29	**	**
San Antonio	Males	26	19	31	28	34	23	51	18	21	**
	Females	23	17	23	28	28	16	45	14	21	**
San Diego	Males	46	28	44	54	51	44	68	17	54	**
	Females	37	26	34	33	47	44	69	18	37	**
San Jose	Males	26	20	25	27	35	26	39	19	29	18
	Females	27	18	23	37	32	18	54	24	22	**
Washington, D.C.	Males	48	21	48	63	58	50	50	22	**	**
	Females	65	53	57	71	82	56	67	48	**	**

Source: National Institute of Justice/Drug Use Forecasting Program

* Positive by urinalysis, January through December 1990

** Less than 20 cases

Males / Females

Update

The drug use charts for the second quarter of 1991 show a breakdown of the different drugs that were tested and the dates of highest and lowest positive results (Tables 8.12 and 8.13). Cocaine was the most commonly used drug.

JUVENILE TESTING

Eleven DUF sites collected data on male juveniles. The percentage of male juvenile arrestees who had used drugs ranged from 10 percent in Kansas City, MO to 31 percent in Los Angeles, CA. Los Angeles also had the highest rate of multiple drug use. In eight of the 11 cities, marijuana was the most commonly used drug. Cleveland, St Louis, and Washington were the only cities reporting higher cocaine use (Table 8.14).

Self-Reported Use

More than 70 percent of the juveniles reported using alcohol beginning at around 13 years old. Except for in Washington D.C.*, anywhere from a fifth to over half of the youth admitted to using alcohol in the past 30 days. Over half of the juveniles reported cigarette use, with nearly all of the group reporting having smoked in the past 72 hours. About 30 percent admitted to feeling dependent on tobacco. Marijuana use (excluding Washington) ranged from 38 percent in St. Louis to a

____

* Reported use was very low for all drugs in Washington, but, urinalysis for cocaine use revealed high drug use, making the accuracy of self-reported use questionable.

high of 77 percent in Los Angeles. (See Table 8.15.)

During the DUF interview, arrested juveniles were asked if they were attending school. Of those who were not, the majority had dropped out. In six of the sites more than 50 percent had dropped out, and in six cities, more than 20 percent had been expelled. The majority of the males were 15 to 16 years old and, except in Indianapolis, less than 10 percent were between 9 and 12 years of age (Table 8.16). The race of the arrestees reflected the population of their cities. Hispanic arrests were high in Los Angeles, San Antonio, TX, and San Jose, CA, while in Portland the majority of juvenile arrestees were white.

DRUG USE AMONG PRISON INMATES

A special report by the BJS (1991, "Drugs and Jail Inmates, 1989," WDC) surveyed inmates in local jails in 1983 and 1989 regarding their crimi-

TABLE 8.12

Drug Use by Male Booked Arrestees*

Adult Males

Site	% Positive Any Drug*	Range of % Positive				2+ Drugs	Cocaine	Marijuana	Amphetamines	Opiates	PCP
		Low	Date	High	Date						
Manhattan	79	69	4/90	90	6/88	29	64	24	0	16	2
Philadelphia	77	72	11/90	84	4/89	33	65	19	**	13	4
San Diego	76	66	6/87	85	1/89	42	45	42	19	15	**
Chicago	75	71	5/90	85	7/88	40	60	26	0	23	11
Miami	65	65	6/91	75	8/88	16	57	20	0	1	0
Houston	64	55	11/90	71	4/90	17	54	19	0	4	0
Atlanta	63	62	10/90	63	4/91	19	56	22	**	4	0
New Orleans	63	54	1/91	76	4/89	24	51	27	0	6	2
Washington, D.C.	63	53	5/90	72	2/89	19	54	13	**	10	4
Los Angeles	62	56	10/90	77	4/88	21	40	23	7	7	4
Birmingham	61	56	8/90	75	7/88	15	52	14	0	6	0
Ft. Lauderdale	60	56	8/90	71	3/88	14	40	28	0	1	0
Detroit	57	45	9/90	69	10/88	17	41	21	0	9	0
St. Louis	57	42	7/90	69	4/89	21	39	29	0	6	3
Cleveland	56	49	8/90	70	8/89	12	42	18	0	2	**
Dallas	56	50	11/90	72	6/88	13	42	21	2	3	**
Portland	56	54	1/89	76	8/88	16	24	32	8	8	0
San Jose	56	49	8/90	65	8/89	22	28	24	7	9	14
Denver	54	35	8/90	58	2/90	11	24	36	**	**	0
Phoenix	50	44	10/90	67	5/90	16	21	32	4	6	0
Kansas City	49	39	9/90	64	5/89	14	34	22	**	2	7
San Antonio	46	43	9/90	63	3/90	17	28	19	0	11	0
Omaha	40	22	8/90	57	7/88	7	9	34	0	1	0
Indianapolis	39	33	9/90	62	9/89	8	19	19	0	4	0

Source: National Institute of Justice/Drug Use Forecasting Program

* Positive by urinalysis, April through June 1991. Drugs tested for include cocaine, opiates, PCP, marijuana, amphetamines, methadone, methaqualone, benzodiazepines, barbiturates, and propoxyphene

** Less than 1%

TABLE 8.13

Drug Use by Female Booked Arrestees*

Adult Females

Site	% Positive Any Drug*	Range of % Positive				2+ Drugs	Cocaine	Marijuana	Amphetamines	Opiates	PCP
		Low	Date	High	Date						
Cleveland	78	67	5/90	88	2/90	15	76	7	0	4	4
Washington, D.C.	78	58	11/90	88	6/89	20	73	5	0	10	1
Los Angeles	77	69	10/90	80	7/89	31	62	14	9	18	2
Philadelphia	75	69	11/90	90	8/89	23	62	18	**	8	**
Manhattan	74	71	4/90	83	2/88	31	65	11	0	18	2
Portland	72	51	5/90	82	8/88	35	32	32	14	18	0
San Diego	71	70	2/90	87	12/87	36	33	23	25	19	3
Detroit	70	67	9/90	85	3/88	17	65	2	0	15	0
Kansas City	67	56	9/90	83	8/89	22	56	20	1	3	4
Atlanta	66	66	4/91	71	10/90	12	63	11	0	3	0
Birmingham	66	43	11/89	77	4/89	31	40	7	1	19	0
St. Louis	62	45	11/88	75	4/89	21	57	12	0	12	2
Ft. Lauderdale	60	54	11/90	79	3/90	14	48	18	0	2	0
Houston	60	48	10/89	68	4/90	22	49	11	**	8	0
Phoenix	60	47	10/90	78	3/89	26	42	17	4	18	**
New Orleans	58	46	11/87	65	1/90	17	47	12	0	7	1
San Jose	56	48	8/90	64	2/90	23	34	14	8	6	14
Denver	54	52	11/90	62	2/90	19	36	22	2	2	0
Dallas	52	42	9/89	71	6/88	12	46	4	4	6	1
Indianapolis	52	26	11/90	57	3/91	25	27	20	1	15	0
San Antonio	39	36	6/90	56	2/91	19	24	10	3	15	0

Source: National Institute of Justice/Drug Use Forecasting Program

* Positive by urinalysis, April through June 1991. Drugs tested for include cocaine, opiates, PCP, marijuana, amphetamines, methadone, methaqualone, benzodiazepines, barbiturates, and propoxyphene

** Less than 1%

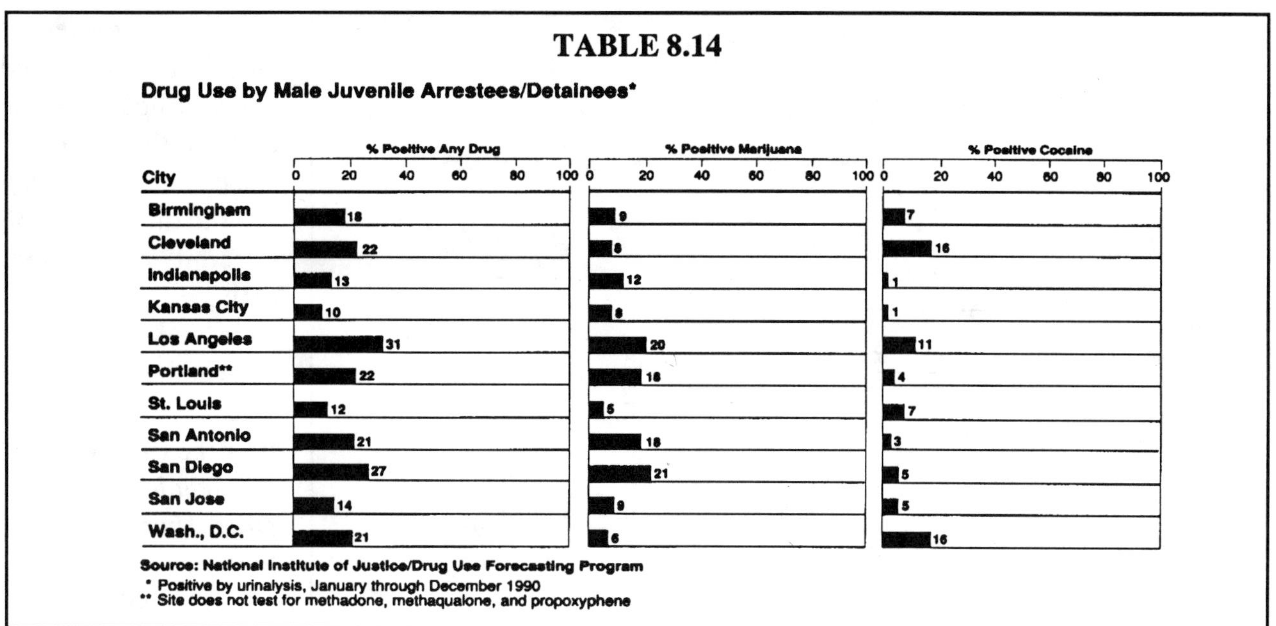

TABLE 8.14

Drug Use by Male Juvenile Arrestees/Detainees*

Source: National Institute of Justice/Drug Use Forecasting Program
* Positive by urinalysis, January through December 1990
** Site does not test for methadone, methaqualone, and propoxyphene

---

nal and drug histories. The percentage of jail inmates charged with drug charges as their most serious offense more than doubled between 1983 and 1989 from 9.3 percent to 23 percent. When multiple charges were evaluated, those with at least one drug charge increased from 11 percent to 25.8 percent (Table 8.17). The number of inmates with a drug charge as their most serious offense rose from 20,479 in 1983 to 87,551 in 1989, a 328 percent increase, while the number of persons held for all other offenses increased 47 percent.

The majority of users of major drugs (heroin, crack, cocaine, PCP, LSD, and methadone) were in jail for either drug crimes or crimes for economic gain. Approximately 65 percent of those who had used a major drug in the month prior to arrest were convicted of robbery, burglary, larceny, drug trafficking, or other drug offenses. In contrast, about half of the inmates who had used drugs at some time in the past and 31 percent who had never used drugs were in jail for these offenses.

TABLE 8.15

Male Juveniles: Self-Reported Alcohol, Tobacco, and Marijuana*

City	% Ever Used	Median Age of First Use	Of Those Who Ever Used: % Ever Dependent	% Used in Past 30 Days	% Used in Past 72 Hours
Birmingham	78	13	5	27	15
Cleveland	82	13	7	22	8
Indianapolis	69	13	7	24	15
Kansas City	86	13	8	30	12
Los Angeles	92	13	6	50	27
Portland	85	12	15	46	16
St. Louis	80	13	3	20	9
San Antonio	80	13	4	36	26
San Diego	91	13	3	40	26
San Jose[A]	90	13	6	52	32
Washington, D.C.	71	14	2	6	4
Birmingham	61	13	34	49	43
Cleveland	58	13	32	44	40
Indianapolis	54	12	42	43	40
Kansas City	61	12	36	38	31
Los Angeles	75	13	34	56	50
Portland	74	12	60	63	57
St. Louis	51	13	24	36	29
San Antonio	57	13	35	48	47
San Diego	77	12	30	53	46
San Jose[B]	72	13	29	49	44
Washington, D.C.	36	14	3	8	6
Birmingham	50	14	7	27	15
Cleveland	46	13	7	22	8
Indianapolis	44	13	11	24	15
Kansas City	66	14	10	30	12
Los Angeles	77	13	9	50	27
Portland	66	13	18	46	16
St. Louis	38	14	6	20	9
San Antonio	55	13	9	36	26
San Diego	75	13	10	40	26
San Jose[A]	60	13	7	32	17
Washington, D.C.	16	14	9	6	4

Source: National Institute of Justice/Drug Use Forecasting Program

* Data based on voluntary self-reports, January through December 1990
[A] Data from San Jose, 1st and 2nd Quarter 1990 are not included in self-reported 30-day and 72-hour use
[B] Data from San Jose, 1st and 2nd Quarter 1990 are not included

TABLE 8.16

Age and Race of Male Juvenile Arrestees/Detainees*

City	Age (In Percent)				Race (In Percent)			
	9–12	13–14	15–16	17–18	Black	White	Hispanic	Other
Birmingham	2	16	45	36	83	16	**	**
Cleveland	4	16	46	33	74	22	3	0
Indianapolis	15	27	37	21	64	35	**	**
Kansas City	**	12	80	7	70	28	1	0
Los Angeles	2	15	53	30	22	12	62	4
Portland	4	22	53	21	36	56	3	5
St. Louis	8	29	55	8	87	12	**	**
San Antonio	3	22	66	10	18	13	68	1
San Diego	4	20	44	31	29	30	34	6
San Jose	6	24	44	26	15	25	48	12
Washington, D.C.	2	20	48	28	96	1	2	**

Source: National Institute of Justice/Drug Use Forecasting Program

* January through December 1990
** Less than 1%

Violent crimes and public order offenses were more commonly committed by non-users. (Alcohol, involved in many public order crimes, was not considered a drug.) (See Table 8.18.)

A higher percentage of convicted inmates who reported being under the influence of alcohol or drugs at the time of their offense had used alcohol (41 percent) than drugs (28 percent). More than half of the inmates reported using one or the other or both. Other than the 93 percent who were arrested for DWI (driving while intoxicated), the most common crime committed under the influence of alcohol was assault at 54 percent. (See Table 8.19.)

Demographics

The demographic characteristics of jail inmates revealed increases in the number of female, black, and Hispanic drug offenders. Women's rates rose from 9.3 percent to 13.7 percent, while Hispanics increased from 19.9 percent to 24.7 percent, and blacks went from 34.6 percent to 48.3 percent over the six year period (Table 8.20.) In 1989, nearly three-fourths of those in jail on drug charges were either black or Hispanic.

About 78 percent of all jail inmates reported using drugs at some point in their lives — 44 percent in the month prior to the offense, 30 percent used them daily, and 27 percent were under the influence at the time of the offense. Based on data from the 1990 *National Household Survey on Drug Abuse* (National Institute on Drug Abuse), jail inmates were twice as likely as the general population to ever have used drugs and seven times more likely to be current users. Only crack (an inexpensive, smokeable form of cocaine) and cocaine use increased among males from 1983 to 1989. All other drug use declined except for amphetamines and barbiturates ("uppers and downers") taken together which remained unchanged. (See Table 8.21.)

Users of crack and cocaine were more likely to be female and black non-Hispanics than were inmates who had used either no drugs or some other drug in the month before their arrest. Users were more likely to be unemployed (47 percent compared to 34 percent of other drug users, and 29 percent of non-users). Three times as many crack and cocaine users reported committing their current offense to obtain money for drugs than did other drug users. About 42 percent of cocaine users had received drug treatment in the past. (See Table 8.22.)

Parental Influence

Jail inmates who reported that their parents had abused drugs and alcohol were more likely to have used drugs themselves. They were also younger when they began their drug use. The children of

TABLE 8.17

Jail inmates charged with drug offenses, 1989 and 1983

Status and drug offenses of jail inmates	Percent of jail inmates 1989	1983
Drugs, most serious charge		
Total	23.0%	9.3%
Convicted	22.5	10.0
Unconvicted	23.8	8.3
Drugs, any charge		
Total	25.8%	11.0%
Convicted	25.5	11.4
Unconvicted	26.1	10.3
Number of jail inmates	380,160	219,573

Note: Excludes an estimated 15,394 inmates in 1989 and 3,979 inmates in 1983 because their offense was unknown.

TABLE 8.18

Convicted jail inmates who committed current offense under the influence of drugs or alcohol, by the most serious offense, 1989

Most serious offense	Number of convicted jail inmates	Percent of convicted jail inmates who were under the influence of drugs or alcohol at the time of offense Total	Drugs only	Alcohol only	Both
All offenses	205,254	56.6%	15.4%	29.2%	12.1%
Violent offenses	34,188	55.6%	8.8%	30.7%	16.1%
Robbery	10,208	53.1	17.7	18.1	17.3
Assault	10,569	58.7	4.5	44.3	9.8
Property offenses	59,858	48.9%	18.2%	17.9%	12.8%
Burglary	20,172	58.3	20.4	20.4	17.5
Larceny/theft	16,905	44.7	18.4	16.5	9.8
Drug offenses	44,325	48.2%	28.6%	7.3%	12.3%
Possession	21,196	56.1	32.9	6.7	16.5
Trafficking	21,051	40.6	23.9	7.8	8.9
Other/unspecified	2,077	44.7	32.1	7.7	4.8
Public-order offenses	64,084	70.1%	6.4%	54.1%	9.6%
DWI	29,791	94.6	1.8	82.7	10.1
Other public-order	34,293	48.8	10.5	29.2	9.1

TABLE 8.19

The most serious offense of convicted jail inmates, by their drug-use history, 1989

Most serious offense	Percent of convicted jail inmates Never used drugs	Used a drug any time in the past	Used a major drug in the month before the offense
All offenses	100.0%	100.0%	100.0%
Violent offenses	19.6%	15.7%	14.1%
Homicide[a]	2.8	1.6	.9
Sexual assault[b]	5.0	2.9	1.9
Robbery	4.4	5.2	7.0
Assault	6.5	4.7	3.5
Other violent[c]	1.0	1.3	.8
Property offenses	24.6%	30.5%	34.0%
Burglary	5.6	11.0	12.9
Larceny/theft	6.5	9.0	10.0
Motor vehicle theft	3.6	2.6	2.7
Fraud	4.9	4.0	4.8
Stolen property	2.2	2.2	2.6
Other property[d]	1.7	1.8	1.0
Drug offenses	15.5%	24.5%	34.7%
Possession	7.4	11.7	18.0
Trafficking	7.8	11.6	14.9
Other/unspecified	.3	1.2	1.8
Public-order offenses	38.8%	27.8%	16.3%
DWI	20.5	12.0	4.3
Other public-order	18.3	15.9	12.0
Other	1.5%	1.4%	1.0%
Number of jail inmates	47,733	170,260	60,368

Source of all tables: *Drugs and Jail Inmates, 1989*, Bureau of Justice Statistics, (WDC, 1991)

Note: For inmates who had never or ever used drugs, the table excludes 494 inmates whose offense or use of drugs was unknown. For inmates who had used a major drug in the month before the offense, the table excludes 804 inmates whose offense or use of drugs was unknown.
[a] Includes murder, nonnegligent manslaughter, and negligent manslaughter.
[b] Includes rape.
[c] Includes kidnaping.
[d] Includes arson.

abusers began use at a median age of 13; first used a major drug at 16; and regularly used a major drug at 17 years old. Among inmates whose parents had not abused drugs, they first used drugs at 16; a major drug at 19 years; and used drugs regularly at 21 years of age (Table 8.23).

Inmates who grew up with both parents had a lower rate of ever using drugs or using drugs regularly than inmates who were reared by a single parent or who were raised in foster homes (Table 8.24). Similarly, inmates who reported being physically or sexually abused were more likely to use drugs (Table 8.25).

The Victim's Drug Use

In 1986, the Bureau of Justice Statistics, in "Violent State Prisoners and their Victims," (1990, WDC), surveyed 245,562 inmates in state correctional facilities about the victims of their crimes. Over half the inmates (54 percent) said they had committed the crime under the influence of drugs, alcohol, or both (Table 8.26). Nearly one-third of the inmates thought their victim was under the influence of alcohol or drugs. In 64 percent of the offenses, drugs or alcohol played a role for either victim or offender or both. Manslaughter was the most common crime for which drug and alcohol use were mentioned, over three-quarters of the time (Table 8.27).

DRUG USE IN RURAL CRIME

Attention often focuses on drug use in the inner city, neglecting substance abuse in rural states like Montana or North Dakota. The Government Accounting Office (GAO) gathered data from the FBI, high school surveys, the

---

TABLE 8.20

Demographic characteristics of jail inmates, by type of offense, 1989 and 1983

Demographic characteristic	Percent of jail inmates charged with			
	Any drug offense		A nondrug offense	
	1989	1983	1989	1983
Sex				
Male	86.3%	90.7%	92.1%	93.3%
Female	13.7	9.3	7.9	6.7
Race and Hispanic origin				
White non-Hispanic	25.5%	43.7%	43.3%	46.8%
Black non-Hispanic	48.3	34.6	39.6	37.8
Hispanic	24.7	19.9	14.6	13.6
Other*	1.6	1.9	2.6	1.8
Age				
17 or younger	.7%	.2%	1.8%	1.5%
18-24	33.6	32.0	32.4	41.4
25-29	25.4	30.2	23.0	22.3
30-34	19.9	19.6	19.0	15.0
35-44	15.9	14.0	17.0	12.2
45-54	3.3	3.0	5.0	5.0
55 or older	1.2	.9	1.8	2.6
Median age	28 yrs.	27 yrs.	28 yrs.	26 yrs.
Education				
8th grade or less	15.2%	14.8%	15.7%	18.0%
Some high school	39.0	36.7	38.3	42.1
High school graduate	32.7	33.3	33.2	28.6
Some college or more	13.0	15.2	12.8	11.4
Number of jail inmates	97,999	24,118	282,161	219,573

Note: Excludes an estimated 15,394 inmates in 1989 and 3,979 in 1983 because their offense was unknown. In 1989 data were missing on education for 0.5% of cases. In 1983 data were missing on race and Hispanic origin for 0.2% of cases and on education for 1.1% of cases.
*Includes Asians, Pacific Islanders, American Indians, Aleuts, Eskimos, and other racial groups.

Source : *Drugs and Jail Inmates, 1989*, Bureau of Justice Statistics, (WDC, 1991)

TABLE 8.21

Drug use history of jail inmates, by type of drug, 1989 and 1983

Type of drug	Percent of jail inmates who had used drugs				Percent of convicted jail inmates who had used drugs					
	Ever		Regularly		In the month before the offense		Daily in the month before the offense		At the time of the offense	
	1989	1983	1989	1983	1989	1983	1989	1983	1989	1983
Any drug	77.7%	76.1%	58.1%	60.8%	43.9%	46.1%	29.7%	32.9%	27.0%	29.6%
Major drug	55.4%	46.2%	37.4%	30.5%	27.7%	18.6%	17.3%	11.0%	18.2%	12.1%
Cocaine or crack	50.4	38.0	30.7	17.8	23.6	11.8	14.2	6.4	13.7	5.5
Heroin	18.2	22.4	11.4	16.0	7.0	7.9	5.1	5.8	4.6	5.6
LSD	18.6	22.3	6.3	8.5	1.6	3.0	.2	.9	.4	1.3
PCP	13.9	15.6	4.6	6.3	1.7	3.0	.6	1.2	1.3	1.9
Methadone	4.8	6.9	1.9	3.1	.6	.8	.2	.4	.5	.6
Other drug	71.9%	74.5%	49.8%	57.9%	31.3%	41.8%	18.9%	28.2%	12.0%	22.8%
Marijuana	70.7	73.0	47.9	55.0	28.1	38.6	16.8	25.6	9.1	16.9
Amphetamines	22.1	32.8	12.1	19.6	5.4	9.4	3.2	5.1	2.2	4.2
Barbiturates	17.2	27.8	7.2	13.9	3.3	5.9	1.4	2.8	.9	2.9
Methaqualone	14.7	23.0	4.2	8.8	.8	3.8	.2	1.5	.3	1.7
T's and blues*	11.0	10.9	5.4	5.9	2.4	3.0	1.3	1.8	.2	1.7

*A combination of amphetamines and barbiturates.

Source : *Drugs and Jail Inmates, 1989*, Bureau of Justice Statistics, (WDC, 1991)

118

TABLE 8.22

Characteristics of convicted jail inmates who had used cocaine or crack, other drugs, or no drugs in the month before their offense, 1989

Characteristic	Percent of jail inmates who in the month before the offense used		
	Cocaine or crack	Another drug	No drug
Sex			
Male	83.6%	92.0%	92.1%
Female	16.4	8.0	7.9
Race and ethnicity			
White non-Hispanic	35.2%	50.2%	42.6%
Black non-Hispanic	45.2	29.6	36.7
Hispanic	18.0	17.0	17.5
Other	1.6	3.3	3.1
Age			
17 or younger	.5%	1.5%	1.2%
18-24	31.7	37.3	28.2
25-29	28.2	26.0	23.0
30-34	22.1	19.5	17.7
35-44	15.3	13.5	19.1
45 or older	2.2	2.2	10.8
Education			
8th grade or less	14.4%	12.4%	18.0%
9th to 11th grade	42.1	41.1	35.3
High school graduate	31.3	36.1	31.1
Some college or more	12.2	10.4	15.6
Employment			
Employed	53.4%	65.8%	70.3%
Full time	43.2	55.8	58.7
Part time	10.2	10.0	11.6
Unemployed	46.6	34.1	28.7
Looking for work	27.4	20.7	17.9
Not looking for work	19.2	13.4	10.8
Sources of income			
Wages	69.6%	76.7%	79.1%
Benefits	20.1	18.8	18.2
Family or friends	21.8	18.7	17.2
Illegal income	25.2	15.8	4.9
Other	2.2	2.7	3.4
Current offense			
Violent	15.4%	15.2%	17.5%
Robbery	7.9	3.8	4.3
Assault	3.4	4.4	6.0
Property	33.7	32.4	26.2
Burglary	12.9	11.5	7.9
Larceny	9.3	10.7	7.3
Drug	34.2	28.6	15.4
Possession	16.0	16.8	6.3
Trafficking	16.4	10.4	8.5
Other drug	1.7	1.3	.5
Public-order	15.9	22.7	39.1
Other	.9	1.3	1.8
Committed current offense for money for drugs	38.6%	12.9%	2.6%
Incarcerated in past	67.3%	63.7%	52.4%
Ever convicted in past	84.3%	84.5%	74.1%
Received drug treatment in past	42.2%	36.5%	13.3%
Number of jail inmates	51,337	44,550	121,962

TABLE 8.23

Median age at which jail inmates began using drugs, by whether parents abused drugs or alcohol, 1989

Jail inmates	Median age for jail inmates whose parents abused			
	Drugs	Alcohol	Drugs or alcohol	Neither
First use of any drug	13 yrs.	15 yrs.	15 yrs.	16 yrs.
First use of a major drug	16	17	17	19
First regular use of a major drug	17	19	19	21

Note: Major drug includes heroin, crack, cocaine, PCP, LSD, and methadone. Any drug includes the major drugs, marijuana or hashish, amphetamines, barbiturates, and methaqualone.

TABLE 8.24

Drug use of jail inmates, by childhood living arrangements, 1989

	Number of jail inmates	Percent of jail inmates who used drugs	
		Ever	Regularly
Who jail inmates lived with most of their childhood			
Single parent	167,248	82.2%	62.1%
Both parents	172,931	74.6	55.0
Other relatives	39,869	78.7	58.2
Foster home or institution	7,889	80.5	62.8
Other	4,016	59.0	50.9
Jail inmates who lived in foster home or institution			
Ever	53,875	87.3%	71.3%
Never	338,079	76.8	56.4

TABLE 8.25

Drug use of jail inmates, by whether they were physically or sexually abused before admission to jail, 1989

	Number of jail inmates	Percent of jail inmates who	
		Ever used drugs	Used drugs regularly
All offenders			
Physical or sexual abuse	62,395	86.4%	71.5%
No physical or sexual abuse	322,484	77.0	56.2
Men			
Physical or sexual abuse	46,198	85.0	69.9
No physical or sexual abuse	302,281	76.9	56.0
Women			
Physical or sexual abuse	16,197	90.3	76.3
No physical or sexual abuse	20,203	77.1	59.5

Source of all tables: *Drugs and Jail Inmates, 1989*, Bureau of Justice Statistics, (WDC, 1991)

TABLE 8.26

Whether State prison inmates committed violent offense under the influence of drugs or alcohol, by characteristics of the victims and victim-offender relationship, 1986

	Total	Percent of inmates who committed offense under the influence of:			
		Drugs	Alcohol	Both	Neither
All cases	100%	13.6%	20.4%	20.3%	45.7%
Sex of victim(s)					
Male	100%	13.9%	20.5%	19.1%	46.5
Female	100	11.0	21.8	21.5	45.7
Both	100	23.7	13.3	22.3	40.7
Race of victim(s)					
White	100%	13.2%	21.2%	22.5%	43.1%
Black	100	11.5	19.6	15.6	53.3
Other	100	19.3	21.6	20.4	38.6
Mixed	100	25.0	9.4	18.6	47.0
Age of victim(s)					
Minor	100%	6.7%	18.5%	18.1%	56.6%
Adult	100	14.9	20.4	20.7	44.0
Both	100	9.6	19.0	25.0	46.4
Relationship					
Close	100%	6.3%	23.8%	16.0%	53.9%
Known	100	10.4	25.1	19.4	45.2
Stranger	100	16.9	17.5	21.9	43.7

TABLE 8.27

Use of drugs or alcohol by State prison inmates and perceived use of drugs or alcohol by their victims at the time of the violent offense, 1986

	Total	Murder	Man-slaughter	Rape	Sexual assault	Robbery	Assault	Other violent
Total	100.0%	100.0%	100.0%	100.0%	100.0%	100.0%	100.0%	100.0%
Offender using only drugs and victim using:	13.4%	9.3%	7.2%	6.8%	5.3%	20.7%	10.7%	13.3%
Drugs	2.1	1.8	2.4	1.2	.6	2.5	2.7	1.7
Alcohol	.8	.7	1.1	0	.5	1.1	.7	1.0
Both	.7	.8	1.2	.4	.4	.6	1.0	1.0
Neither	9.8	6.1	2.4	5.2	3.8	16.5	6.4	9.8
Offender using only alcohol and victim using:	20.1%	23.6%	32.4%	24.7%	20.9%	13.4%	24.5%	20.9%
Drugs	1.2	1.3	1.5	2.4	1.0	.8	1.7	1.0
Alcohol	4.9	7.3	14.1	5.0	3.0	1.8	7.6	2.7
Both	1.8	2.7	5.1	2.2	.7	.5	3.0	2.2
Neither	12.1	12.3	11.8	15.2	16.1	10.3	12.1	15.0
Offender using both drugs and alcohol and victim using:	20.0%	19.0%	12.8%	25.2%	19.8%	21.2%	17.9%	22.1%
Drugs	1.9	2.9	1.3	2.8	1.3	1.7	1.4	1.7
Alcohol	2.6	3.2	3.5	3.6	2.7	1.8	2.9	2.7
Both	3.0	4.2	3.3	4.2	3.4	1.4	4.2	3.4
Neither	12.5	8.8	4.7	14.7	12.2	16.3	9.4	14.3
Offender not using drugs or alcohol and victim using:	46.5%	48.1%	47.6%	43.3%	54.2%	44.7%	46.9%	43.6%
Drugs	4.3	5.7	6.5	2.3	1.5	3.7	6.7	1.6
Alcohol	4.3	5.2	10.4	2.4	1.6	3.3	7.0	1.4
Both	2.1	2.5	6.5	2.0	.9	1.0	3.5	1.4
Neither	35.8	34.7	24.3	36.7	50.2	36.8	29.8	39.2
Number of offenders	245,562	50,552	14,421	19,047	20,280	98,838	36,191	11,253

Note: When offenders reported they did not know whether the victim had been using drugs or alcohol, the victim was assumed not to have been using either.

Source of both tables: *Violent States Prisoners and Their Victims,* Bureau of Justice Statistics, (WDC, 1990)

1988 *Household Survey,* and interviewed officials and experts for their report, *Rural Drug Abuse: Prevalence, Relation to Crime, and Programs* (1990, WDC). (A rural state is one of 18 with a population density of 50 persons or less per square mile including: AK, AR, AZ, CO, ID, IA, KS, ME, MT, NE, NV, NM, ND, OK, OR, SD, UT, and WY.) The report found that total substance abuse (alcohol abuse and other drug abuse) was about as high in rural as nonrural areas. While alcohol abuse is very high for both, it is higher in rural areas, while cocaine abuse is lower (Figure 8.1). Table 8.28 shows the same pattern for treatment admissions and arrests. Alcohol abuse is higher in rural areas and other drugs are more prevalent in nonrural states, but the overall differences are small.

Drugs and Rural Prison Inmates

A survey of substance abuse in four state corrections systems found that the vast majority of prison inmates in Arkansas, Iowa, Montana, and North Dakota have substance abuse problems. The largest group has abused both alcohol and other drugs. Table 8.29 reveals that total abuse ranged from 71 percent in Arkansas to 91 percent in Montana. The high levels of combined drug and alcohol abuse indicate it is a mistake to focus attention on the effect of any one drug on criminal activity.

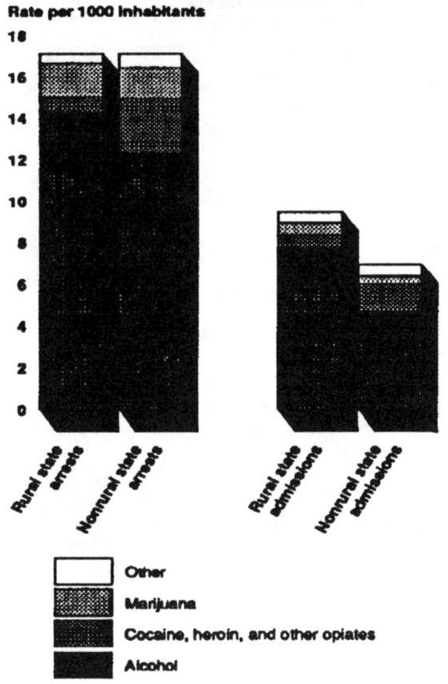

Source: Treatment admissions data in W. Butynski, D. Canova, and S. Jenson, State Resources and Services Related to Alcohol and Drug Abuse Problems, Fiscal Year 1988: An Analysis of State Alcohol and Drug Abuse Profile Data, a report for the National Institute on Alcohol Abuse and Alcoholism and the National Institute on Drug Abuse (Washington, D.C.: National Association of State Alcohol and Drug Abuse Directors, 1989), pp. 22 and 36; arrest data in U.S. Department of Justice, Crime in the United States, 1988 (Washington, D.C.: Federal Bureau of Investigation, 1989a); and U.S. Department of Justice, unpublished data, Federal Bureau of Investigation, 1990f.

TABLE 8.28

Alcohol and Other Drug Treatment Admissions and Arrests by Rural and Nonrural States and Counties, 1988[a]

	Alcohol[b]	Other drugs[c]	Total
Treatment admissions[d]			
Rural states	7.7	1.7	**9.4**
Nonrural states	4.7	2.2	**6.9**
Arrests[e]			
Rural states[f]	14.3	2.8	**17.0**
Nonrural states	12.3	4.8	**17.1**
Rural counties[g]	12.6	2.4	**15.0**
Nonrural counties	11.3	3.0	**14.2**

[a]Rate per 1,000 inhabitants.

[b]Arrests for alcohol include driving while under the influence, liquor law violations, and drunkenness

[c]Treatment data for other drugs include abuse of legal substances (such as over-the-counter produc and tranquilizers); all arrests involve illegal use.

[d]Treatment admissions include only programs that received some funds administered by the state alcohol and drug agency during the state's fiscal year 1988. Rural states that did not submit data included New Mexico and Wyoming; Washington was the only nonrural state that did not report the data.

[e]Arrest data based on agencies submitting 12 months complete data. Kentucky and Florida did no submit data.

[f]Includes the 18 states with population densities of 50 persons or fewer per square mile.

[g]Rural counties are outside SMSAs. Counties in SMSAs are designated suburban counties

Source: Treatment data in W. Butynski, D. Canova, and S. Jenson, State Resources and Services Related to Alcohol and Drug Abuse Problems, Fiscal Year 1988: An Analysis of State Alcohol and Drug Abuse Profile Data, a report for the National Institute on Alcohol Abuse and Alcoholism and the National Institute on Drug Abuse (Washington, D.C.: National Association of State Alcohol and Drug Abuse Directors, 1989), pp. 22 and 36; arrest data in U.S. Department of Justice, Crime in the United States, 1988 (Washington, D.C.: Federal Bureau of Investigation, 1989a); and U.S. Department of Justice, unpublished data, Federal Bureau of Investigation, 1990f.

DRUGS AND CHILD ABUSE

The National Committee for the Prevention of Child Abuse reports that drug abuse plays a major role in child abuse and neglect reports. The Committee has found that almost every state in the country has cited substance abuse as a major problem in family cases. The increased use of drugs and alcohol by caregivers was reported by six states as the primary cause for increased abuse reporting levels. Only 14 states provided estimates of the number of substantiated (proven) cases involving substance abuse. On average, 32 percent of the cases in these states involved substance abuse.

Currently there is no proven causal link between drug abuse and child abuse. There is, however, substantial evidence that chemical dependence and child abuse are very often found together. Few statistics on the relationship between the two are available because the connection has only been recently recognized and because Child Protective Services agencies have focused on the abuse and neglect of the child, rather than the behavior of the caretaker that might have caused the abuse. Nonetheless, as drug use has increased in certain segments of society, the caseloads of CPS agencies have increased. In addition, the number of boarder/abandoned babies (babies, most often born with addictions or AIDS or both, left at the hospital after birth because the mother is incapable of caring for the infant or cannot even be located) is soaring.

TABLE 8.29

Substance Abuse Among Inmates Recently Admitted to Four State Corrections Systems

State	Alcohol abuse	Other drug abuse	Alcohol and other drug abuse	Total substance abuse	No abuse	Total
Arkansas[a]						
Number	584	492	678	1,754	714	**2,468**
Percent	24%	20%	27%	71%	29%	**100%**
Iowa[b]						
Number	1,044	521	2,175	3,740	1,222	**4,962**
Percent	21%	10%	44%	75%	25%	**100%**
Montana[c]						
Number	58	45	212	315	31	**346**
Percent	17%	13%	61%	91%	9%	**100%**
North Dakota[d]						
Number	106	[e]	298	404	151	**555**
Percent	28%	[e]	54%	73%	27%	**100%**

[a]In 1989, 3,657 persons were admitted into the Arkansas corrections system. Approximately one third (1,189) of the inmates did not fill out the reports concerning substance use; these individuals have been omitted from the table.

[b]Iowa data for calendar year 1988.

[c]Montana uses several different methods to assess the substance abuse problems of persons in the state prisons. (See table VI.10 in appendix VI for a presentation of these different assessments.) Montana data are from December 1989 to June 1990.

[d]North Dakota does not record a separate category for other drug abuse and the categories of alcohol abuse and alcohol and other drug abuse overlap. Total substance abuse thus is not the sum of the first three columns. North Dakota data from June 1989 to June 1990.

[e]Not available.

Source: Arkansas, unpublished data, Department of Corrections, Pine Bluff, July 2, 1990b; Iowa, Iowa Strategy for Drug Control and System Improvement, 1990, (Des Moines: Department of Public Health, Governor's Alliance on Substance Abuse, January 1990), table 8, p. 16; Montana, unpublished data, Chemical Dependency Program, Montana State Prison, Deer Lodge, July 1990; North Dakota, unpublished data, Department of Corrections, North Dakota State Prison, Bismarck, July 1990.

Drug Use and the Pregnant Woman

Should a pregnant woman be charged with child abuse when she takes drugs during pregnancy which will threaten the well-being of the fetus? Questions of rights to privacy and fetal rights are fiercely debated. If a woman can be arrested for using cocaine during pregnancy on the grounds of child abuse, this would give her fetus status as a human being. This would have serious implications for current abortion laws. Many welfare workers believe that threatening to arrest women will drive drug abusing women away from the help they need. On the other hand, those in favor of prosecution maintain that prosecutors can help a pregnant woman get treatment and that these women must be held responsible for their behavior. Under present laws, drug and alcohol use alone are not enough to justify a charge of child abuse.

DRINKING AND CRIME

The consumption of alcoholic beverages is an accepted part of American culture, even though it sometimes leads to driving while intoxicated or becoming violent. Drinking is illegal for anyone under 21 years of age. Among high school age students, drug use has declined to about half the level of a decade ago, but drinking has been decreasing more slowly. In 1992, the University of Michigan's Institute for Social Research at Ann Arbor reported that 30 percent of high school seniors admitted recent occasions of heavy drinking (five or more drinks in a row within the last two weeks), down from a high of 41 percent in 1983. Fifty-four percent of seniors reported having consumed at least some alcohol in the last 30 days, down from 72 percent in 1980. College students continue to drink heavily; three-quarters have drunk in the last month (down slightly from the peak of 83 percent in 1982) and 43 percent admit to binge drinking (five or more drinks consumed in a short period with the intention of getting drunk), a rate that has been about the same ever since the Institute's surveys began.

Drinking and Driving

An estimated 5 to 10 percent of drivers are intoxicated late on Friday or Saturday night. Ac-

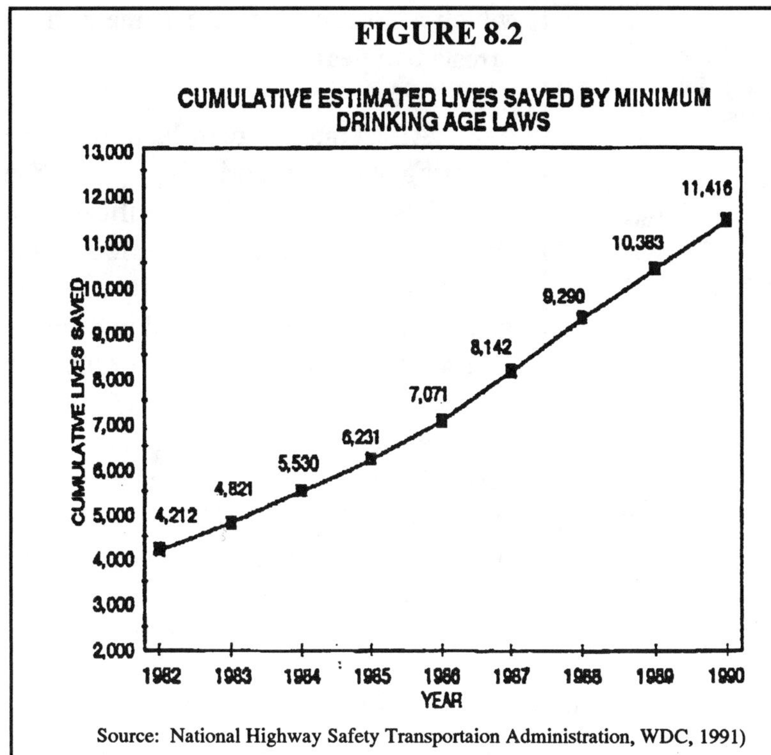

Source: National Highway Safety Transportaion Administration, WDC, 1991)

cording to the National Highway Traffic Safety Administration (NHTSA), 22,084 persons died in alcohol-related traffic accidents in 1991, half (49.6 percent) of the 44,529 people who died in traffic fatalities. This is a decrease from the 57.3 percent of alcohol related fatalities in 1982.

The downward trend leads experts to hope that the government goal of 8.5 alcohol-related fatalities for every 100,000 people by the year 2000 might be reached. In 1991, the rate was 8.9 per 100,000 persons compared to 9.8 in 1987. New Year's Eve is the holiday with the most alcohol-related accidents. In 1990, 62 percent of the 130 traffic deaths were alcohol related; in 1982, these deaths were 83.5 percent of the 187 fatalities.

Arrests for drunk driving have been decreasing since 1982. Repeat offenders account for a disproportionate number of fatal accidents. Drivers with a past record of convictions for drunk driving are 4.6 times more likely to be involved in these accidents than are those with no record. Experts put some of the blame on problems with the criminal justice system. Judges frequently do not know the offender's complete record of alcohol-related crimes when they sentence the offender, and too often they are lenient in sentencing because the judges do not take drunk driving as seriously as violent street crime.

Blood alcohol concentrations (BAC) measure the level of alcohol in a person's blood stream. These levels can be influenced by how rapidly the alcohol was consumed, the size of the drinker, and whether the person ate any food while drinking. In most states, the legal BAC is under 0.10 (over this amount a person is legally drunk) although studies show that important driving skills are impaired at a level of .08 and that there is already measurable impairment at .05 BAC. A recent study by the AAA Foundation for Traffic Safety (1992, "The Effects of Blood Alcohol Levels on Driving Simulator, Coordination, and Reaction Time Tests in a High Risk Population," WDC) found that the true blood alcohol level was not reached until 50 minutes after the last drink. It would, therefore, be impossible for someone who had rapidly consumed alcohol to accurately judge how intoxicated he or she was. The young men in the study believed they were not impaired and were willing to drive. This study did not include women who absorb alcohol far more quickly into the blood stream than men do.

The NHTSA has estimated that approximately two in every five Americans will be involved in an alcohol-related crash at some time in their lives. Each year nearly half a million people are injured in these accidents, in other words, one person hurt every minute and a half, one-quarter of whom are seriously injured. The estimated economic cost of drunk driving ranges from $11 billion (National Highway Traffic Safety Administration, 1985) to $24 billion (Federal Bureau of Investigation, 1989) each year.

TABLE 8.30

ROLE OF 18,500 FATALITIES IN DRUNK DRIVING CRASHES

	Number	Percent
DRIVERS WHO WERE DRUNK AND WERE KILLED	10,210	55
NON-DRUNK DRIVERS WHO WERE KILLED IN A DRUNK DRIVING CRASH	1,280	7
PASSENGERS WHO WERE KILLED IN A DRUNK DRIVING CRASH	3,970	21
NON-OCCUPANTS WHO WERE DRUNK AND KILLED	2,180	12
NON-OCCUPANTS WHO WERE NOT DRUNK AND WERE KILLED IN A DRUNK DRIVING CRASH	860	5
	18,500	100

Source: "Alcohol Involvement in Fatal Crashes, Recent Trends: 1982-1988," National Highway Traffic Safety Administration, undated release

In 1990, 30.8 percent of fatally injured 16 to 20 year olds drivers were intoxicated (BAC of .10 or more). The proportion of drivers in this age category who were involved in fatal crashes and were intoxicated dropped from 31.1 percent in 1982 to 21.2 percent in 1990. All states and the District of Columbia have a 21 year old minimum drinking age law (see below). This restriction is estimated to have cut traffic fatalities in this age group by 13 percent and saved over 11,000 lives since 1975 (Figure 8.2).

Arrest Rates

The FBI reports that 1,771,400 arrests were made for DUI (driving under the influence of an intoxicant, which can include drugs or alcohol compared to DWI which refers to driving while intoxicated by the effects of alcohol) in 1991, which accounted for 12.5 percent of all arrests that year.

Arrest rates were influenced by the lowering of the legal drinking age to 18 in the 1970s in response to the ratification of the 26th Amendment, which extended the right to vote to 18 year-olds. By 1983, 33 states had lowered the drinking age to below 21. However, because of the high number of youths between 15 and 19 involved in fatal crashes, the laws were reversed and every state now bans drinking under 21 years old. (The federal government informed the states that this was required to be eligible for federal highway funding.) While there are fewer young DUI's, there has also been a change in attitude toward drunk driving which has increased arrest rates — the public has generally become less tolerant of drunk driving and the police have become more stringent in enforcing the law. Furthermore, driving drunk is no longer socially acceptable.

Who Died?

Drunk drivers kill themselves, their passengers, people in other vehicles, and pedestrians. The NHTSA surveyed 18,500 people killed in drunk driving accidents: 1,280 (7 percent of the total fatalities) non-drunk drivers were killed; 3,970 (21 percent) non-drunk passengers were killed; and 860 (5 percent) non-vehicle occupants (pedestrians, bicycle riders, etc.) who were not drunk were killed (Table 8.30).

CHAPTER IX

PUBLIC OPINION OF CRIME

THE FEAR OF BEING A VICTIM

The fear of becoming a victim is often much greater than the likelihood of victimization and has permeated our society so completely that it plays a daily role in our lives. In the "Statement of the Chairman," Lois Haight Herrington in the *President's Task Force on Victims of Crime* (1982, WDC) stated, "Every citizen of this county is more impoverished, less free, more fearful, and less safe, because of the ever-present threat of the criminal. Rather than alter a system that has proven itself incapable of dealing with crime, society has altered itself." Fear of crime undermines community relationships. People withdraw, physically and emotionally, losing contact with their neighbors, weakening the social fabric of their lives. Rather than deal with the roots of criminality, citizens cope by adapting their lives to avoid dangerous situations.

TABLE 9.1

How about at home at night — do you feel safe and secure, or not?

	Yes	No
1992	89%	11%
1990	90	10
1989	90	10
1983	84	16
1981	84	16
1977	85	15
1975	80	20
1972	83	17

Source: The Gallup Poll, (Princeton, NJ, 1992)

A 1992 Gallup Poll showed that 89 percent of Americans thought there was more crime than in 1991, up slightly from the 84 percent who thought there was more crime in 1990 than in 1989. Forty-four percent were afraid to walk alone at night, about the same as the 45 percent who were afraid in the years 1975 through 1983, but significantly higher than the 31 percent who claimed to be afraid in 1967. Eleven percent said they did not feel safe in their homes at night, about half the 20 percent who did not feel secure in 1975 (Table 9.1).

Who is Afraid?

When asked about walking alone at night, more than twice as many women (59 percent) as men (28 percent) and more non-whites (58 percent) than whites (42 percent) were afraid. Those over 65 years old were the most fearful age group (55 percent), followed by 18 to 29 year-olds who were afraid 48 percent of the time, while the least afraid were 30 to 49 years old (40 percent). The poor with incomes under $20,000 were much more likely to be fearful than were those with incomes over $50,000 (57 percent as compared to 33 percent).

Where and how someone lives influences his or her fear of crime. The respondent least likely to be fearful was a white, middle-aged male, living in a rural area of the Midwest (the area of the country with the lowest crime rates), with a college degree and an income over $50,000. In contrast the respondent most likely to be fearful was a non-white, older woman, living in the city in the South, without a high school diploma and having an income below $20,000. (See Table 9.2.)

TABLE 9.2

How Safe Is Your Neighborhood?

QUESTIONS: Is there more crime in your area than there was a year ago, or less?

Is there any area near where you live — that is, within a mile — where you would be afraid to walk alone at nigl

| | More crime this year? | | | | Unsafe to walk at night? | | |
	More	Less	Same (vol.)	No opinion	Yes	No	No opinion
National	54%	19%	23%	4%	44%	56%	•
Sex							
Male	49	22	25	4	28	72	•
Female	58	17	21	4	59	41	•
Age							
18-29 years	54	23	16	7	48	52	0
30-49 years	55	18	22	5	40	60	0
50 & older	53	18	27	2	46	53	1
65 & older	55	22	22	1	55	44	1
Region							
East	53	20	24	3	47	53	0
Midwest	45	23	27	5	34	55	•
South	60	17	19	4	51	49	•
West	54	18	22	6	42	57	1
Community size							
Large city	64	15	16	5	60	40	0
Medium city	57	21	17	5	56	44	0
Suburbs	46	21	28	5	42	57	1
Small town	47	23	27	3	36	63	1
Rural area	58	14	24	4	31	69	•
Race							
White	52	19	25	4	42	57	1
Non-white	66	23	6	5	58	42	0
Education							
College grads.	53	14	28	5	37	62	1
College inc.	56	17	22	5	45	55	0
High school grads.	53	21	22	4	43	57	•
Not H.S. grads.	52	27	19	2	53	46	1
Politics							
Republicans	52	23	19	6	40	60	•
Democrats	56	18	23	3	53	46	1
Independents	52	17	27	4	40	60	0
Ideology							
Liberal	54	22	19	5	51	49	0
Moderate	53	17	26	4	42	58	0
Conservative	54	21	21	4	44	55	1
Registered voter							
Yes	56	18	23	3	45	55	•
No	44	26	22	8	41	59	0
Income							
$50,000 & over	53	16	27	4	33	67	•
$30,000-49,999	51	19	26	4	42	58	•
$20,000-29,999	56	17	24	3	37	62	1
Under $20,000	56	23	16	5	57	43	•
Religion							
Protestant	55	19	22	4	44	56	•
Catholic	55	19	24	2	44	56	0
None	49	18	29	4	37	63	0

• Less than one percent

Source: The Gallup Poll, (Princeton, NJ, 1992)

Crime in the Neighborhood

In both 1990 and 1992, Gallup Polls asked people whether they thought there was more crime in their neighborhood than there had been a year before. The national rate of those who thought there was more crime increased from 51 percent to 54 percent, a rate as high as the previous all-time high in 1981 (the year that the Bureau of Justice Statistics reported the highest rates of crime — see Chapter III) (Table 9.3).

In 1990, Gallup Polls asked whether respondents thought certain American cities were safe to live in or to visit. New York was perceived to be the most unsafe (85 percent), followed by Miami with 76 percent. Seattle and Minneapolis were seen as the most safe with 68 and 66 percent who thought they were safe as compared to 16 and 11 percent, respectively, who thought they were not. (See Table 9.4.)

WHAT TO DO ABOUT CRIME

Factors Responsible for Crime

In 1981, only 13 percent of respondents thought that drug use was a cause of crime. Over one-third cited unemployment, one out of five thought the courts were too lenient, and 13 percent thought punishment was too lax. In 1990, 60 percent blamed drugs, by far the most frequently given answer, while the lenient courts and lax punishment were cited by only 2 percent of the respondents. The breakdown of family values was named 19 percent of the time in 1981 and 6 percent of the time in 1990 (Table 9.5).

How Can Crime be Reduced?

The poll asked what was the most important thing that could be done to help reduce crime? People most frequently chose cutting the drug

	More	Less	Same (vol.)	No opinion
1992 Feb	54%	19%	23%	4%
1990 Sep	51	18	24	7
1989 Jun	53	18	22	7
1989 Jan	47	21	27	5
1983	37	17	36	10
1981	54	8	29	9
1977	43	17	32	8
1975	50	12	29	9
1972	51	10	27	12

Source: The Gallup Poll, (Princeton, NJ, 1992)

supply (17 percent), which was a tremendous drop from the over half (51 percent) of those polled who thought so in 1989. A decade ago harsher punishment was the remedy of choice (38 percent of the time) which, in 1990, was mentioned almost as often (15 percent) as cutting drugs. One in 10 thought education could help reduce crime (Table 9.6).

The Police and the Courts

In 1989, the public did not have a positive opinion of either the police or the courts. Overall, half of the people polled had little or no confidence in the police's ability to protect them from violent crime, exactly the same proportion as in 1981. Seventy-three percent had little or no confidence in the court's ability to convict and properly sentence criminals. This was a little higher than in 1981 (70 percent), despite court reforms of more determinate sentencing, greater rights for victims, and an increasingly "get-tough" attitude over the past decade. (See Table 9.7.)

Those who were most likely to have the most confidence in the police were women who were 50 years or older living in small towns or cities (52 percent for all three categories). Over half (53 percent) of those who earned $15,000 or less had either a great deal or quite a bit of confidence in the police. As is shown in Table 9.8, the public was even less approving of the courts than the police. Between two-thirds to three-quarters of those polled thought that the courts had little to no ability to properly convict and sentence criminals. Although the differences were not very large, blacks (64 percent), dropouts, and those with incomes under $15,000 (69 percent for both) were the least negative.

Eight out of 10 people thought the courts were not harsh enough in the treatment of criminals. This is a 20 percent increase since 1968 and a 10

TABLE 9.4
Perceived Safety in Major U.S. Cities

QUESTION: Now thinking about large cities, both those you have visited and those you have never visited, from what you know and have read, do you consider each of the following cities to be safe to live in or visit, or not?

	New York		Miami		Washington, DC		Detroit		Chicago	
	Safe	Unsafe	Safe	Unsafe	Safe	Unsafe	Safe	Unsafe	Safe	Unsafe
National	11%	85%	17%	76%	22%	71%	18%	68%	26%	65%

	Los Angeles		San Francisco		Philadelphia		Atlanta		Boston	
	Safe	Unsafe	Safe	Unsafe	Safe	Unsafe	Safe	Unsafe	Safe	Unsafe
	26%	64%	44%	43%	40%	40%	45%	39%	53%	29%

	San Diego		Dallas		Houston		Seattle		Minneapolis	
	Safe	Unsafe	Safe	Unsafe	Safe	Unsafe	Safe	Unsafe	Safe	Unsafe
	56%	28%	55%	26%	55%	25%	68%	16%	66%	11%

<table>
<tr><td colspan="2" align="center">TABLE 9.5</td></tr>
</table>

In your opinion, what factors are most responsible for crime in the US today?

	1981	1989	1990
Drugs	13%	58%	60%
Unemployment	37	14	4
Breakdown of family social values	19	13	6
Courts too lenient	20	4	2
Punishment too lax	13	4	2
TV violence	3	2	1
Lack of education	NA	NA	2
Guns	NA	NA	2
Poverty	NA	NA	2
Justice system	NA	NA	•
Other	17	19	11
No opinion	8	6	7

• Less than 0.5 percent

TABLE 9.6

What is the most important thing that can be done to help reduce crime?

	1981	1989	1990
Cut/eliminate drugs	32%	51%	17%
Harsher punishment	38	24	15
Teach values and respect for law	13	12	7
Reduce unemployment	22	10	5
More police	11	5	8
Try cases faster	6	2	•
Legalize drugs	NA	NA	1
Education	NA	NA	10
Tighten judicial system	NA	NA	2
Community watch or involvement	NA	NA	1
Gun control	NA	NA	1
Death penalty/ kill drug dealers	NA	NA	3
Other	13	21	16
No opinion	11	14	12

Note: Adds to more than 100% due to multiple answers

TABLE 9.8

Confidence in Police, Courts

QUESTIONS: *How much confidence do you have in the ability of the police to protect you from violent crime?*

How much confidence do you have in the ability of the courts to convict and properly sentence criminals?

June 8-11, 1989 (telephone)

	Police					Courts					
	A great deal	Quite a bit	Not very much	None	No opinion	A great deal	Quite a lot	Not very much	None	No opinion	Number of interviews
NATIONAL	14%	34%	42%	8%	2%	5%	20%	59%	14%	2%	1235
SEX											
Men	13	32	43	10	2	4	21	56	17	2	611
Women	16	36	41	6	1	6	19	61	12	2	624
AGE											
18-29 years	9	36	45	9	1	4	24	56	15	1	284
30-49 years	13	35	41	10	1	5	21	57	16	1	508
50 & older	20	32	41	4	3	5	16	65	11	3	429
REGION											
East	13	36	43	6	2	4	19	66	10	1	294
Midwest	14	33	44	7	2	5	22	56	14	3	316
South	17	34	38	10	1	6	23	54	15	2	364
West	13	34	44	8	1	4	14	62	19	1	261
RACE											
White	13	36	41	8	2	4	20	60	14	2	1097
Non-whites	25	17	49	8	1	12	22	51	13	2	127
EDUCATION											
College grads.	13	36	44	8	1	5	22	62	9	2	344
College inc.	10	31	48	10	1	3	21	60	16	•	267
High school grads.	16	37	38	7	2	6	17	60	15	2	469
Not H.S. grads.	18	28	42	11	1	6	21	54	15	4	145
POLITICS											
Republicans	14	39	39	6	2	5	22	60	11	2	427
Democrats	17	30	45	8	2	5	20	58	14	3	386
Independents	13	33	43	10	1	5	18	59	17	1	422
HOUSEHOLD INCOME											
$50,000 & over	15	35	40	9	1	3	22	61	13	1	250
$30,000-$49,999	13	35	44	7	1	7	20	59	13	1	306
$15,000-$29,999	13	35	43	8	1	2	19	60	17	2	258
Under $15,000	17	36	37	7	3	5	22	56	13	4	168
PLACE											
Large city	18	22	52	6	2	5	23	56	14	2	244
Suburb	14	36	43	6	1	6	17	61	16		252
Small city/town	14	38	39	8	1	6	19	59	13	3	518
Rural	12	35	38	12	3	2	22	59	16	1	210

TABLE 9.7

Confidence in Police — Trend

	1989	1985	1981
Great deal	14%	15%	15%
Quite a bit	34	37	34
Not very much	42	39	42
None	8	6	8
No opinion	2	3	1
	100%	100%	100%

Confidence in Courts — Trend

	1989	1985	1981
Great deal	5%	8%	5%
Quite a bit	20	22	23
Not very much	59	54	59
None	14	12	11
No opinion	2	4	2
	100%	100%	100%

Source of above tables: The Gallup Poll, Princeton, NJ

TABLE 9.10

Severity of Punishment

QUESTIONS: *In general, do you think the courts in your area deal too harshly, or not harshly enough with criminals?*

Which are you more worried about: That some criminals are being let off too easily, or that the constitutional rights of some people accused of commiting a crime are not being upheld?

June 8-11, 1989 (telephone)

	Courts' treatment of criminals				More worried about:			
	Too harsh	About right (vol.)	Not harsh enough	No opinion	Criminals let off too easily	Abuse of Constitutional rights	No opinion	Number of interviews
NATIONAL	3%	8%	83%	6%	79%	16%	5%	1235
SEX								
Men	3	10	81	6	78	19	5	611
Women	2	6	85	7	82	14	4	624
AGE								
18-29 years	3	9	82	6	74	23	3	284
30-49 years	3	9	82	6	80	16	4	508
50 & older	2	6	85	7	81	13	6	429
REGION								
East	3	6	86	5	80	14	6	294
Midwest	3	11	77	9	77	20	3	316
South	4	6	85	5	79	16	5	364
West	1	9	83	7	80	16	4	261
RACE								
White	2	8	84	6	81	15	4	1097
Non-whites	.6	6	79	9	68	27	5	127
EDUCATION								
College grads.	2	14	77	7	82	14	4	344
College inc.	2	7	83	8	80	16	4	267
High school grads.	2	8	86	4	80	17	3	469
Not H.S. grads.	6	3	.84	7	74	19	7	145
POLITICS								
Republicans	2	10	84	4	86	10	4	427
Democrats	4	8	80	8	75	19	6	386
Independents	2	6	85	7	76	20	4	422
HOUSEHOLD INCOME								
$50,000 & over	2	11	82	5	85	13	2	250
$30,000-$49,999	2	7	86	5	82	13	5	306
$15,000-$29,999	3	9	84	4	78	18	4	258
Under $15,000	5	5	84	6	79	16	5	168
PLACE								
Large city	2	6	83	9	76	17	7	244
Suburb	2	6	89	3	84	13	0	252
Small city/town	3	9	80	8	78	17	5	518
Rural	2	11	83	4	79	19	2	210

TABLE 9.9

Courts' Treatment of Criminals — Trend			
	1989	1988	1965
Too harsh	3%	2%	2%
About right (vol.)	8	13	19
Not harsh enough	83	75	63
No opinion	6	10	16
	100%	100%	100%

Source: The Gallup Organization, Princeton, NJ

---

percent decrease in the number of respondents who had no opinion on the issue (Table 9.9). College graduates (77 percent) and those with incomes over $50,000 (82 percent) were the least likely within each group to feel that the courts were not harsh enough (Table 9.10).

Judicial Changes

The Gallup polltakers asked whether people approved (18 percent) or disapproved (79 percent) of allowing the police to search a home without a warrant. The majority did favor making it more difficult for violent criminals to be paroled (82 percent in comparison to 16 percent who opposed it) and for violent criminals not to be released on bail while awaiting trial (68 as opposed to 29 percent). Support for gun control was almost twice as great as opposition (60 percent to 34 percent) and was most strongly supported by women, the well-educated, and the well-to-do. See Table 9.11 for further details of the responses.

In 1990, Gallup asked if people supported a ban on handguns, except for the police and other authorized persons. Overall, 41 percent supported a ban: females (48 percent), those 50 years and older (47 percent), blacks (45 percent), college graduates (49 percent), and Democrats (49 percent) favored the ban. A large majority (81 percent) favored registering handguns. See Table 9.12 for the details of the poll.

TABLE 9.11

Anti-Crime Measures

QUESTION: *For each of the following, please tell me whether you favor or oppose each as a way of dealing with crime in the U.S. Do you strongly favor, favor, oppose or strongly oppose:*

June 8-11, 1989 (telephone)

	Making it more difficult for those convicted of violent crimes like murder and rape to be paroled?					Prohibiting plea bargaining — whether the defendant agrees to plead guilty to a reduced charge?					
	Strongly favor	Favor	Oppose	Strongly oppose	No opinion	Strongly favor	Favor	Oppose	Strongly oppose	No opinion	Number of interviews
NATIONAL	54%	28%	8%	8%	2%	16%	27%	33%	17%	7%	1235
SEX											
Men	53	31	9	6	1	14	30	35	18	5	611
Women	55	26	8	9	2	17	24	32	17	10	624
AGE											
18-29 years	51	28	12	8	1	12	34	35	14	5	284
30-49 years	57	29	5	7	2	16	27	34	18	5	508
50 & older	53	28	9	9	1	18	21	33	16	12	429
REGION											
East	57	27	7	7	2	16	25	32	19	8	294
Midwest	49	29	10	10	2	15	27	36	16	6	316
South	58	24	10	7	1	17	26	33	16	8	364
West	52	34	6	8	*	14	31	32	15	8	261
RACE											
White	56	29	7	7	1	16	27	34	16	7	1097
Non-whites	44	19	20	14	3	16	24	29	21	10	127
EDUCATION											
College grads.	59	28	6	4	3	14	33	32	14	7	344
College inc.	65	21	7	7	*	18	27	32	17	6	267
High school grads.	51	29	9	9	2	16	26	33	18	7	469
Not H.S. grads.	43	33	11	12	1	14	22	39	15	10	145
POLITICS											
Republicans	52	30	10	6	2	12	28	38	17	5	427
Democrats	53	28	9	9	1	16	28	34	14	8	386
Independents	57	27	6	8	2	19	24	29	19	9	422
HOUSEHOLD INCOME											
$50,000 & over	58	31	5	5	1	16	32	32	16	4	250
$30,000-$49,999	61	26	6	7	*	13	26	34	20	7	306
$15,000-$29,999	52	31	8	8	1	16	33	32	13	6	258
Under $15,000	50	26	12	10	2	18	21	31	20	10	168
PLACE											
Large city	58	26	8	8	*	17	30	32	12	9	244
Suburb	61	25	6	8	*	16	26	36	17	5	252
Small city/town	49	31	10	8	2	14	27	33	17	9	518
Rural	54	29	6	8	3	19	23	33	20	5	210

(Continued on following page)

Deterrence and Punishment

In 1989 nearly half of those polled felt that rehabilitation was the goal for those in prison, while 38 percent felt that punishment was the purpose of a prison term. In 1982, 59 percent supported rehabilitation and 30 percent wanted punishment (Table 9.13). Almost two-thirds (61 percent) polled felt that the way to lower crime was to invest more money in correcting social problems

Anti-Crime Measures
(continued)

QUESTION: *For each of the following, please tell me whether you favor or oppose each as a way of dealing with crime in the U.S. Do you strongly favor, favor, oppose or strongly oppose:*

June 8-11, 1989 (telephone)

	Enacting tougher gun control laws?					Not allowing those accused of violent crimes like murder and rape to get out on bail while awaiting trial?					Allowing the police to search a home without a warrant?					
	Strongly favor	Favor	Oppose	Strongly oppose	No opinion	Strongly favor	Favor	Oppose	Strongly oppose	No opinion	Strongly favor	Favor	Oppose	Strongly oppose	No opinion	Number of interviews
NATIONAL	28%	32%	23%	11%	6%	42%	26%	17%	12%	3%	6%	12%	43%	36%	3%	1235
SEX																
Men	20	32	27	16	5	37	29	19	12	3	5	11	40	41	3	611
Women	34	34	18	7	7	47	25	14	12	2	6	14	46	31	3	624
AGE																
18-29 years	25	38	21	11	5	40	30	17	12	1	5	18	40	35	2	284
30-49 years	27	33	24	13	3	44	28	13	13	2	5	8	44	41	2	508
50 & older	30	28	22	10	10	41	23	20	12	4	7	13	44	30	6	429
REGION																
East	28	38	17	9	8	46	25	15	12	2	4	14	41	37	4	294
Midwest	29	33	24	11	3	39	27	20	11	3	9	10	46	33	2	316
South	29	28	25	11	7	42	23	18	14	3	5	11	40	40	4	364
West	24	32	24	15	5	42	33	12	10	3	4	15	46	32	3	261
RACE																
White	28	32	23	12	5	43	27	16	11	3	5	13	44	35	3	1097
Non-whites	28	34	18	10	10	35	22	22	19	2	6	7	40	46	1	127
EDUCATION																
College grads.	35	34	19	8	4	43	35	13	7	2	4	11	41	42	2	344
College inc.	30	31	22	12	5	46	27	12	14	1	5	11	43	40	1	267
High school grads.	25	34	24	12	5	42	25	17	14	2	6	12	45	34	3	469
Not H.S. grads.	22	31	24	14	9	38	20	25	13	4	7	18	41	30	4	145
POLITICS																
Republicans	24	34	24	13	5	43	27	15	13	2	6	14	45	32	3	427
Democrats	33	31	20	8	8	40	27	1	13	3	6	12	43	36	3	386
Independents	26	32	24	13	5	44	25	17	11	3	5	12	41	40	3	422
HOUSEHOLD INCOME																
$50,000 & over	32	32	21	12	3	41	30	17	9	3	5	10	43	39	3	250
$30,000-$49,999	27	38	20	10	5	48	26	11	14	1	4	13	39	42	2	306
$15,000-$29,000	24	31	28	13	4	42	29	16	11	2	6	9	44	37	4	258
Under $15,000	27	26	26	12	9	41	19	24	14	2	5	14	47	33	1	168
PLACE																
Large city	34	32	20	7	7	45	24	15	14	2	3	10	43	41	3	244
Suburb	32	34	18	12	4	48	24	14	12	2	5	11	40	41	3	252
Small city/town	24	35	22	12	7	37	28	20	12	3	7	14	44	32	3	518
Rural	25	23	34	15	3	45	28	12	12	3	5	13	45	36	1	210

Source: The Gallup Organization, Princeton, NJ

through better education and job training rather than spending money on improving law enforcement with more prisons, police, and judges. This was supported by all categories of people, although high school drop-outs were the least in favor of this remedy (51 percent) (Table 9.14). In 1990, confidence in social remedies appeared to drop slightly (57 percent), while providing more money for the police, prisons, and judges gained favor (36 percent) (Table 9.15).

TABLE 9.12

Possession and Registration of Handguns

QUESTIONS: Do you think there should or should not be a law that would ban the possession of handguns except by police and other authorized persons?

Would you favor or oppose the registration of all handguns?

	Ban civilian handguns?			Register handguns?			
	Should	Should not	No opinion	Favor	Oppose	No opinion	No. of interviews
National	**41%**	**55%**	**4%**	**81%**	**17%**	**2%**	**1031**
Sex							
Male	32	65	3	78	28	1	508
Female	48	47	5	84	13	3	523
Age							
18-29 years	37	62	1	85	14	1	224
30-49 years	37	61	2	82	17	1	438
50 & older	47	46	7	75	20	5	357
Region							
East	54	44	2	85	14	1	258
Midwest	36	58	6	79	19	2	261
South	35	60	5	79	18	3	304
West	38	60	2	81	17	2	207
Race							
White	39	57	4	81	16	3	909
Black	45	52	3	78	22	0	68
Other	58	40	2	76	24	0	47
Education							
College grads.	49	49	2	89	10	1	296
College inc.	39	59	2	82	17	1	224
High school grads.	38	59	3	82	16	2	376
Not H.S. grads.	39	53	8	66	28	6	126
Politics							
Republicans	36	60	4	80	16	4	360
Democrats	49	48	3	85	13	2	335
Independents	38	58	4	77	22	1	309

	Ban civilian handguns?			Register handguns?			
	Should	Should not	No opinion	Favor	Oppose	No opinion	No. of interviews
National	**41%**	**55%**	**4%**	**81%**	**17%**	**2%**	**1031**
Ideology							
Liberal	44	55	1	89	10	1	311
Moderate	41	56	3	84	16	0	79
Conservative	37	59	4	80	19	1	488
Income							
$50,000 & over	43	55	2	87	13	0	238
$30,000-49,999	35	62	3	86	13	1	275
$20,000-29,999	41	57	2	81	17	2	189
Under $20,000	42	53	5	73	23	4	259
Religion							
Protestant	36	60	4	80	18	2	570
Catholic	49	47	4	86	13	1	275
None	41	59	0	66	27	7	73
Gun Owners							
Yes	22	76	2	78	21	1	479
No	58	37	5	81	16	3	543
Residence							
Large city	50	46	4	79	19	2	183
Medium city	47	50	3	88	11	1	189
Suburban area	43	55	2	80	18	2	202
Small town	39	57	4	80	16	4	288
Rural area	27	69	4	77	23	*	158

Source: The Gallup Poll, Princeton, NJ

Deterrence and Punishment

QUESTIONS: *To lower the crime rate in the U.S., some people think additional money and effort should go to attacking the social and economic problems that lead to crime, through better education and job training. Others feel more money and effort should go to deterring crime by improving law enforcement with more prisons, police and judges. Which comes closer to your view?*

In dealing with those who are in prison, do you think it is more important to punish them for their crimes, or more important to get them started "on the right road?"

| | June 8-11, 1989 (telephone) | | | | | |
| | Crime Deterrence Preferences | | | Punishment vs. Rehabilitation | | |
	Attack social problems	Improve law enforcement	No opinion	Punish	Rehabili-tate	No opinion	Number of interviews
NATIONAL	61%	32%	7%	38%	48%	14%	1235
SEX							
Men	58	34	8	39	48	13	611
Women	63	30	7	37	49	14	624
AGE							
18-29 years	68	27	5	40	48	12	284
30-49 years	63	32	5	42	45	13	508
50 & older	53	36	11	31	53	16	429
REGION							
East	63	32	5	40	46	14	294
Midwest	65	27	8	34	53	13	316
South	54	40	6	38	47	15	364
West	62	28	10	39	48	13	261
RACE							
White	61	32	7	37	49	14	1097
Non-whites	61	35	4	42	46	12	127
EDUCATION							
College grads.	67	26	7	37	53	10	344
College inc.	69	28	3	37	50	13	267
High school grads.	59	34	7	40	46	14	469
Not H.S. grads.	51	39	10	35	48	17	145
POLITICS							
Republicans	58	35	7	41	49	10	427
Democrats	61	32	7	35	51	14	386
Independents	62	30	8	38	45	17	422
HOUSEHOLD INCOME							
$50,000 & over	63	30	7	41	52	7	250
$30,000-$49,999	61	36	3	43	45	12	306
$15,000-$29,999	64	29	7	32	51	17	258
Under $15,000	54	38	8	37	46	17	168
PLACE							
Large city	61	31	8	34	53	13	244
Suburb	59	35	6	39	52	9	252
Small city/town	63	29	8	38	47	15	518
Rural	60	36	4	40	44	16	210

TABLE 9.13

Punishment vs. Rehabilitation — Trend

	1989	1982
Punish	38%	30%
Rehabilitate	48	59
No opinion	14	11
	100%	100%

Source: The Gallup Organization, Princeton, NJ

TABLE 9.15

To lower the crime rate in the U.S. some people think additional money and effort should go to attacking the social and economic problems that lead to crime, through better education and job training. Others feel more money and effort should go to deterring crime by improving law enforcement with more prisons, police and judges. Which comes closer to your view?

	1989	1990
Spend money on social and economic problems	61%	57%
Spend money on police prisons and judges	32	36
No opinion	7	7
	100%	100%

Source: The Gallup Poll, Princeton, NJ

Robert Rich and Robert Sampson, in "Public Perceptions of Criminal Justice Policy: Does Victimization Make a Difference?" (1990, vol 5., no 2., *Violence and Victims*, New York: Springer Publishing), polled residents of Chicago to determine if having been a victim influenced attitudes towards criminal justice. Respondents were asked how many years of incarceration convicted criminals received for different violent crimes and how many they should receive. Generally, all categories of people felt that criminals were sentenced to one-quarter to one-half the term they should receive. Women thought rapists served 8.13 years in prison, but that they should be sentenced to 34.11 years for their crimes. There were no real differences between the perceptions of victims and non-victims. Those with some college education fa-

TABLE 9.16

Views on Imprisonment: Mean Number of Years Offenders Will Get and Should Get, by Socio-Demographic Characteristics

Socio-demographic Variables	Rape will get/years	Rape should get/years	Murder will get/years	Murder should get/years
Gender				
Female	8.13	34.11	28.57	59.79
Male	9.08	25.50	38.77	69.34
Race				
White	8.56	29.36	32.75	64.97
Nonwhite	8.42	33.73	34.62	58.82
Age				
18–31	8.83	34.51	36.60	66.77
32–46	7.87	25.10	33.44	64.84
47–99	8.78	30.99	28.62	59.93
Education				
<HS graduate	8.77	37.03	25.94	58.15
HS graduate	9.72	34.90	24.40	59.01
Some college	7.99	26.68	38.70	67.12
Victimization				
Non-victim	8.61	30.26	31.89	62.61
Victim	8.23	30.17	37.30	67.09

Socio-demographic Variables	Burglary will get/years	Burglary should get/years
Gender		
Female	4.41	7.73
Male	4.36	6.91
Race		
White	4.06	6.46
Nonwhite	5.36	10.69
Age		
18–31	4.87	6.75
32–46	3.44	7.06
47–99	4.56	8.39
Education		
<HS graduate	5.50	8.89
HS graduate	4.00	7.39
Some college	4.42	7.10
Victimization		
Non-victim	4.52	6.86
Victim	3.95	9.11

Source: "Public Perceptions of Criminal Justice Policy: Does Victimization Make a Difference?" Robert Rich and Robert Sampson, *Violence and Victims*, 1990, Springer Publishing Company, Inc., New York 10012. Used by permission.

vored fewer years of incarceration for rape and burglary than did those with less education. On the other hand, the college educated approved of longer sentences for murder than did those without college. (See Table 9.16.)

Nearly two-thirds of respondents thought that reducing poverty and improving family discipline were the most important factors in reducing crime. Only one-quarter favored longer prison sentences, implying that the longer sentences they had favored (above) may have reflected the desire to remove criminals from the streets or to punish them. Respondents were not clear on their attitudes towards rehabilitation. Although only 13 percent thought putting more effort into rehabilitation would reduce crime, 70 percent thought the failure to rehabilitate was a somewhat to very important reason for high crime rates. An equal percentage (57 percent) thought that while the emphasis on imprisonment was on protecting society, the emphasis should be to rehabilitate. (See Table 9.17.)

TABLE 9.17

Attitudes Toward Rehabilitation and Prison Policy

A. Which of the following would be *most* important in reducing crime?
a. Giving longer prison sentences to criminals 24%
b. Putting more effort into rehabilitating prisoners 13%
c. Getting parents to use stronger discipline on their children 38%
d. Getting rid of poverty 25%

B. How important do you think the failure of prisons to rehabilitate convicted criminals is in explaining why we have so much crime in this country?
a. Not at all important 10%
b. Not very important 20%
c. Somewhat important 30%
d. Very important 40%

C. What do you think the *main* emphasis *is* in most prisons—punishing the person convicted of a crime, trying to rehabilitate the person to become a productive citizen, or putting the person in prison to protect society from future crimes the person might commit? What do you think the main emphasis *should be?*

	Emphasis is	Emphasis should be
Punishing	23%	13%
Rehabilitating	20%	57%
Protecting society	57%	29%

Source: "Public Perceptions of Criminal Justice Policy: Does Victimization Make a Difference?" Robert Rich and Robert Sampson, *Violence and Victims,* 1990, Springer Publishing Company, Inc., New York 10012. Used by permission.

INDEX